THIRST

THIRST

A STORY OF REDEMPTION, COMPASSION, AND A MISSION TO BRING CLEAN WATER TO THE WORLD

SCOTT HARRISON

Founder and CEO of charity: water

———

with
LISA SWEETINGHAM

CURRENCY
NEW YORK

Currency books are available at special discounts for bulk purchases for
sales promotions or corporate use. Special editions, including personalized
covers, excerpts of existing books, or books with corporate logos, can
be created in large quantities for special needs. For more information,
contact Premium Sales at (212) 572-2232 or e-mail specialmarkets@
penguinrandomhouse.com.

Library of Congress Cataloging-in-Publication Data is available upon
request.

ISBN 978-1-5247-6284-1
Ebook ISBN 978-1-5247-6285-8

Printed in the United States of America

*Jacket design and photograph by charity: water in collaboration with Baas
Creative*

Photo insert credits: pages 1–2: Courtesy of the author; page 3: (top and
bottom) Scott Harrison/Mercy Ships, (middle) Courtesy of Mercy Ships;
page 4: Scott Harrison/Mercy Ships; page 5: (top left and bottom) Scott
Harrison/Mercy Ships, (top right) Erin Blinn; page 6: Courtesy of the
author; pages 7–8: charity: water; page 9: (top) Lynnette Astaire, (bottom)
charity: water; page 10: (top and bottom left) Scott Harrison, (bottom
right) Water for Good; page 11: (top) charity: water, (bottom) © Esther
Havens Photography; page 12: (top and bottom right) charity: water,
(bottom left) Samantha Bouche; page 13: charity: water; page 14: Scott
Harrison; page 15: charity: water; page 16: Cubby Graham

10 9 8 7 6 5 4 3 2 1

First Edition

For Viktoria,
who continues to inspire and challenge me.
You make everything better.

For Mom and Dad,
who never gave up on me and taught me
how to fight for what's right.

For Jackson and Emma.
I love you both so much,
and I can't wait to see who you become.

Contents

I

PURE

1

———

Numb

NEW YORK CITY, FALL 2003

It started in my arms and legs. The nerve endings would go dead for twenty or thirty minutes, like I'd woken up on a limb that fell asleep. Sometimes the fingers of my right hand lost sensation, and then a prickly blanket of numbness would spread to my wrist and up my arm. I could've banged on my hand with a hammer and still felt nothing.

At first I thought there must be a simple explanation, like a pinched nerve. I was twenty-eight years old, with no history of serious illness. But when the episodes became more frequent, I got the name of a neurologist in Manhattan and made an appointment.

Sitting in the dingy waiting room, I nervously flipped through a half-dozen dog-eared magazines, hoping to take in some news from the real world. It was mostly bad. Bombings in Istanbul, suicide attacks in Iraq, the passing of Johnny Cash.

A nurse called me to the reception window and handed me a stack of forms to fill out. Name, age, height, and weight were easy—Scott Charles Harrison, twenty-eight, six foot one, and a slim 170 pounds, thanks to a steady diet of Marlboro Reds—but the long list of questions about my lifestyle wasn't so simple. Looking through the packet,

I realized that I didn't dare answer truthfully, lest the doctors think the presentable college grad in front of them was some kind of degenerate.

Do you smoke cigarettes? (Two to three packs a day. Is that too much?)

Do you consume alcohol? How many drinks per day? (Up to ten drinks, but I try not to mix. My current favorites, in order: Champagne, beer, and vodka and Red Bull.)

Do you use recreational drugs? If so, how frequently? (Well, that really depends on how much I've had to drink. Cocaine, two to three times a week; Ambien to come down; MDMA whenever I can get my hands on it.)

Anyone who knew the full extent of my partying would've said it was no wonder I was finally having health problems. But I'd come here for a brain scan and a quick diagnosis, not a lecture. And the fact was, getting wasted every night was my *job*.

For the last ten years, I'd climbed the ranks of New York nightlife to become one of the top club promoters in the city. Most nights, you'd find me at the hottest party in town, sitting at the owner's table with beautiful women, drinking expensive Champagne (or occasionally spraying it), and looking like the guy who had it all. And for a while, I did.

I was making about $200,000 a year but living like a millionaire, thanks to the perks. The place I called home was a big, industrial Midtown loft with a baby grand piano in the living room, a killer stereo system, and a private rooftop patio. Bacardi and Budweiser each paid me $2,000 a month just to be seen drinking their brands in public. On my wrist, I wore a Rolex Oyster Perpetual, which I loved to flash at club photographers with a knowing smirk. The watch had been a gift from my then-girlfriend, a nineteen-year-old Danish model whose face graced the covers of *Vogue* and *Elle*.

I hadn't always lived like this. Ten years earlier, when I moved to the city and began collecting these superficial markers of success, one of my first mentors in nightlife said, "Scott, you're too nice. If you're going to do this right, you need to be seen out every night, spending money, with a hot model on your arm."

Mission accomplished. But somewhere along the way, the sameness of nightlife—booze, drugs, girls, repeat—made me restless. I wanted change, and the more things stayed the same, the more booze, drugs, and girls I'd needed to force my mind and body to show up for work with a smile. It's like what Ernest Hemingway said about going bankrupt: It happened gradually, then suddenly. For me, "suddenly" would involve a gun, a bottle of Scotch, and a cobalt-blue Mustang. But that comes later.

Over several weeks in the fall of 2003, I endured a battery of medical tests, searching for the cause of my numbness. Technicians examined my brain and spinal cord with an MRI and a CT scan, looking for possible culprits: tumors, blood clots, bone and tissue irregularities. Doctors put sensors on my arms and legs, monitoring the electrical activity from my brain to my muscles and nerves. Nurses stuck me with needles, drew blood, and ordered me to urinate in small plastic cups.

But in the end, all my tests came back normal. They couldn't find anything wrong with me. I was simply going numb.

"Maybe it's the cigarettes?" I said to my business partner, Brantly Martin, as I fumbled to open my third pack of Reds for the day. We were on our way to a club.

"Why don't you try to cut down to two packs and chill on the booze?" he offered.

We joked about it, but inside, I was gripped with a quiet certainty that I was dying of some terrible disease that the doctors and their tests had missed. I used to find humor in darkness. I even laughed in the face of death once. It was a few years back. I was high on ecstasy and trying to get a friend's attention, and I crashed my hands through the floor-to-ceiling windows of a building at New York University. The pane shattered into pieces, and shards of glass rained down, making cuts all over my face and hands. I bled all over the backseat of the cab on my way to the ER, but I couldn't stop laughing about it. I didn't care. At twenty-five, you think you're going to live forever. Until one day, you don't.

———

Alone in my loft later that night, I typed "numbness" into Google, trying to self-diagnose my condition. Trying to find a solution that the doctors couldn't. There, high in the results, among the generic medical advice, I was surprised to see a religious essay. I clicked the link and got lost in a sermon about spiritual numbness, about how one's conscience can become seared to the point where it no longer works. Near the end of the sermon, the author asked, "Are you right with God?"

As a child, I'd heard that question a hundred times from the pulpit, but now it filled me with existential terror. I wondered what would happen if I actually died. Would a childhood full of fervent bedtime prayers, Bible study, and church band still count? I wasn't so sure. I turned off my computer and climbed into bed, my right arm still tingling like a pincushion being poked by a thousand needles.

My father's worried voice filled my head. "Please pray for our son. He's gone prodigal," Dad would tell his friends at church.

It was true. When I left home at nineteen, I'd turned my back on faith, virtue, and just about everything else that mattered most to Chuck and Joan Harrison. I still called my parents every few weeks, though. Mom would always ask about my spiritual life. Dad would ask how the nightlife business was going, and then he'd pass along words of wisdom from the Bible, trying to reignite my interest in faith. "Uh-huh," I'd say, before changing the subject. That's how our conversations went for almost ten years. But now, at twenty-eight, although I'd never have admitted it to my father, I knew I had to change.

Just start over, I'd think to myself. *Do something different with your life.*

But I was too numb to make a move. And what would I do, anyway? You don't just leave nightlife and become a successful doctor or lawyer or banker. I felt trapped in the shallow end of the pool.

And so, every night, I'd snort another line of cocaine and pass the rolled-up bill to another pretty girl and think to myself, *This is not who I am. This is not who I want to be. This is not how I thought my life would turn out.*

2

Poison

On New Year's Day 1980, my mother collapsed in her bedroom, unconscious. I was four years old and asleep in my own room, so I have no memory of my father lifting her to her feet as she briefly regained consciousness and then passed out again.

It would take another year before my parents figured out what was wrong with her, twelve more months before they learned that an invisible gas was spreading throughout our two-story Colonial home, robbing Mom's body of oxygen and vitality.

Long-term, low-level exposure to carbon monoxide works like a steady drip of poison, with symptoms so subtle that doctors miss it all the time. For Mom, the effects came in the form of nausea; tight, throbbing headaches; and muscles that were too sore to lift a coffee cup. She figured she had the flu or was stressed out from having set up our new home.

We'd moved to Moorestown two months earlier so that my dad, Chuck, a sales manager for a manufacturing company, could shorten his one-hour commute to twenty-two minutes. The drab gray house wasn't love at first sight, but my parents liked that it was on a cul-de-sac in a quiet, tree-lined neighborhood, and that there was a respected elementary school at the end of the block. Pragmatism won out.

My mom, Joan, thrives on order. She wanted everything to be perfect in time for Christmas, so she spent weeks inside our polluted house, unpacking, organizing, and hanging paintings on the walls. When she passed out on the floor, Dad called our neighbor, Dr. Joe Winston. He gave Mom a physical exam, and she scheduled a series of appointments with an infectious disease specialist and an allergist. They discovered that she was mildly allergic to mold and pollen, but they couldn't find anything to explain the fatigue, soreness, or dizziness she was feeling. She kept looking for answers.

In the back of her mind, Mom wondered if chasing after me was just tiring her out. After all, ever since I learned to walk and talk, I'd been a strong-willed, curious kid with fast legs, a loud mouth, and boundless energy. Mom still tells the story about the time she took me with her to the bakery and I stuck my fingers into a fruit pie to find out if it tasted as good as it looked. She apologized to the baker and bought the pie. Next, we went to a bookstore, where I ripped the pages from a pop-up book. She bought the book. Next stop, a hardware store, where she rescued me seconds before I whipped a chainsaw off the shelf. That was the last time she took me shopping for a while.

The medical tests continued all throughout the spring, summer, and fall. But by winter, Mom was still sick and getting sicker. One day, she almost passed out making me oatmeal on the gas stove. Every time the heater in our house fired up, her heart would race.

"Joan, you do seem to feel better when you're outside," Dr. Winston said after reviewing another batch of inconclusive test results. "I wonder if something *inside* your house is making you sick?"

That clue sent Dad to the library to do research on indoor pollution. He called the Environmental Protection Agency, and spent hours talking to experts about asbestos, formaldehyde, radon, and other common household pollutants. He had the gas company inspect our furnace, stove, and water heater. A chimney expert examined the fireplace flue. But everything checked out okay.

"What's *happening* to me, Chuck?" Mom asked Dad one night in despair. "It's been a year, and I'm only getting worse. I'm scared." My dad, forever the optimist, is a consummate problem solver, but nothing he tried was helping her. Pretty soon his coworkers started questioning her illness. "Some women don't take to change well," they told him. "She's probably just upset with you about having to move."

Another colleague put it more bluntly: "Maybe it's all in her head."

If you ask Dad what first drew him to Mom, he'll grin and tell you, "Her long legs." In the summer of 1967, Dad spotted a pretty girl in a miniskirt at a party and walked up to introduce himself.

Mom took one look at the dark-haired naval officer in the crisp white uniform and knew exactly what she wanted. A few dates later, Joan Kleppinger informed her mother that she'd met the man she was going to marry. Chuck Harrison possessed all her "must-haves" for a husband. He was ambitious, smart, educated, tall, and good-looking. His sense of humor, she said, was a bonus.

At twenty-four years old, Mom had just earned a master's degree in English. She was kind and caring, smart but gullible, and easy to bring to laughter—the kind of girl who remains a virgin until her wedding night. Dad was twenty-six, a hard-drinking, hard-smoking former naval officer who served on a 370-foot U.S. Navy destroyer while putting himself through business school. They dated for a year, spending Thanksgiving with Mom's family and Christmas with Dad's. By New Year's Eve, Mom had practically picked out her wedding dress.

They got married in August of the next year, 1968, in a candlelight service. Mom walked down the aisle in a simple bridesmaid gown, arm in arm with her father. Mendelssohn's *Wedding March* filled the chapel. Traditional music, followed by traditional vows.

"Do you take this woman to be your lawful wedded wife, to love her in sickness and in health, for richer or for poorer, until death do you part?" the minister said.

"I do," Dad said, never taking his eyes off Mom—not knowing just how fiercely this vow would be tested.

Seven years later, on September 7, 1975, I came along, and then we were three. On the night I was born, Dad wasn't content to sit on the sidelines. Instead, he stood by Mom's side, watching the fetal monitor and coaching her through the contractions.

"Come on, now . . ." he said. "Okay. You're almost at the top. You've got it now! There you go!" The nurses called Dad the Howard Cosell of the delivery room.

At the time, Mom had been working as a feature writer and photographer for a suburban Philly newspaper, but she felt torn about going back to work. While second-wave feminism swept through the country and *Time* magazine awarded its 1975 Man of the Year cover to "American Women," Mom decided this wasn't her fight. She told my dad, "Jobs can wait, babies can't."

I can tell from family photo albums that this was the happiest time for her. She took me to the zoo and the children's museum, to parks and family gatherings. I don't have the memories to call upon, but I know that these were the only years in my life when Mom got to be a normal parent.

Around the time I turned two, Dad became reacquainted with an old fraternity brother who'd gotten married and become a born-again Christian. Something about this couple (how they lived their lives, how they treated one another with love and respect) intrigued Mom. She started reading the Bible and praying more regularly, and she encouraged Dad to attend a Tuesday-night Bible study in the couple's home. Out of curiosity mostly, he agreed to go.

"We may think that we are good people," the group's leader said one night, "but the Bible says that our good deeds are like filthy rags. Every one of us is sinful. We want to run our own lives, be our own boss. We don't want anyone telling us how to live, especially God."

Every Tuesday night, my parents would come home a little shaken up.

"Chuck, are we good people?" Mom would ask. They would lie

in bed talking for hours about their sins: envy, greed, impatience, selfishness.

Nine weeks into the Bible study, Mom and Dad dropped to their knees in their bedroom and gave their lives over to Jesus. From that day on, Dad stopped swearing—not an easy habit for a former naval officer to break. He also pulled out his checkbook and confronted something that had been nagging at his conscience. A few years back, he'd spent $400 on a wedding present at a store, but they lost the check and it was never cashed. Every time Dad balanced his checkbook and saw that extra $400, he felt lucky. But integrity was an important part of living like a Christian, so he wrote another $400 check and mailed it to the store with a note of explanation.

For me, our new Christian life meant that honesty, respect, and obedience were now the sacred bylaws of our household. I instantly became a Sunday school regular, and loved it. The pastor would share these fantastic stories from the Bible (Noah's ark, David and Goliath, Jonah and the whale) and hand out felt characters that we'd stick to a flannel board.

"Scott, you get up here and put the whale in the ocean," he'd say. "And Jill, can you take the sun down and put up the moon?"

Being a Christian family now—a family that read the Bible together, prayed together, and lived in service to Jesus—was everything to my parents. It's what inspired the move to suburban Moorestown. If we lived closer to Dad's work, it would help us do something else that Christian families do: spend more time together.

Dark clouds filled the skies on the day we pulled our moving van into the driveway of our new home, but the rain held off. Every piece of furniture seemed to fit in its place, and Mom was already imagining what a coat of paint and some landscaping could do to make the house beautiful. We had such high hopes for our new life.

3

___

Family

"I don't care what the gas company says!" Dad yelled. "Just rip it out! Get rid of it!"

Of all the experts dispatched to investigate Mom's illness, it was a plumber who finally solved the mystery. In early January 1981, a family friend who ran a plumbing/HVAC business went down to the basement and, on a hunch, pulled back the casing of the gas furnace. And there it was: three or four pinholes in the heat exchanger. Every time the heat came on, he explained, low levels of carbon monoxide had been escaping and circulating through our tightly sealed, energy-efficient home. Somehow the gas company had missed it. The friend helped Dad tear the heavy steel machine from the wall and throw it on the front curb, where it lay mangled and disarmed.

To confirm a diagnosis of carbon monoxide poisoning, Dr. Winston ordered a carboxyhemoglobin test, which would show the saturation level in Mom's blood. An amount over 2 percent in a nonsmoker is a classic indicator of CO poisoning; over 24 percent, and you risk cardiac arrest.

Mom's results came back at 25.

"I've never seen anything like this," Dr. Winston said.

We later learned that it's common for the homemaker to be hit hardest by a carbon monoxide leak. In our case, Dad spent most days at his office, breathing clean air, and I was at preschool or running around in the backyard with friends. But Mom worked inside all day, battling dizziness, headache, and fatigue. And the worse she felt, the more she stayed in the house.

With the mystery now solved, Dad sent me and Mom to live with a neighbor while he worked quickly to detox our home. He bought and installed a new gas furnace and electric water heater. Friends from church helped him rip out two thousand square feet of wall-to-wall carpeting, which might have contained formaldehyde or other chemicals that would trigger Mom's dizziness. They then worked their way through the house collecting rugs, cushions, and furniture pillows— anything with a chemical odor or under suspicion—and piled them in an upstairs guest room, a place we dubbed "the abandoned room." It all had to be stashed away until Mom got better.

But despite Dad's hard work, as soon as we moved back into our purified house, Mom got sick again. Even with the new furnace, her heart raced whenever the heat came on. So Dad turned the heat off. It was the dead of winter, and in order to keep warm, we slept in scratchy wool sweaters and hats, underneath layers of heavy blankets. It felt suffocating; to this day, I hate the feel of wool.

"What are we going to do?" Mom asked Dad one night, clearly in distress.

"I don't know," he said. "But it's freezing, and we can't stay here if the house is still making you sick."

He decided that we'd stay a few days at Mom's parents' place in Bethlehem, Pennsylvania, where he'd make more calls and dig deeper into home-purification research. If the situation didn't resolve itself, we'd stay with Dr. Winston's family until Dad figured out our next move.

My grandparents' house smelled like mothballs, musty carpets, and onions. Still, it was cozy and warm, and I loved it there. My feisty grandmother, who went by Garni, was always padding about her white linoleum kitchen floor, cooking savory stews and talking with her hands. After dinner, she would scold Mom for depriving me of sweets, and then sneak me handfuls of plastic-wrapped hard candies that made me hyperactive.

For as long as I can remember, sleep has been my enemy, action and constant movement my allies. And bedtime at Garni and Pop-Pop's house would arrive at the worst times—often in the middle of a James Bond movie. Hopped up on sugar, I'd sneak out of my bed in the attic and tiptoe down the stairs, secretly listening to Sean Connery persuade beautiful women to do things I didn't yet understand.

Pop-Pop, my grandfather, was quieter than Garni, with a big smile and a hidden mischievous streak. He taught me how to fish in a nearby limestone stream and gave me piano lessons on an old three-tiered organ in the house. My legs were too short to reach the foot pedals, but I pressed the keys with intensity.

"You don't have to bang them, Scott," Pop-Pop would say. "Gently does it!"

The pipe was Pop-Pop's one vice. He'd light up in the basement while rigging our fishing poles, and a whisper-thin trail of smoke would waft upstairs to Mom, plaguing her with chronic headaches. Other times, the smells of hairspray and perfume would assault Mom when Garni returned from the salon, or the neighborhood ladies dropped by for tea and biscuits. At the first hint of a vapor, Mom's head would tighten, and she'd get fidgety and nervous because she knew the pain was coming. After a while, even the aroma of Garni's kitchen became too much for her.

"Mother's cooking with onions again," she'd complain to my dad on the phone. "She knows how sick they make me, but she keeps using them."

She tried opening the bedroom window and stuffing rolled-up towels under the door, but nothing really worked. She'd leave the house and go on long aerobic walks in the nearby woods, angry about her predicament, angry that her parents didn't understand her illness. But then she'd remember that the Bible and her new faith told her to thank and praise God for everything.

"Praise you for that onion, Lord. Praise you for the onion," she'd repeat, pacing a new path in the tall grass at a furious clip.

By mid-January 1981, Mom still hadn't found relief, so we moved again—this time to the home of Dr. Winston and his wife, Arlita. We stayed with the Winstons for six glorious weeks while Dad worked to fix our toxic house once and for all.

The Winstons were a gold-medal Christian family: loyal and kind to one another, firm with rules and expectations. They assigned each of their five kids thirty minutes of chores a day (dishes, laundry, bed making), and they kept a list on their refrigerator door of other jobs the children could do to earn extra money (washing windows, mowing, polishing silver). I was five years old, my parents' adored only child, and had few responsibilities—that is, until the Winston kids taught me how to sweep a porch, rake leaves, and empty a trash can.

Every morning, as the Winston kids bounded down the stairs with full backpacks and marched off to school, I would do my best just to keep up. After school, the boys would throw me over their shoulders and roughhouse with me. They were athletic kids, and at any given moment, one of them would be heading off to a baseball tournament or wrestling match.

The Winstons taught me things about family and teamwork that have stayed with me to this day. And my parents learned that their only son could stand some firm discipline every now and then. It all started one bone-chilling cold day, when Arlita and Mom decided to take me on a walk.

"Get your jacket on, Scott," Mom said for the fifth time.

"But Mommy," I said, batting my eyelashes at her. "I don't neeeeeed to."

"Scott, please, just put it on," she pleaded.

"But I don't get cold when I'm walking and running!"

Mom chased me around the house, upstairs, downstairs, holding out my little red coat with extended arms, begging me to wear it. I wasn't the type of kid to throw a tantrum or pout. I knew that persuasion and charm went a lot further than whining. I also knew that Mom rarely had the energy to outlast me.

Arlita Winston, however, was different. After watching this dance for thirty minutes, she spoke up. "Joan, *stop*," she said. "Are we going for a walk or aren't we?"

"But he won't get his jacket on," Mom said.

"And *who's* in charge?"

Mom looked at me and crumpled into tears.

"Joan, I know you want to be a perfect mother," Arlita told her. "And Scott is a bright, creative child. But you have to teach him to obey you immediately. Delayed obedience is disobedience."

Arlita totally had my number. Mom used to call me a pint-size lawyer, as I guess most kids are. But Arlita and Joe were like Supreme Court justices, presiding over their five kids. Whatever parenting magic they seemed to possess, it worked. And before they knew it, my parents were watching in awe as I got right in line behind the Winston kids, welcoming the discipline, the chores . . . and the music lessons.

The Winstons required each of their children to learn an instrument, so there'd always be a cello, recorder, or clarinet lying around the house. When we moved in, I gravitated to their grand piano, though rarely playing it gently as Pop-Pop had instructed. Soon, I was pounding the keys at Sunday school, leading one hundred little worshippers in rousing renditions of "Jesus Loves Me." Years later, I got barred from the church band for a whole month because I kept sneaking up the volume on my keyboard amplifier.

"Scott, this isn't about the music," the pastor said. "This is about worshipping God."

I tried, unsuccessfully, to explain to him why the keyboard was the most important part of the ensemble and therefore should be the most audible. I was certain God agreed.

In the evenings, Dr. Winston would build a roaring fire and we'd all sprawl out on the couches or pillows on the living room floor. Arlita would bring out trays of cookies and hot cocoa, and we'd take turns reading aloud from *The Hobbit, The Chronicles of Narnia,* Sherlock Holmes stories, or Shakespeare's plays.

Although I never dared tell my parents, I secretly wanted to be adopted by the Winstons. To me, they were like the Brady Bunch: a perfect, all-American family of seven. In comparison, we were a weird threesome who lived in a cold house with a sick mom and no couch cushions.

One night toward the end of our six weeks with the Winstons, I heard Dad asking Joe and Arlita to pray for us. "I'm thinking about whether to sue the gas company," he said. He ticked off all the costs he and Mom had taken on: a new furnace, a new hot water heater, medical bills with no end in sight. As a matter of principle, shouldn't the company have to pay? Dr. Winston listened patiently and then asked Dad if he was ready to endure months or even years of litigation if the gas company decided to fight back.

"The effect that could have on Joan's health and on your family's spiritual well-being—it may not be worth it," he said.

Dad took Dr. Winston's advice. When it came to Mom's illness, he didn't want to be bitter. "God will provide for our expenses," he told my mom later that night.

In exchange for not suing the gas company, my parents received a settlement check in the mail for $1,500. When I was old enough to understand how little we received for our pain and suffering, I was offended. *Oops, we're so sorry we poisoned you and ruined your life! Don't spend it all in one place!* For Dad, though, the matter was settled forever.

"Now, Joanie," he said. "We simply have to *forgive* them." He meant it, too.

Shortly after my parents proclaimed their forgiveness, Dad and I were approached by a local photographer to model for an ad campaign. Dad said yes, thinking it would be a fun father-son activity. For about an hour, the guy took a bunch of shots of me holding a football and talking to Dad as he pretended to read his newspaper. When it was all over, I got $50.

Weeks later, my parents picked up the local paper and were shocked to see our photo in a full-page ad for . . . a *gas company.*

Dad held the paper up and laughed out loud. "You know, God!" he said. "What a sense of humor you have."

4

Getting Pure

By March 1981, we had moved out of the Winstons' house. For the rest of that spring, Mom's symptoms remained frequent and unpredictable. An urgent new rhythm had entered our lives, one of constant retreat from invisible attackers.

Whenever Mom's headaches or dizziness flared up, we'd climb into her white Ford Taurus station wagon and drive until we found an open field or a park. If her symptoms came at night, we'd camp in our car as a family, rolling our windows all the way down so Mom could breathe in the clean air.

One evening, the wind blew in our direction off a nearby four-lane highway. Just after midnight, Mom woke up sick, and asked me to come with her on an adventure. We drove a few miles "upwind" to a friend's barn, on the other side of the highway. As we unpacked our sleeping bags, a big horse with a thick brown mane let me get close enough to stroke its muzzle. I could feel its hot breath on my face. I remember tossing my bag down in a pile of scratchy hay and never feeling happier. But minutes later, Mom smelled exhaust from the highway. The wind had changed direction again, and we had to keep moving.

I loved being Mom's traveling companion. I loved the long hikes with her in the woods, listening to the loud whish-whish-whish of her red snow pants, watching her hands cut through the air like a soldier's. I loved wandering through strangers' homes, and meeting new kids who had new toys to play with. If we couldn't lead a normal life like the Winstons', then I'd embrace our nomadic existence. I was happiest anywhere but inside our cold, contaminated home.

Dad never gave up trying to find a solution to Mom's illness. After dinner one night, in May of 1981, four months after we'd discovered the carbon monoxide leak, he announced a new plan: "I think we should try seeing a doctor who specializes in environmental and food allergies—a clinical ecologist." Dad had just learned of a twenty-one-day program at a small hospital in Pennsylvania run by a doctor known for treating people with problems like Mom's. Clinical ecology was a new and controversial science, Dad said, but Dr. Winston had looked into the program and agreed that it was worth a try.

"You'll be in a chemically pure room for three weeks," Dad said. "You'll have to fast for the first five days, but then you'll get to eat one type of food at every meal, so they can measure your reaction and figure out which foods you're allergic to."

"But I don't have food allergies," Mom protested.

"Apparently, that's what a lot of patients with environmental illness think."

Clinical ecology works on the assumption that our bodies are like rain barrels, with a finite capacity for allergens. Most of us can process the day-to-day offenders—smog, pollen, animal dander, pesticides, dust—but if you suffer a massive chemical exposure as my mom did, your barrel fills up, and any new allergens can cause an overflow. The idea was that if the doctors could identify and eliminate Mom's food triggers, her body would have fewer allergens in the barrel, and she'd start to feel better.

"Do you really want me to do this?" Mom said.

"I'm not sure," Dad said. "But nothing else seems to be working."

The following Monday, Dad dropped me at Garni and Pop-Pop's, and checked Mom into the ecology unit of a small redbrick hospital three hours away, in Montrose, Pennsylvania. Mom had packed stationery, knitting needles, and a stack of Christian books to keep herself occupied during her stay.

Under a doctor's supervision, she drank nothing but springwater for the first five days, purging her body of food and chemicals. On day six, they brought her a bowl of dates, but she had the appetite to eat only four. After every one of these "single-food meals," Mom had to rank the severity of her reactions. She soon learned that beef gave her diarrhea, milk messed with her concentration, corn produced muscle aches, and lamb triggered migraines. These foods were now off-limits.

Each night over the next two weeks, Dad would call and cheer Mom on at the discovery of a new "safe food."

"She's got buckwheat!" he'd yell to me and Garni.

Another night, it was potatoes: "Oh, that's *great*! Potatoes are filling!"

Still, every time a new food was declared unsafe, Mom became paralyzed with fear. How could she possibly be a normal wife and mother when she couldn't even bake her son a birthday cake or roast a Thanksgiving turkey? She'd open her Bible, hoping to find a verse that revealed God's will.

Well, God knows that I need at least twelve safe foods to follow this diet, she'd say to herself. *So I'm not going to worry.*

By the end of the program, Mom had tried forty-eight foods and identified exactly twelve she could eat, including fish, organic rabbit, quinoa, cashews, and buckwheat. Dad found a health food store and stocked up. And because tap water, with its fluoride and chemical additives, was no longer safe, he tracked down the Artesian well that the ecology unit used to source spring water for their patients.

The well was located a couple miles from the hospital, on the side of the road, under a cracked wooden trellis. Dad backed up to it in the station wagon and spent twenty minutes filling heavy glass bottles with the pure, ice-cold liquid.

"Joanie, this water is a gift straight from God!" he said.

I remember thinking how cool that was. I'd never really thought about where water came from, and I certainly never imagined it was hiding in the ground, deep beneath our feet.

By the time Mom came home from the hospital in June, Dad and I were so happy to see her that nobody said anything about the dark circles under her eyes, or about how frail she looked at five foot seven and 106 pounds. Things got even worse as she followed her new diet. Her weight dropped to a dangerously low 96 pounds, and she was soon all pointy hips and sharp cheekbones. But while this new way of eating did decrease the intensity of some symptoms, she still couldn't get relief. A strict diet clearly wasn't enough. Purifying our home wasn't enough. Moving around from place to place wasn't enough.

In October 1981, Dad went to a clinical ecology convention in Pennsylvania, where he attended seminar after seminar on environmental allergies. He came home with sobering news.

"Joanie, you're just going to have to isolate yourself from everything that gives you a reaction," he said.

"Everything?" she said. "Do you mean I can't get together with my friends or go to the store?"

It was actually worse than that. It meant no more Bible study group, no more grocery shopping, holiday parties, or driving the car. Mom's immune system needed to be completely quarantined in order to build it back up to fighting level.

Mom looked shocked. Her world was getting smaller and smaller. She felt cornered. But she had no other choice.

Scientists say that the average human nose can detect a trillion different smells. By the age of eight, I'd honed my olfactory system to protect my mother. Common odors that you or I might find mildly unpleasant—a mist of hairspray, black tar baking on the road, freshly cut grass mingled with gas-mower fumes—would hit Mom like a toxic tidal wave. So, with bloodhound accuracy, I learned to sniff out cologne on someone's handshake and warn Mom to keep away. If I noticed a new-plastic smell on one of my toys, I'd quickly throw the toy in the yard to outgas. To this day, I have a visceral revulsion for the scent of fabric softener sheets and nail polish remover, two things that brought on some of Mom's worst symptoms.

At one point, Mom even began reacting to the TV, radio, microwave, and computer—basically anything that emitted electromagnetic radiation. She couldn't talk on the phone for more than five minutes without getting dizzy, so she covered the receiver in tinfoil and kept a small minute timer nearby to limit her calls.

When she lost the energy to cook or do laundry, we relied on the kindness of friends from church. At one point, an army of fourteen different women took turns cleaning our house, grocery shopping, and babysitting me while Mom hunkered down in her bedroom. Anyone who wanted to come in close contact with her would receive a list of instructions on how to prepare:

1. Shower and bathe with Ivory soap.
2. Wash hair with Almay hypoallergenic shampoo or Ivory soap.
3. Be naturally beautiful: no makeup, deodorant, perfume, or hand/body lotions.
4. Launder your clothes in baking soda.

Dad and I had to "get pure" as a matter of ritual. Ivory soap's singsong slogan, "99.44 percent pure," could have been written for the Harrisons. Before getting near Mom, I always showered and changed into fresh clothes to get rid of the scents I'd picked up at school. But some of the volunteers didn't get pure enough. They'd slip up and use scented lotion on their skin or dryer sheets on their clothes, so eventually Mom banished all visitors from our home. There was no way to know if they'd followed the purification rituals correctly.

From then on, most of the cooking, cleaning, and laundry fell to me. Each day, Mom made a list of chores (empty dishwasher, clean kitchen floor, make bed, etc.) and stuck it to the fridge. I could take on extra work for more money: fifty cents for cleaning the bathroom, a dollar or two for vacuuming and mopping all the rooms, or a few bucks more for washing windows inside and out. Like the Winston kids, I took on my new jobs with gusto.

By nine years old, if I wasn't practicing piano or playing soccer in the backyard with friends, I'd be scrubbing our bathroom walls and making them sparkle. I'd tie a yellow balloon to the kitchen mop, watching it bounce and bob as I swabbed the linoleum with Basic H, a safe, biodegradable household cleaner. I didn't always enjoy doing chores, but I tried finding ways to make them fun.

I learned how to cook, too. Mom's rotation diet was easy to prepare, often no more than a bowl of string beans for breakfast, walnuts for lunch, and fish for dinner. Because the oven triggered symptoms, I'd cook her cod in the microwave for six minutes until the lifeless slab of white flesh oozed in its own congealed gravy. No seasoning, no lemon—just stinky, slimy nuked fish. I'd carry it to her room at arm's length with a smile. If it looked like she was feeling down, I'd bring my portable keyboard upstairs and play music for her while she ate.

At first, I felt a deep sense of pride at being so necessary to my mother. How many of my friends could say they did this much for their family? Plus, having my own money gave me freedom. I'd ride my bike alongside the abandoned train tracks and buy Fun Dip and Skittles at the local 7-Eleven. By age eleven, I was earning pocket change by knocking on neighbors' doors and selling them Christmas cards, raking their leaves, and mowing their lawns. I learned how to greet strangers with a smile, make them laugh, and get them to like me. Mom said I had a knack for it.

When Dad got home at the end of his day, the two of us would sit at the dinner table to eat steaming hot Hungry-Man microwave dinners, the kind with Salisbury steak, mashed potatoes, and apple crumble, each in its own little compartment. I'd always try to eat the dessert first. Hoping to have some hand in parenting me, Mom made me a cardboard sign listing eight "Mealtime Manners," including "Chew with mouth closed," "Don't use fingers," "Napkin on lap," and "Don't clank teeth with utensil." She was determined that her son would learn proper etiquette, even if she wasn't there to enforce it.

Though we lived like bachelors, Dad always tried to make the best of it. He'd put plastic cups over his ears and stick out his tongue to make me laugh. After dinner, if it was still light out, we'd bike around the neighborhood together or fire BBs into phone books in the back-yard. Or he'd challenge me to an epic Ping-Pong battle in our base-ment, playing left-handed to give me a chance at scoring a few points.

When I think of Mom, she's always wearing a large carbon filter face mask to protect her from the evil smells and chemicals she couldn't see. All I could see were her big green eyes, brown wavy hair, and the charcoal-gray cover that hung like a catcher's mask over her mouth and nose. Sometimes, I'd stick my own face in one of her masks, to see what it felt like to be Mom. It smelled like damp, gray sickness.

For a long while, Mom's protective veil had been unremarkable to me, as natural as seeing another mom in pearl earrings. But by the time I became a teenager, her mask was a constant reminder of the burden we carried as a family. I loved my mother. I knew she was miserable from living in a body that was in a continual state of civil war. But the older I got, the more I tired of being her foot soldier in that endless battle. I felt like our family was stuck in the trash compactor from *Star Wars*, knee-deep in muck and metal as the giant walls slowly closed in. Except, there was no one to call for help. No one to save us from being crushed.

5

Slide

Sneaking across the hall late one night with a portable radio, I stopped in front of the bathroom where Mom slept. It was her safe room, and she always kept the door closed. After fumbling in the darkness and finding the grooves of the wall outlet, I plugged the radio's power cable into the socket.

The speakers squawked with white noise, and I quickly turned the volume all the way down. Had she heard me? I held my breath and waited. Hearing nothing but crickets chirping outside, I slowly raised the antenna and pushed the speakers flat against the bathroom door, blasting radio waves straight into Mom's body.

This is a test, I thought. *This is only a test.*

Back in my room, I crawled into bed, excited to wake up in eight hours and claim a moral victory over my mother. *See, Mom? You're not allergic to radio waves. And you're probably not allergic to the TV, either. It's all in your head.*

At almost sixteen, I was pushing toward full-blown teenage angst. A couple of years earlier, we'd finally moved from Moorestown and found a two-story home in rural Stockton, New Jersey. Set on four acres, far from the auto fumes of the highway, and bordered by lush woods, the house had been Dad's last-ditch hope for Mom's recovery. But on the day we moved in, she immediately got sick, and Dad began the all-too-familiar environmental detective routine again.

He discovered that the polyurethane coat on our hardwood floors emitted fumes that could take two years to outgas. So, for now, Mom would spend her time between an outdoor shelter and the upstairs bathroom, her safe room. She slept on an old army cot sandwiched between the tub and toilet. One afternoon, Dad and I wrapped the bathroom door in shiny aluminum foil to trap any lingering scent of wood varnish.

Outside in the backyard, a friend's father built Mom a crude plywood lean-to. Most days, she would sit out there on a folding chair, with a small red Igloo cooler by her side, filled with her special food. Dad would come home after work, pull up a chair downwind, and cheerfully ask, "How was your day, dear?" as if Chuck and Joan Harrison were like every other family in rural New Jersey. Mom tried to stay positive, but sometimes it took all her strength to reach across the pain and mental fog and report that the highlight of her day had consisted of watching a tiny bug land on her leg and then crawl up and down her arm before flying away.

Sometimes, when Mom yelled across the yard to me, I'd pretend not to hear. In some ways, I'd become her biggest antagonist. I got sloppy around the house, leaving my clothes on the floor, lights on in empty rooms, and faucets running—risking the $1-per-item fines my parents eventually instituted as punishment. I posted a sign on my door warning them to STAY OUT, and fought them constantly over the house rules.

"*Normal* parents let their kids stay up past ten p.m.," I'd argue. "And *normal* parents let their kids watch R-rated movies."

But Dad never budged, at least not on the movies. One time, he found a forbidden videotape hidden under the living room couch. I don't recall the exact title, but I do remember watching Demi Moore's sex scenes in *St. Elmo's Fire* and *About Last Night* over and over again in secret, finding them both shocking and wonderful. When Dad discovered my contraband, he took me to the garage and made me watch as he shoved the video in a vise and turned the handle until the tape exploded. Black R-rated plastic flew in the air, almost blinding us both.

Mom and Dad were a unified front. Without discipline, they reasoned, I would grow into a man of low moral character, my own worst enemy. But to me, their rules felt suffocating, meant to make my world as small as Mom's. So when Mom started saying that I couldn't listen to the radio nearby or watch TV because it made her sick, I began to wonder if her symptoms were even *real*. What if she was nuts? What if she was making this all up just to make me miserable? That's when I decided to test her.

The radio waves silently bombarded Mom as she slept. I couldn't wait to see her face in the morning when I told her what I'd done.

How're you feeling, Mom? Huh? You're fine? Guess freaking what? I blasted you with the radio all night long!

But instead of proving me right, she woke up feeling hyperactive and scared. She didn't understand why she was having a severe reaction in her safe room, or what she'd done wrong. Ashamed, I never questioned her illness again.

Not that this changed my rebellious trajectory. While Mom slowly made peace with a life behind tinfoil-covered walls, I was pounding against walls of my own. I dreamed of escaping our small town for a new and bigger life. In particular, I dreamed of escaping my tiny Christian school.

New Life Christian School was a K–12 private school housed in the basement of a church. It had only about five classrooms, with nine kids to a class, and we learned by VHS tape. They would literally roll our "teachers" in on metal TV cabinets, the ones with the gray ribbed mats. A class monitor would pop in a tape and press Play, and our math, biology, or English class would begin. Those forty-five-minute videos felt like they lasted forty-five hours. Even worse, we didn't have a proper playground or cafeteria. We played kickball in the parking lot and ate lunch in the church's fellowship hall. It was bad enough that my home life felt so weird. Did my school have to be so strange, too?

At New Life, students wore a mandatory uniform of dark-green pleated chinos, a plaid tie, and a collared shirt the hue of dark urine. Instead of buying the standard-issue shirts, I made Mom and Dad get me ones that were a slightly lighter yellow, just so I could feel original. I even kept a secret stash of street clothes under the sink in the boys' bathroom. When the final bell rang at 2:50 p.m., I'd race to the bathroom, rip off my uniform, and waltz past my classmates in regular clothes as if I were Superman.

By the time I turned sixteen in the summer of 1991, I'd had enough. One night at dinner, I announced to my parents that I was done with New Life and was going to public high school in the fall.

"Scott, you have a lot of love and support at New Life," Mom said.

"I know the teachers really care about you," Dad added.

"I don't care," I said. "I want to go to Central High."

"You know what happens to kids who go there and fall in with the wrong crowd," Dad said. "They experiment with drinking, sex, maybe even drugs. And they never find their way back to God." Classic Dad, always preaching his warnings to me.

"You simply cannot make me go back to New Life," I pleaded. "I'll run away from home if you try to stop me."

They didn't. As much as they wanted me in a "safe" Christian environment, my parents knew that having a TV for a teacher wasn't challenging me. They knew the academics at Central were a world apart, so they just prayed, hoping that God would keep me on the straight and narrow.

It took exactly one day at Hunterdon Central Regional High for me to lose my status as the cool, rebellious kid. This was a real high school, with jocks, cheerleaders, skaters, thespians, and rockers. Here, without my uniform, I was the quintessential skinny nerd in ironed L.L.Bean khakis and a mock turtleneck. There were one thousand kids in my grade alone, an exhilarating upgrade. But I felt invisible and hungry for attention.

Walking between classes one day, I overheard two seniors talking about a band they were trying to form. One of them looked like he lived at the gym, and the other guy had more facial hair than I had body hair.

"We just need a good keyboard player," said the ripped one with tattoos and a Metallica T-shirt. I snapped to attention.

"Hey!" I said, tapping his shoulder. "*I'm* a keyboard player!"

They turned around and stared at me blankly.

"*Thirteen years* I've been playing piano!" I said in a voice easily one octave higher than theirs. "*Thirteen years!*"

I kid you not, I was wearing a thin polyester black-and-white keyboard tie that day. A tie. At high school. Maybe it persuaded them, or perhaps my timing was just good. In any case, it felt like fate.

"*Oh*. Okay, cool," said Metallica. "What's your name, kid?"

They invited me to their next band practice, and I was in. From that day on, the band became everything to me. We'd practice in Metallica's sweaty, 105-degree garage with frayed Oriental rugs covering the walls, and perform at drunken college frat parties in New Jersey and Pennsylvania. I brought a Bruce Hornsby/Billy Joel influence to the other guys' '90s alt-rock sound. Imagine Counting Crows meets Live meets Pearl Jam. We called ourselves Sunday River, after a ski resort we'd heard of in the Northeast. I don't think any of us had ever been there.

We were an odd mix. These guys were nothing like my Christian school friends, who studied hard and dated nice girls whom they hoped to marry in a proper church wedding. The Sunday River guys smoked pot, swore like sailors, cut class, and got laid. As the youngest guy in the band, I was the sober virgin. I wrote soulful ballads and dutifully drove the band's gear to our shows in the family station wagon.

But I hustled, too. As soon as we had ten original songs, we recorded a demo in a studio, and I distributed our CDs far and wide. I cold-called managers and club owners from New York to LA: *You'll be so packed, you're going to have to turn people away at the door . . . Brian's got a killer voice, and you need to hear it . . . There's no Top Forty band with keys so strong!* I was a little surprised when my pitches actually worked and I landed us professional gigs in the city, at places like CBGB, the Wetlands, and the Bitter End, and at battle-of-the-bands competitions.

As Sunday River took off, I became a ghost at Central High. Classes no longer held my interest, and I cut so many days of school that I almost didn't graduate. To this day, my parents tell people that on the morning of my graduation, they had no idea whether I'd be on the dais.

At home, I was constantly exploding in anger, so Dad started taking me to a Christian counselor—a kind, balding guy named Bob Wendt. With Dad sitting alone out in the waiting room, Mr. Wendt would usually talk to me first. I'd unload all my grievances: *I want to go out with my friends on weeknights instead of studying and I want to be allowed to drive into New York City to promote the band and I don't need a bedtime anymore and why on earth should I still have to show up at mealtimes?* Put simply, I wanted total freedom.

Then Mr. Wendt would ask Dad to come in. Having used the time waiting to carefully compose a battery of his own complaints, Dad would fire them off one by one. I was disrespectful, irresponsible, self-centered. I was sullen and evasive. I lied. The counselor tried to play peacemaker and help each of us see the other's position. And while counseling may have kept our family from imploding during my senior year, it certainly wasn't changing me.

Once, during our weekly session, Dad and I were talking about my future when Mr. Wendt drew symbols on two slips of paper and asked me to choose one. The first paper had a cross; the second had a dollar sign. I quickly chose the second.

Dad looked down, defeated. I think something deep inside him changed in that moment. He later told me that he pleaded with God to guide me, because he just didn't think he had the will to do it anymore.

As a sign of my allegiance to the almighty dollar, I bought my first car: a cherry red 1980 BMW 318i with 185,000 miles on it. My parents warned that it would cost more to keep it running than what I'd paid for it. Whatever. I needed that car. I loved the sunroof, the orange analog lights, and the stick shift with the custom leather ball. Racing her into the school parking lot each morning felt like showing up with the prom queen.

My parents disapproved, but that was nothing compared to how they felt when I rejected the Christian colleges that Dad had selected for me to visit. They'd picked two: Wheaton College, in Illinois, which Dad called the "Harvard" of Christian schools, and Gordon College, in Boston.

"*Ugh* . . . Why do I even *need* to go to college?" I'd said with typical youthful arrogance. "The band is going to make us all rich and famous."

"Scott," Mom said, "you'll regret it if you don't get a college degree."

I went through the motions, visiting both schools, but Dad didn't even bother to join me for the Wheaton tour because he knew I wasn't serious. I actually liked the campus, until I came across Wheaton's "virtue covenant," which all students were expected to sign: No premarital sex or pornography or drunkenness or gossip or bad language. More boundaries.

I came home delighted to deliver the bad news to Dad. "I could never go to a place like that," I said. "I just wouldn't be able to sign that thing and follow all those rules."

Dad, being a man of integrity, actually supported my decision. He couldn't bear the thought of his son spending four years there, lying through his teeth while breaking the virtue covenant.

We were at an impasse. Having barely graduated high school, and with no plans for college, I knew I couldn't live with my parents much longer. Nor did I want to. From their perspective, my disregard for the house rules was aggravating Mom's condition and adding stress to Dad's already challenging life. Mom listened to Christian tapes for strength: *Immature teenagers can be frustrating, but don't give in to your anger by kicking him out. He'll come under bad influences that could affect the course of his entire life.*

Maybe so, she thought. But something had to give.

———

At nineteen, I declared that I was moving to New York City to pursue a record deal for Sunday River. Given how tense our relationship had become, I think my parents were relieved to get me out of the house but disappointed that I wouldn't be going to college. Dad had been saving for it since I turned four, and had $100,000 ready for my education.

Still, in December 1994, after four months of looking for an apartment, he helped me move into a $650-a-month sublet in a six-floor walkup on Christopher Street, in the West Village. The apartment was 350 square feet.

That first night, I took a walk by myself around my new neighborhood. I soaked in the drunken laughter of couples ducking into bars, and strolled along wet sidewalks littered with cigarette butts. I peeked through the big windows of the S&M shops that lined my block. The stuff inside blew my mind. There were latex toys on display that actually scared me. I'd never seen anything like it.

The next morning, excited to have my first breakfast as a New Yorker, I headed across Sheridan Square to a bagel shop I'd read about in a city guide. But before I got there, a man holding a Sony 3CCD video camera box stopped me.

"Hey, kid," he said. "I'll give you a great deal. It's $700 new at Best Buy, but I'll sell it to you for $150 cash."

I'd really wanted one of the new Handycams, and this felt like too good a deal to pass up.

"Okay," I said. "Wait here?"

I ran to the ATM for the money, came back, and made the exchange. Scrapping my breakfast plans, I climbed the stairs back to my apartment and set the box down on the kitchen table, excited to charge my new toy. Grabbing a knife, I opened the box up to find a large gray rock wrapped in newspaper.

"What?" I yelled out.

Furious, I ran down the steps and back to the square, but the man was long gone. Welcome to the city, kid.

A few weeks later, I got a part-time job selling keyboards and synthesizers at the Sam Ash megastore in Times Square. I figured I could get discounts on musical gear for the band, and maybe even meet fellow musicians. One night after the store had closed, Stevie Wonder came in and bought $50,000 worth of gear. The manager let me look after him personally as he tried out synth after synth. Stevie was larger than life: flowing braids, genius hands, pearly-white smile. I couldn't believe it. Me and Stevie "Master Blaster" Wonder together in the keyboard section!

Life was good. I had a job and even found a manager for Sunday River, a guy named Daniel Belard. When he learned that I had a college fund I wasn't using, he encouraged me to take part-time classes at NYU to give the band "some class." I did, and broke the news to my parents like I was doing them a big favor.

Sunday River continued to play gigs in beer-stained rock 'n' roll venues. But I got my first taste of a proper New York City dance club at age nineteen, when Daniel brought me out to Club USA, a notorious Times Square hotspot. On the street outside, hundreds of people pushed against the red velvet ropes, trying to get noticed by the bouncer. Daniel walked straight to the front, made eye contact with the doorman, nodded in slow motion, and then watched the ropes part like the Red Sea before Moses.

Inside, half-dressed girls towered and spun over us on round pedestals, writhing for the crowd as house music blasted at earsplitting levels. Red and gold laser lights slashed and twisted in the fogged-up air. Drinking, smoking, dancing, sweating, and grinding—this place assaulted the senses. It was everything my parents had feared, all in one place and all at once.

But in the strangest way, as I climbed the stairs to the mezzanine level to take it all in, it felt like home. A long, twisting, Plexiglas slide connected the upper level of the club to the dance floor. (Decades later, it would be the only thing people remembered about the place.) I waited my turn for the slide, and when I finally got to the front of the line, I sat on the ledge, took one look at the giant, pulsing mass of humanity on the dance floor beneath me, and threw my body down the chute.

6

—

"Wishy-Washy, Twinkly-Twinkly Piano, Soft-Rock American Garbage"

Bands always seem to break up for the same reasons: drugs, alcohol, clashing personalities, and varying commitment levels. Sunday River was no different.

Looking back, the beginning of the end came in January 1995, when we played a gig for Music Box Live, a showcase at a supper club called Tatou. It was produced by a singer and dancer named Patrick Alan, who got his start as a casting director for the TV show *Star Search*. He'd worked with everyone from Michael Jackson and James Brown to Pharrell Williams. The energy and talent at the club were amazing, and when I saw people paying $20 a head to get in the door, I called Patrick.

"Hey, man, do you need an assistant? I'll work for free . . . I just want to learn more about the business."

"Really?" he said. "You're gonna work for free? *Okay*."

Patrick taught me how to create guest lists, work the crowd, and keep the acts moving. After paying the house band, he'd clear around $700, and he'd toss me $100 for my help.

In February, a few weeks after Patrick and I met, a legendary club on Fourteenth Street called Nell's invited him to produce an R & B open-mic night.

"You can come along," he said. "I'll cut you twenty percent."

I was in.

The night—which Patrick named "Voices at Nell's"—quickly took off. Months later, we were running the most talked about open-mic night in the city. Whitney Houston, Chaka Khan, Brian McKnight, and, yes, Stevie Wonder would show up unannounced to perform. Patrick taught me how to be a nightclub promoter—how to bring top talent to the stage and paying customers into Nell's. I worked hard, and he trusted me.

Voices at Nell's grew. But then, Patrick was invited to sing on a world tour for a musical called *Smokey Joe's Cafe*. We made a deal: For the next eighteen months of his tour, I'd run the showcase and put aside $200 a week for him. When he returned, I'd give him the cash and go back to being his assistant.

You can probably imagine where this story is headed. I was an immature nineteen-year-old, and eighteen months was an awfully long time. It didn't help that the manager of Nell's, a puckish punk rocker who went by the pseudonym Tex Axile, was constantly whispering in my ear, daring me to seize what was mine.

"Patrick? That guy's trouble," he said. "He expects you to do all the work for a year and a half and pay him? Pay him for what? Ditch him, and we'll do our own thing."

So I did. And when the *Smokey*'s gig ended, Patrick came home to find there was no money and no more Nell's for him. I don't think I even told him I was sorry.

Tex, who was almost twenty years older than me, became my new best friend and corrupter. He'd grown up in a small factory town in Sussex, England, and like me, had escaped to the big city (London, in his case) to earn fame and riches playing keyboard in a series of punk bands. Except Tex actually did it, collectively selling six million records in the '80s. His real name was Anthony Doughty; his stage name was a play on the words *tax exile,* a concept he considered when he didn't pay his for a couple years.

Tex had the foulest mouth of anybody I'd ever met, like a character in a Guy Ritchie movie. In addition to the frequent F- and C-words I already knew, I learned at least five or ten British swearwords I'd never heard before. Language that would've scandalized my parents or the teachers at New Life Christian School became shorthand between me and Tex.

As different as we were, Tex and I complemented each other. He was cynical, with no patience for prima donna types, while I was animated and deferential, eager to please any A-lister who walked in the door.

"Prince, what a pain in the *arse,*" Tex would say whenever the singer's two black limos pulled up outside Nell's. Meanwhile, I'd eagerly unscrew the lightbulb above The Artist's favorite corner booth—he liked to sit in the dark—and then lead him inside, pulling up a chair for his bodyguard, who'd sit facing the crowd to keep people away.

When the club shut down at 4 a.m., Tex would invite me and some friends to his apartment, a run-down loft above Nell's, where we'd blast music in his home recording studio and get hammered.

Tex *hated* my taste in music. "Wishy-washy, twinkly-twinkly piano, soft-rock American garbage," he'd say whenever I played the solo from Hornsby's "That's Just the Way It Is" for the umpteenth time just to annoy him.

A sophisticated cook with a sommelier's certification, Tex loved hosting impromptu four-hour dinner parties, with fresh bread, pasta, and expensive wine. Twice a year, a group of us would travel to his place in the French Pyrenees, a magical 1930s forester's home that he'd bought as a tranquil escape from his rock 'n' roll lifestyle.

Once, when I casually mentioned to my dad that I was traveling to Tex's house with a girlfriend, he sent me a four-page letter expressing his disappointment. "The reality hit me that you have completely abandoned your Christian upbringing and are not even ashamed of your behavior re: fornication," he wrote. I was twenty-four at the time and didn't have the heart to tell Dad that saving myself for marriage had been off the table for some years now.

Eventually, I think he figured this out, because when I asked him later about bringing a new girlfriend home, he laid down the law. "If you're going to sleep in our house, you'll follow our rules and sleep in separate bedrooms," he said. "There won't be any fornicating here."

"No problem, Dad," I said. "We'll just stay at a bed-and-breakfast in New Hope. Why don't you drive out and meet us for breakfast tomorrow?"

The next morning, he fumed over my lousy directions as he spent thirty minutes walking around New Hope, Pennsylvania, looking for the white Tudor manor where his son had just spent the night in sin.

But I didn't care. I was living out my teenage freedom fantasy. I could eat with my hands, slurp my soup, and leave all the lights on in my apartment if I wanted to. I kept my clothes in loose piles on the floor. My cash was piled in stacks of tens and twenties in the fireplace because, well, where else would you keep your cash if you had a non-working fireplace? And my mom, if she'd been well enough to visit, would have cringed at seeing how the walkway to my ground-floor apartment was littered with the cigarette butts I'd flicked out the window. It was messy because I was *living*.

Of all the changes instigated by my friendship with Tex, perhaps the most important was my decision to leave him and Nell's behind.

"You're a young man, and this is an old man's club," he said one night, after we'd been working together for five years. He knew me well enough to know that I was always reaching for the next rung. "Scott, once in a while, you have to break everything and move somewhere else," he said. "And if you want to get to the top, you need to work at Lotus."

Lotus, an Asian-inspired ten-thousand-square-foot supper club in Manhattan's Meatpacking District, was a mecca for fashion designers, supermodels, artists, media moguls, and the kind of people who actually *read* the articles in *Italian Vogue*. When it opened down the street from Nell's in the summer of 2000, the four owners landed on the cover of *New York* magazine.

I took Tex's advice and left message after message on the club's voicemail, pleading, "Let me promote for you. I can bring great people. Give me a shot."

After weeks of persistence, I finally got a break. One of the owners called me back and said, "Fine, you can promote Mondays"—the dead night. Still, I took that opportunity and made a career out of it. At Nell's, I'd looked after the needs of R & B superstars. At Lotus, *I* would be treated like a superstar.

7

Lord Scott Harrison

NEW YORK CITY, 2001–2003

Two bouncers lifted Brantly Martin's limp body off the dance floor. A few minutes earlier, we'd been celebrating my business partner's twenty-fourth birthday with bottles of Champagne, beautiful girls, and two hundred of our closest friends. Now he was passed out, and his lips were turning blue.

The bouncers carried Brantly away from the guests, across the lounge, and past a set of swinging doors into the kitchen. I followed them, briefly blinded by the harsh fluorescent lights. Brantly's long legs dangled lifelessly as they laid him on the cold cement floor. I dialed 911 as the owner of the club got down on his knees and started doing CPR.

Hang on, Brantly, I thought. *Please hang on.*

It was June 2001, and we'd been in business together for a year, promoting parties at Lotus and this venue, Halo, whose kitchen we had now conspicuously occupied. I knew Brantly was becoming a garbage head (club lingo for the kind of guy who'd take any drug you put in front of him), but he also had a tremendous tolerance. He could dance all night fueled by cocaine, vodka, and tequila shots, go home with two or three different women at once, and then shake off the morning paranoia with a hot coffee from Balthazar.

"I don't feel good or bad about it," Brantly would say whenever I tried to shame him over his all-night benders. "It's moral-neutral, Scott. Your internal guilt clock is exaggerated."

Maybe. Tonight, however, Brantly had gone too far. He'd snorted heroin thinking it was coke, or maybe just not thinking at all. Minutes later, I found him twitching and convulsing on the floor. And now, watching the club owner frantically perform CPR, I was sure Brantly was going to die.

"C'mon, man!" we were all yelling at him. "Wake up, bro!"

Just as the paramedics burst through the kitchen door, Brantly sputtered and coughed. He was alive. I took a deep breath and realized just how fast my heart had been pounding. Someone put a cold compress on Brantly's neck, and he slowly gained consciousness.

"Just another night at the club," the owner growled, as he washed his hands in the sink.

When Brantly came to, he looked up to see a circle of friends and medics standing over him. His eyes lit up, and he seemed amused, like we were all about to break out in a rendition of the "Happy Birthday" song. He laughed so hard, you'd have thought he was having the time of his life. That was Brantly. That was us. Invincible.

When we first met in the summer of 2000, Brantly was a twenty-three-year-old doorman at Lotus. He'd grown up in Houston, gone to college in Austin, and then had moved to New York to find adventure. Tall and athletic, he had clear blue eyes, long brown hair, and a dark, brooding wit. I was twenty-five, skinny and a bit slump-shouldered, but I ran my mouth with a cocky confidence.

The moment we met, I knew Brantly would make a great business partner. Gregarious and articulate, he could talk with authority about David Lynch films, then switch gears and quote Charles Bukowski. He'd riff on Henry Miller, then say in Spanish, "Comprende, cabron?"—all while never losing the thread of the conversation. Girls flocked to him, which was a definite plus. We instantly hit it off, started hanging out, and decided to promote together.

Nightclub promoting is an unusual occupation. You don't own the brick and mortar, and you don't pay the liquor and electricity bills. It's asset-light, so to speak. At high-end venues like Lotus, there are two categories of promoter. Filler promoters, or "subs," pack the place with ordinary paying customers and make it look busy. I was the other kind of promoter, an image promoter, tasked with upholding Lotus's status as the coolest club in Manhattan. Image promoters bring in the people whom the rest of the room wants to look like. Check out any Saint Laurent or Calvin Klein ad and you'll get an idea of whom I'm describing: six-foot-plus seductresses in miniskirts, guys with wavy hair and perfect teeth, rock 'n' rollers in skinny jeans and leather jackets.

Every week, Brantly and I would call a hundred people—going down a phone list of models, modeling agency contacts, women we met at parties—and ask *Hey, wanna come out tonight? We're having a pool party,* or *It's Tara's birthday,* or *We have an epic DJ in from Paris spinning tonight.*

To succeed as promoters, to really *work* a party, we needed to get people wasted and show them a great time, a formula that revolved around "models and bottles." Any wealthy banker can buy a good bottle of Champagne for $60 and drink it at home. It was my job to persuade him to spend $600 on that same bottle for the privilege of drinking it alongside a coterie of beautiful people with exotic names.

At the end of the evening, for all our promoting efforts, Brantly and I were entitled to a percentage of the night's liquor sales, and often all the cash at the door. For example, if the club sells $50,000 worth of liquor on a Saturday, that's at least five grand in your pocket for a night's work of partying.

Brantly and I reveled in shutting down the hedge fund guys in suits who tried to buy their way to a VIP table. To be included in the parties we were throwing, you couldn't just be rich. You had to be vetted by us. You had to kiss the ring and prove that you could be trusted to spend money and behave yourself. The girls—that's what we called them—always had to feel comfortable. Bring in some new rich guy who drinks too much and tries to get handsy with the girls, and that'll be his last night.

For those on the inside, a typical night went like this: You'd join me and Brantly, a few other wealthy guys, and maybe a dozen models and socialites—the "jewelry," as Tex called them—for dinner at 10 p.m. (The restaurant would comp our entire meal as a thanks for bringing the eye candy.) Then, just after midnight, we'd all head to Lotus, where a crowd would already be gathered outside. A doorman would usher us past the dance floor to the VIP section, a raised platform at the center of the club, protected by another doorman and another velvet rope. It was there that we'd watch our girlfriends dance on the tables and bask in the spotlight without being bothered by the "B-listers" below.

Sometimes we'd all slip up to the "secret room," a private lounge behind a hidden door on the mezzanine level. The heavy door had a digital keypad lock with a code that changed daily, and a special pass-through window for the bartender to send in drinks. A lot of sex, drugs, and madness went down in *that* room. We'd emerge the next morning, pass the cleaning crew mopping the sticky floors on our way out, and joke, "Where did everybody go?"

By 2001, Brantly and I were running the hottest Thursday-night party in Manhattan. Peter Beard, Heidi Klum, and Sean Penn were regulars, mixing fluidly with the socialites and starving artists. On a good night at Lotus, you'd see Puff Daddy seated at Table 1, Jay-Z at Table 3, and Brantly and me sandwiched between them at Table 2.

We were "young, flashy bucks," in the words of veteran club owner and nightlife queen Amy Sacco. But beneath all the fun, we were dead serious about our business. We'd built a mailing list of fifteen thousand names and became one of the first promoter teams to send mass invitations via email. Back then, email was such a novelty that our "open rates" were almost 100 percent.

As our partnership boomed, I became obsessed with excellence and growth. Maybe my mother's perfectionism and my father's discipline had left a mark on me after all. I was the guy who came to every meeting on time with a line-item budget already prepared. Once, I convinced Lotus management to throw away thousands of expensive invitations because the printer had misspelled the word *recommended.*

Brantly cared less about meetings and typos, but we both enjoyed coming up with creative ways to build buzz around the club. We once filled Lotus with a hundred beach balls, hired a lifeguard to sit at the top of a big white stand, and billed the whole thing as a pool party. Everyone showed up in bikinis and flip-flops. Another time, we threw a pajama party and let in only the people who'd come wearing their pj's. As we moved from club to club, we'd partner with top modeling agencies, fashion magazines, and well-known photographers, leveraging their brands to create more hype.

And just so they'd never miss a moment of their prodigal son's escapades, I put my parents on our mailing list. Every time she received a flyer in the mail with a half-dressed Vargas girl or a nude model wrapped in an American flag, Mom would roll her eyes and handwrite notes to God on them—"180-degree turn, please Lord" or "Dear Lord, Let us all 3 celebrate when Scott's eyes and heart are opened to You and Your Kingdom." She saved the cards in boxes next to the Mother's Day cards I gave her as a kid.

By 2001, Brantly and I had started our own S corporation—creatively named Brantly&Scott Inc.—and opened up a joint bank account, which never had more than a few hundred dollars in it. I'd drain the account on travel expenses, Brantly on drugs, and we'd fight about money like an old married couple—that is, until we'd get drunk, forget about it, and jump on a friend's plane to the Formula One race in Montreal or Fashion Week in Milan. Brantly and I once stamped through our entire passports in a single year.

When we flew on our own dime, it was always coach. So I changed all my frequent flier names to *Lord* Scott Harrison, in the hope that my experience in economy would improve.

Would you like a mimosa in seat 36E, Lord Harrison?

Why, yes. Yes, I would.

One time, Brantly and I spent two sleepless nights in Paris. On our last morning, we did some blow and then drank tall glasses of beer in a café by the Seine, like we were tortured souls following in the footsteps of Hemingway and F. Scott Fitzgerald. A lot of my memories from the Lotus years bleed into one another, so I have trouble drawing out the exact moment when things started to get ugly. But I know that by the time we showed up at the Air France ticket counter for our return flight, we were coked up and reeking of booze. I was a mess, yelling at the desk clerk in French—butchering the language, as Brantly always liked to point out—and demanding that Lord Scott Harrison be given the exit row window.

When they finally let us board, I crawled into one of the bathrooms, curled up in the fetal position on the floor, and passed out for the entire flight back to New York. I remember the look of shock on the flight attendant's face as she roused me at the start of the descent and asked, "Were you in there the whole time?"

By 2003, Brantly and I were club royalty, but I was starting to feel the weight of the crown. Officially, we worked two to three parties a week, but our days off were spent taking clients to dinner, bouncing from club to club to show our faces, and meeting new people who could be useful in our inner circle.

The nights felt endless—and they often were. After hitting the clubs, instead of going home, we'd head to an after-hours joint in the East Village called Brownies, which didn't even open until 4 a.m. (and you had to know the secret knock just to get in). We'd approach the tiny bar first to buy a couple dime bags of blow, and then settle at a booth in the back. Invariably, someone would try to cut the coke with a credit card right there at the table, and the manager would yell, "Only in the bathroom! You know the rules!" We'd wait until he turned his back, and then the girls would laugh and take turns snorting through a rolled up hundred-dollar bill. Not wanting to wait, I'd pour a little on the base of my thumb to bump.

Brantly and I had developed a few tricks over the years to stave off the brutal hangovers that came with the job. We'd try hard to stick to one kind of booze, and then chase three Advil before bed with a half gallon of water. But nothing could cure the gnawing shame I felt each time I stumbled out into the sunlight after a long evening.

The more successful we got, the more I polluted my body, and the darker my cloud of guilt became. By September 2003, the bizarre bouts of numbness had started. I was a mess. But for some reason, I kept calling my parents every few weeks—and they kept answering the phone. They never gave up on me.

One night, not long after my twenty-eighth birthday, Dad inquired, as he always did, about my drinking. I finally blurted out, "Dad, you don't get it. I *have* to get drunk just to put up with the same inane conversations every night."

"*Oh,*" he said, an uptick in his tone. "It's starting to wear thin, huh?"

There was a time when I reveled in tormenting my parents. I'd pick up the phone and joke, "Oh, hi, Dad. Hold on. Let me turn off the porno I was watching. Ha ha!" Or after he'd innocently asked how I was doing, I'd say, "Not great, I'm sooo hungover."

But instead of writing me off, he and Mom kept trying to win me back. Dad even signed me up for the mailing list of a ministry called Models for Christ, figuring I might go to church if it meant meeting hot Christian girls. (I had to hand it to him, he always *was* a problem solver.) Mom commandeered an army of church ladies to pray for me. They practically wore holes in the rugs with their knees, pleading my case to heaven night after night.

Maybe all their appeals were finally working, because lately I just didn't have it in me to twist the knife when we talked. What was the point? It wasn't funny anymore.

One morning in November 2003, I had an epiphany. It was around 9 a.m., and I was crashing at Brantly's after a typical cocaine-fueled evening. Hazy sunlight poured through the windows of his apartment on Houston Street, keeping me from the sleep I so desperately needed. I popped an Ambien and dragged a chair to the window.

When you're a promoter and you need to turn day into night, duct tape and blankets are your best friends. As I stood there at the window, struggling to secure a duvet to block the sun, I looked out over the street below and saw regular people hurrying past in suits, uniforms, and gym clothes. They were on their way to work and school and yoga class, their days just starting. Everyone looked so healthy, so full of purpose. My jaw was tight and a sore on the inside of my cheek was growing into a raw spot I'd been chewing all night.

When that familiar numb feeling rose up my arm, I could no longer ignore what was all too obvious. I was twenty-eight, and I'd had an amazing run. But the last eight years of partying had been like a constant injection of adrenaline to my overworked system. My body was dulling. My conscience was cooked. I couldn't remember the last time I'd laughed without being high or cried about losing someone or something important to me. I couldn't remember the last time I'd prayed. It took about ten years to pull it off, but somehow I'd managed to become the worst version of myself.

Too tired to think about it anymore, I jammed the edge of the blanket onto the window frame, taped it up as best I could, and crashed. In eight more hours, I'd have to wake up and start the same day all over again.

8

Pursuit

Tourists take note: New York City might be your idea of fun on New Year's Eve, but for those who live here, December 31 is the one time of year when our beloved city betrays us. With out-of-towners flooding the streets and packing elbow to elbow in Times Square, club owners happily let them buy their way past the velvet ropes for sparklers and a free glass of fake Champagne at midnight. It's the one night every year when I took a pass on nightlife.

In December of 2003, Brantly and I rounded up a few of our friends and went in on a seven-bedroom compound near the beach in Punta del Este, Uruguay. We booked the place for ten days over New Year's Eve, and told other friends to rent homes nearby. All I wanted was to relax with my girlfriend and let my head clear, get a fresh start to 2004.

Before leaving, I spent Christmas with my parents. As usual, we went to the Christmas Eve candlelight service at the local community church. Each year, the lights would dim, and everyone would sing and hold lit candles while I lowered my head and pretended to be in communion with God. Usually I would spend that time thinking about how I couldn't wait to party somewhere warm with my friends. Or how, if I twirled my candle just right, I could make the wax drip onto its circular paper base until the whole thing was covered. But this year was different.

Ever since I'd tried to self-diagnose my numbness online, my mind had been spinning. In church that night with my parents, I bowed my head and asked for help. *God, please help the doctors figure out what's wrong with me. Please help me feel healthy again.* I wasn't sure if anyone was listening, but it felt good to pray again.

A few days after Christmas, I packed a suitcase for Punta: T-shirts, sandals, bathing suits, a few books to read by the pool. Dad had given me a thin paperback for Christmas, *The Pursuit of God: Finding the Divine in the Everyday.*

"It's a quick read," he'd said. "A guy named A. W. Tozer wrote it in the late forties during a train ride from Chicago to Texas."

When Dad told me that reading Tozer could help me find a deeper relationship with God, I recoiled. *You mean that thing I quit a long time ago?*

Still, I threw the book in my bag and dumped a stack of mini-DV tapes into my carry-on. I'd finally gotten my expensive Sony video camera, and I was excited to break it in by shooting our trip.

We arrived at our destination in Punta, a sprawling retreat with spacious stone-and-wood villas stationed around the property's rolling green lawns and ivy-covered porches. The main house, where we'd come together for meals, was decorated like a Spanish country mansion, with white couches and chairs. An elderly Uruguayan woman showed up each morning to cook us breakfast. A maid and a caretaker cleaned our rooms, did our laundry, and looked after the grounds. There was a giant heated pool and a Jacuzzi to lounge in, and even a luxury yacht we could rent to explore the coast and swim with sea lions.

On our first day, I waved my video camera and loudly proclaimed that I'd be our official historian.

"I'll send you all DVDs. You're going to love it," I said.

When you capture a moment on film, it *proves* that you were there, that these things happened. In this case, I was setting out to prove what a great time we were all having. But that's not the movie I would end up with.

On New Year's Eve, we threw a little party at our compound—or, at least, the party started off little. We dressed in white linens, and met at the main house at 8 p.m. We dined at a long candlelit table. The girls picked at their food, and the guys emptied magnums of Dom Perignon and went for thirds.

At seven minutes to midnight, we moved to the courtyard, opened another bottle of Dom, and blew up $1,000 worth of fireworks. I pressed Record and set the camera down to join my friends, arm in arm, as the explosions sounded off around us, lighting up the sky in gold, white, and green. More friends trickled in after midnight, and a DJ took his place at the rented booth outside.

"Happy New Year, Scotchy," my friend Adam said, using his favorite drunk nickname for me.

The next day, I woke around 10 a.m. and wandered outside to find the music still blasting. Dozens of people were dancing around our pool. We'd flown thousands of miles for a vacation only to find ourselves hosting another party with no end in sight. *Punta, meet Lotus.*

This was not the peaceful escape I'd been dreaming about. But I was a slave to my bad habits, and when someone handed me an ecstasy pill, I popped it in my mouth. Thirty minutes later, with my pulse and spirits artificially lifted, I jammed a new battery into my camera and joined the fray.

"Scotty on camera!" a friend yelled.

"Yo, look, Scorsese's back!" another said with a laugh.

I moved my lens from person to person, group to group, capturing conversations being yelled over the music in staccato bursts:

"You raging alcoholic!"

"Bro, check out your crazy hair!"

"Scott, come here, bro!" another friend yelled. "Document *this*! *This* only happens once in a lifetime!"

I watched him through the viewfinder as he spoke, trying to capture the moment, but there was no *this*. There was just a patio full of drunk girls and coked-up guys consuming copious amounts of high-quality drugs, everyone pretending we'd found paradise.

By noon, my girlfriend had joined the pool party. She rarely drank, and she hated the club scene—even though *being seen* was a necessary evil of her industry. She looked bored, unimpressed.

A few days later, our group would be sipping cocktails on a yacht in the South Atlantic Ocean. I would turn the camera toward her. "Hey, look happy!" I'd yell, zooming in on her face. She would muster a fake smile for me, but it would be obvious that she wasn't happy. And why should she be? We were in a shallow, loveless relationship. We never really talked about our dreams or hopes or fears. Later, I would have the painful realization that I didn't really know her at all. And I knew she could say the same about me.

On the day of the pool party, though, I guzzled a Corona and kept moving through the crowd, playing my role, laughing, and out-bro'ing the next guy. But I kept the video camera close, like a shield between myself and the action. The theme song from *Trainspotting*—"Drive boy dive boy / Dirty numb angel boy"—droned on in my head long after day turned back into night and the guests finally stumbled home.

By my third day in paradise, I craved solitude. I woke up at dawn, long before everyone else, and slipped out of our cottage to walk the grounds alone. Everything was peaceful except for the low hum of a lawn mower in the distance. Dew covered the grass, and I walked past a giant black scar where our fireworks had burned a hole in the earth. Down by the pool, the cigarette butts and cocktail glasses were gone and fresh towels had been placed on the chaises. The staff had put everything back in order while we slept. *If only it were this easy to clean up my life*, I thought.

I walked to the boundary of the property to find horses grazing in open fields. A chestnut mare with a dark brown mane looked up at me, unafraid, and then went back to her grass. Watching the horses and breathing in the cool coastal air, I felt healthy for the first time in days. *This is how a place like this is supposed to be enjoyed*, I thought, as I turned my camera on and panned the landscape. Document *this*.

The others would be getting up soon, but I wasn't ready to part with the moment. Back at the room, I fished Dad's book from my suitcase and took it to the pool. I cracked open the pages, looking for some kind of spiritual nourishment, and read this: "Where faith is defective the result will be . . . numbness."

Numbness.

I kept reading. In *The Pursuit of God,* Tozer writes about God as a real person who loves, desires, and suffers just like us. He says that God is always there, patiently pursuing us, and waiting for us to love him back. I reread that passage again and again, until the words were seared on my heart. I felt like Tozer was speaking directly to me when he spoke of the danger of hungering for material possessions.

Things, Tozer said, can *never* satisfy our hearts. But we continue to pursue them with a passion only God deserves.

For years, I'd been pursuing the wrong things—from the BMW I'd bought as a teenager to the designer clothes I now wore, to the drugs I took and the hip cities I bragged about visiting. But where had it left me? With a numb body, a drug habit, and fingernails bitten down to ugly nubs. I'd been partying with some of the richest people I'd ever known, guys who'd gamble $10,000 on a hand of blackjack while looking indifferent as to whether they'd win or lose. I'd watched middle-aged men torch their marriages so they could date girls younger than their own daughters, only to see those relationships fall apart, too. And I'd enabled and curated all of it in the name of fun and money.

So this is how it all plays out, I thought to myself. *There will never be enough.* Someone else would always have more money, a nicer car, a prettier girl. The evidence was all around me.

The antidote to a life of emptiness, Tozer writes, is to become as "simple as a little child." Sitting there, in the quiet by the pool, I tried to imagine what that even looked like. It sounded like the exact opposite of the life I'd created for myself.

And yet, as a child, I *had* cared about others. I looked after the needs of my mom. When my church youth group planned a trip to help vulnerable children in North Philly, I was the first to raise my hand to volunteer. Mom helped me collect clothes, books, and toys for families who had none, and I remember feeling so proud. Like what we did there actually mattered.

The only charitable act I could remember performing as an adult was throwing a party with Brantly for a nonprofit called New York Cares. We slapped the group's logo on our invitation and promised to donate a percentage of the door money. But when it came time to turn over the cash, we decided to give New York Cares a grand total of 1 percent. And I'm not sure we even followed through.

I felt ashamed at who I'd become.

Hearing the others begin to rise and stumble toward another day, I put the book in my bag and joined them for breakfast. I'd spend the rest of my vacation pretending to be the same Scott Harrison who enjoyed house music and tequila shots. But deep inside me, something had broken open.

9

Captured

NEW YORK, 2004

When I got back from Punta, I resolved to cut back on my vices: drugs, cigarettes, booze, and gambling. For the first time I could remember, I longed for a different life. The problem was, I still had to promote clubs, get people wasted, and be the life of the party in order to pay the bills. I was like a compulsive gambler who'd vowed to quit the slots but still worked in a casino.

"*Please*, God," I'd pray out loud, pacing around my loft. "Show me a way out of here. Please show me a new life."

To steel my resolve, I'd come home after a long night at Lotus and fall asleep listening to sermons on my iPod. Dad, thrilled with my new-found direction, had turned me on to Chuck Missler, a military veteran and businessman who'd quit his job and devoted his life to teaching the Bible chapter by chapter. Missler sounded smart and confident, and his voice soon became as addicting to me as the drugs I'd sworn off. I spent hundreds of dollars on mp3 downloads of his sermons, listening to him riff on Genesis and the Book of Ruth as I walked around the city. At some point, I noticed that I wasn't going numb anymore. The episodes faded out as gradually as they had begun.

I also began to feel guilty about sleeping with a girlfriend I had no intention of marrying. I'd gotten so used to the idea of our being together, to what having a beautiful woman on my arm signaled about me. I loved walking the streets with her as guys stared, and seeing her on the runway, all eyes on her as the camera lights flashed. But I didn't love *her*. She deserved better than a boyfriend who saw her as a piece of jewelry.

Trying to be a virtuous club promoter was a lonely exercise, and I imagined how ridiculous it would sound if I told my friends about my newfound faith.

Hey, Brantly. Want to listen to some hymns?

How about a sermon?

Wanna hit up church with me on Sunday?

Scott, I imagined Brantly saying with a smirk. *I don't do poorly lit self-help gatherings.*

I couldn't share my experience with my club friends, because my life didn't look much different from the outside. And there's nothing worse than listening to a religious hypocrite.

Still, I needed some kind of positive community, so on Sundays, I went looking for a church. I'd find services that met in the afternoon or evenings, and then show up by myself, hoping to be comforted by the music and sermons. But my bar for aesthetics was impossibly high. When your whole life is million-dollar sound systems, smoke machines, and brushes with A-list celebrities, it's hard to feel at home in a church that meets in a fluorescent-lit basement, with a volunteer band playing bad praise music on a cheap PA system. I felt so out of place. I was like the drunk who walks into his first Alcoholics Anonymous meeting and immediately decides he's better than everyone else.

In late June 2004, I was about to give up looking when I got a flyer in the mail about a Models for Christ meeting, the ministry Dad had hoped I might visit. The organization was founded by a model named Jeff Calenberg in 1984 as a place for Christians in the business to meet and share their experiences without being judged. DJ Brant Cryder was scheduled as the next featured speaker.

"I know this guy!" I told my dad. "He used to work for me at Lotus."

As the story went, Brant had learned how to spin by accident. After returning home from an all-night desert rave one morning, he started rummaging through his roommate's record bin and found an old children's Bible on vinyl. Still feeling fuzzy from the drugs he'd taken, he put the record on his roommate's turntable and played a drum-and-bass track over it to make a cool blend of beats, layered with a deep voice intoning, "In the beginning . . . God said, Let there be light." Brant went on to DJ parties in Los Angeles and New York, mixing Bible albums with house music as part of his style.

The night I went to hear Brant speak, he'd just finished a thirty-day water-only fast, something he did once a year to stay spiritually connected. He was about my age and dressed from head to toe in Prada. He walked with the same swagger I'd learned from nightlife over the years, except that his looked more convincing.

During his talk, Brant described growing up in Ohio as a child of divorced parents. As a teenager, he partied and drank with his friends—typical rebellious behavior—but around his eighteenth birthday, his Christian stepmother convinced his father to send Brant off to a forty-five-day rehab program.

"I resented them for that," he said. "I was sober throughout college, and then I *really* started doing drugs. I actually developed a drug problem *after* finishing treatment."

Brant eventually left Ohio for California. By day, he worked selling high-end fashion clothing at Armani, climbing the ladder from the sales floor to management. By night, he DJ'ed at Moontribe raves, where crowds of up to five thousand would gather on mountaintops to take ecstasy, dance to house music for hours, and seek spiritual nirvana.

Every party was amazing in the moment, Brant said. "But then the sun came up, and I started to feel responsible and heavy, looking at the faces of all these people trying so hard to find an answer. It was rough in the morning. No one found the answer."

Around this time, Brant's dad called him out of the blue and invited him to a meeting of the Promise Keepers, an evangelical men's ministry. It wasn't Brant's idea of a good time, but he agreed to go. In

July of 1996, he and his dad traveled together to Mile High Stadium, in Denver, Colorado, where they sat on a grass field alongside sixty thousand other men in oversize khakis and flannel shirts.

"It was a total dork fest," Brant said with a laugh. "It was super weird for me." But then something unexpected happened. "The music stops, and the founder, Bill McCartney, who'd been a football coach, comes out."

As McCartney spoke, Brant looked into the distance and saw a tall white figure atop the stadium scoreboard. It was a statue of a majestic white horse, nostrils flaring and mane flowing as it reared up on its back legs. It reminded him of the story of the Second Coming in Revelation, where Jesus rides a white stallion, leading heaven's armies to vanquish evil. It caught Brant off guard.

"I don't even remember what Bill was saying, but I'm standing on this field, and I start to cry," he continued. "I literally feel my heart and my whole body start to crack. So I'm sobbing, and I hear a booming voice say, 'I am the answer that you've been looking for.'"

Brant was "captured"—that's how he explained it. After all the years of pain and searching, he suddenly felt at peace, like God was telling him, *I'm always with you. I've got you.* From that point on, Brant started pursuing a relationship with Jesus.

All throughout Brant's talk, I held back tears. Here was someone in my world who was smart and successful. He was killing it in fashion and had a beautiful wife and three kids. After years of chasing down drugs, alcohol, and nightlife, he'd found what Tozer wrote about: a more meaningful life. I couldn't wait to go up and talk to him.

"Scott!" he said. "You came! It's great to see you here, man." He welcomed me with genuine warmth and friendship. I felt like I'd found my long-lost brother.

Seeing Brant in this new light was a rush of adrenaline. But as much as his example had inspired me, in some ways it had discouraged me even more. Why wasn't I getting that same voice-of-God moment that

Brant had had? I craved a lightning bolt from the sky that would leave an indelible mark on *my* heart. Instead, I zombie-walked through the clubs each night, pretending to be present.

Ever since I'd come home from Punta, my body and soul had been in constant conflict. I felt polluted, but powerless to change. I'd been entrenched in nightlife since the age of nineteen, and hadn't developed any other skills. It was all so depressing.

And when that lightning bolt didn't strike and my world didn't change, the old rhythms and habits kicked back in. The passed-around tray of coke—*Okay,* I'd think, *maybe just one bump. What does it matter? I'm already a few drinks in.*

I ramped the cigarettes back up, too. At first, I'd smoke a half-pack of Marlboro Reds and throw the rest away. But then, hours later, I'd wake up in the middle of the night craving the fire in my throat and rummage through the garbage can to find them. I had to start drowning the cigarettes in the sink before I tossed them, just so I wouldn't be tempted to light them later.

I wasn't even brave enough to break up with my girlfriend. I felt like a total hypocrite. Like I was letting God down—and maybe that's why He hadn't answered my prayers. But really, I was letting everybody down. I would show up at Lotus with a scowl on my face and the worst attitude.

One of the club's owners, Jeffrey Jah, started teasing me: "Scott, are you coming in today as the angry drunk or the hungover drunk?" Even he could see that I was miserable and had one foot out the door.

"Look, I started out as a promoter and I became an owner," he told me one day, trying to help. "That's the next step for you and Brantly. You need to up your game. You need to graduate."

He was right, I guess. Nobody quits the scene and becomes an astronaut or brain surgeon. And I wasn't going to start over at a minimum-wage job, either. I had no savings and a huge monthly nut to cover: rent, travel, clothes, dining.

So, in the midst of my darkest inner turmoil, Brantly and I decided it was time to graduate and start down the path to club ownership. We zeroed in on a place in West Chelsea called Milieu. The owner, Peter Rabasco, was a talented young designer who'd set out to develop an old diner space into a high-end restaurant with an upstairs VIP lounge. In May, Brantly and I hosted a twenty-person private dinner there, had a great time, and struck a deal with Peter: we'd bring the beautiful people and build buzz, and in return, he would give us a percentage of the business. Promoter turned nightclub/restaurant owner sounded prestigious to me.

In other words, nothing much had changed. Seven months after vowing to get out of nightlife, I was going in deeper. On the surface, it was business as usual, but underneath I raged against myself, ashamed at my lack of courage. Even as Brantly and I moved forward with Peter, I prayed for some angel to come down, rip my world open, and shine a light.

10

Escape

NEW YORK CITY, JULY 2004

"Amy, it's Scott. You have got to fire this guy!"

It was 4 a.m. and I was pacing angrily outside Amy Sacco's club and leaving a voicemail about one of her bouncers.

"He just shook down my business partner for money!" I yelled. "This should *not* be happening at your club. You need to deal with this."

Two hours earlier, I'd shown up at Bungalow 8 with Peter. We'd officially been partners for about two weeks and I'd invited him to hang out after a meeting at Milieu one night. It was a chance for us to have a drink and talk in a quiet lounge where we didn't have to yell above thumping music.

While we were sitting across from each other, talking about where we'd grown up and how we'd gotten into the business, I noticed that a bouncer twice my size was hovering near our table. He'd been acting aggressive ever since we'd arrived, repeatedly walking up to Peter with his hand out, like a train conductor impatiently waiting for a passenger to fish out his ticket. I couldn't hear what the bouncer was saying, but I was annoyed that he kept interrupting our conversation.

"What's your problem?" I finally said to the guy.

He gave me an icy stare and then walked away.

"He wants me to pay him money," Peter said. "A hundred dollars."

"What?" I said, enraged. "For what?"

"Sometimes when I've come here, we'll tip the doorman," he explained. "But this guy is relentless."

"No," I said, my blood pressure rising. "Don't let him do that to you. Bro, it's not right."

"Yeah, I know." Peter shrugged.

"This is not okay. I'm calling his boss."

I knew nothing about this bouncer's life—if he was married, had kids to support, or took care of a sick parent. I wasn't interested in who he was. I just wanted to unleash my anger on someone who'd had the nerve to walk into my line of fire.

Lately, I'd raged over the smallest slights: the taxi driver whose inefficient route cost me an extra few minutes, the waiter who got my order wrong, the delivery guy who asked me to sign a receipt but had no pen on hand.

There was nothing particularly unusual about that night at Bungalow 8. I'd mouthed off to plenty of bouncers before. I'd defended my share of them, too. But, in retrospect, I handled the situation recklessly, like I had nothing left to lose. When Amy listened to her messages the next morning, she immediately fired the guy.

The next night, while I was riding home in a cab from our Saturday-night party, my phone buzzed. It was a text from Eddie, the doorman at the club I'd just left.

Don't go home. Call me.

I called him back and found out that minutes after I'd left, the bouncer from Bungalow 8 I'd just gotten fired had shown up at the door. He had a gun. He knew where I lived. And his rage towered over mine.

"Hey, change of plans. Can you take me to Little Italy instead?" I said to the driver.

I rang my girlfriend to let her know I was on my way over. No answer. I rang again. She picked up after I dialed her number for the fifth time.

"Do you know what *time* it is?" she said in a sleepy voice.

"Babe, I'm coming to stay at your place tonight. My life is in danger. I'll explain later."

"Okay," she said and hung up.

When I got there, she buzzed me up, unlocked the door, and was back in bed by the time I walked in. I slid into bed next to her, much to the annoyance of her now-displaced dog. She wanted to sleep, but I needed to talk.

"I have to tell you something," I said. "I got some guy fired, and he turned up at the club with a gun tonight."

"Oh, no," she said, holding me close. "I'm sorry. I'm sure it'll be all right."

I hoped she was right, but I was scared, even more than I'd been when my body started going numb, more than when Brantly overdosed—probably more than at any other time in my life.

The next morning, Peter called to say that the bouncer had just shown up at Milieu looking for me. I couldn't believe it. This guy was hunting me.

"I told him that he needed to just relax," Peter said. "That he'd brought this trouble on himself." He'd been acting so aggressively, Peter tried to reason, it was only a matter of time before someone fired him. But the bouncer wasn't listening.

"Scott, he's really pissed," Peter told me. "He said he wants to kill you."

I was shocked. For so long, I'd been living like I didn't care what happened to me. But now that someone *else* wanted me dead, life suddenly felt precious. I couldn't go home; and I couldn't go to work, because he might be waiting there.

"Okay," I said to Peter. "Do you have his number?"

As much as I wanted this problem to disappear, I had to talk to the guy, try to explain my side. Dialing *67 to block the caller ID, I then punched in the bouncer's number. He answered right away.

"Hey, bro. I'm really sorry," I said. "I was drunk. I was just trying to stand up for my business partner."

"Where are you?" he said.

"Out of town."

The guy spoke with calm menace. His voice came through the receiver clear and sharp. It felt like there was no one else in the world but him and me.

"I am *not* a guy to mess with," he said. As a child, he'd watched a woman in his family get stabbed. He'd just gotten out of prison and, as he told me, he wasn't afraid to go back.

"I believe you," I said. "I'm sorry."

We talked for another ten minutes, and I offered to help him find his next job, give him leads, be a reference for him—anything that might placate him. By the time we hung up, I wanted to believe him when he said he'd accepted my apology. But I wasn't sure, and even if we never met again, I'd always have to watch my back.

For the first time in years, I had clarity. I knew what I wanted. I wanted to live. And I felt absolutely sure about what to do next. Sometimes, as Tex once said, you have to break everything and move somewhere else. What if I just left New York, took a long road trip, and figured out my next move? Maybe *this* was my way out, my sign that it was time to go.

The next morning, I snuck into my loft to pack a bag, grabbing only the essentials: clothes, cigarettes, cash, my iPod. I also grabbed a leather-bound Bible. Locking the door behind me, it was the last time I set foot there.

I took a train to Newark Airport, rented a cobalt-blue Mustang on a month-long contract, and bought a bunch of maps of the Eastern Seaboard, the kind you can never quite fold back up properly. I didn't know exactly where I was going, but driving out from the rental place and onto the highway, I felt relief watching the New York skyline get smaller and smaller in my rearview mirror.

At first, I traveled south, to Atlantic City, where I met up with some friends and watched them gamble. I told them what had happened with the fired bouncer and explained that I was okay, just traveling for a while. Clearing my head. They laughed at my story and sent me back on the road the next morning with a bottle of Dewar's Scotch and $1,000 in winnings. From there, I headed north.

Passing through northern New Jersey, I called my parents and breathlessly told them the story. "Dad, you'll never believe this. I got this bouncer fired and he came after me and we just missed each other at the club and he's an ex-con and I think he might be following me. I'm getting out of town for a bit."

"Where are you going?" he asked.

"I don't know. North. I'm on the lam." It was my weak attempt at a joke, but Dad wasn't buying it. He knew that I was scared. He said he and Mom would pray for me while I was on the road, and they'd get others to pray, too.

Brantly saw through my front, too. "You're not taking a break," he said when I called to assure him that the trip was only temporary. "You're *done*, bro. It's fine. I'll keep Milieu warm for you if you lose your nerve."

It felt scary to think about leaving behind everything we'd built, everything we were still building. But at the same time, taking off felt exhilarating. I'd been numb for so long, and this felt like an adventure, a journey with no boundaries or rules. Just like getting in the car with Mom in the middle of the night to find a better place. A place where I could breathe easy.

I continued up Route 95, staying in bed-and-breakfasts and eating at greasy diners as I logged miles and signposts: Connecticut . . . Vermont . . . New Hampshire . . . Maine. Watching TV one night at a tiny inn near Bar Harbor, Maine, I listened to a young senator from Illinois address the Democratic National Convention. He said that the audacity of hope was God's greatest gift to us, the gift of belief in things unseen. I jumped to my feet when he said those words. Staring at the TV, I remember feeling totally certain, and saying out loud, "That guy is going to be president one day."

In the car, wandering up highways and backroads with no plan, I spent hours listening to the Bible on my iPod. I quickly reached the story of Lot, the gatekeeper of Sodom, whose life was saved when angels plucked him from the burning city, just before God destroyed it.

For months, I'd been praying for a way out of my own personal Sodom. What if my angel had been a bouncer with a gun?

A verse from James kept coming to mind. "Pure religion is this. Look after orphans and widows in their distress, and keep yourself from being polluted by the world."

I'm 0 for 2, I thought. For the last ten years, I'd polluted my body and the bodies of others. I'd looked after no one but myself. This verse from James painted a picture of the exact opposite of my life, the thing I'd been looking for. And that's when inspiration hit. I said it out loud, to no one but myself and God: "I'm going to tithe a year of my life." One year for the ten I'd wasted.

Tithing is something my parents did: they gave away a tenth of their income to the church and the poor. I didn't have much money in the bank. In fact, after a decade of work in nightlife I'd saved literally nothing. But I could give time, I thought. I could give 10 percent of the last ten years and find a way to help people.

The next day, I parked at a dial-up internet café in Greenville, Maine, and started researching my options. I wrote emails and sent volunteer applications to all the humanitarian organizations I could think of—Oxfam, UNICEF, World Food Programme, Save the Children, Samaritan's Purse, Médecins Sans Frontières. These organizations didn't make it easy to apply online—there were lots of broken forms, missing information, and dead links. After a particularly frustrating experience, I unloaded on some poor staffer who'd emailed me trying to help me through the process:

> PLEASE fix your online application form. I've battled with it for 25 minutes, and cannot get it to submit. Please look into this!

Not exactly the best way to win them over.

In the applications, I described myself as a New York City professional looking to dedicate a year of his life abroad. I had a communications degree from NYU. I had high-powered clients in fashion and music, and I knew how to get people to turn up wherever I said they should. I was ready to drop everything and serve at a moment's notice.

After applying to about a dozen charities, I took a deep breath and shut down my internet session. It was done. Now I just had to wait for the answers and pick the best fit.

A few days later, I called my DJ friend Brant Cryder. I was planning to drive home to New Jersey, and I asked him if there was any way he could take off work and meet me there for a hike on the Appalachian Trail. I'm sure I sounded crazy. The last time we spoke had been a few months earlier, at Models for Christ. But perhaps curiosity got the better of him, because the next day he drove about an hour and a half out of the city and met me in a parking lot at the bottom of the trail.

It was a clear, sunny day, and we hiked uphill, passing ferns and fallen logs. Four miles later, we climbed onto a set of boulders overlooking Sunfish Pond, a giant glacial lake on the Kittatinny Ridge. The place was deserted. Brant and I tossed stones into the glassy water as I told him about my plan.

"I think God is calling me to something," I said. "I'm not quite sure how this is going to work, but I just know that I need to do it."

"Scott," he said, "when we first met, I knew you wanted to accomplish big things, to make an impact. I'm the same way, so I know you're onto something. Just follow that voice. I'll do whatever I can to help you."

We looked out over the lake and prayed. Before he left, Brant offered to write a letter of recommendation if I needed it. As it turned out, I definitely would.

After three weeks of wandering, I was ready to get off the road.

"I'm coming home for a few days," I told my dad.

"Okay. What's the latest on your situation?" he asked.

"I'm not going back to nightlife. I'm going to give a year of my life to the poor," I said. "I've applied to a ton of organizations, and I'm going to hang out in France and decompress while I wait to see who responds."

"Scott, that's a great idea," Dad said. I could almost hear Mom cheering in the background.

"I want to come home for a few days and wrap up some things," I said. The right assignment could come quickly, and I needed to figure out what to do with my stuff in New York, the lease on my apartment.

A couple of nights later, I came home to my parents' place in Stockton, New Jersey. As I stepped onto the gravel driveway, I felt that familiar crunching sensation beneath my feet. Greeted by warm summer air and the familiar din of cicadas, I headed into the garage, the concrete chapel where the ritual of "getting pure" happens.

Inside, I took off my shoes and socks like I'd done countless times before, standing barefoot on the cool cement floor. Mom had left me a set of blue hospital scrubs on the clothes tree. I took off my shirt and pants and slipped them on. I'd performed this tedious drill so often—this crossover from the outside to the inside world—that it was part of my muscle memory by now. But, this time, as I climbed the bare wooden steps and opened the door to our living room, it felt different.

Upstairs, the hallway was dark. I dropped my bag on my bed and headed for the shower. As the water got hotter, I got undressed again and then stepped in. Closing my eyes, I lifted my face toward the shower and let the water wash over me.

11

—

Mercy

Thank you for your interest in our organization. Kindly be advised that at this time we cannot accept your application . . .

Another rejection! My third this week. Ever since coming home, I'd learned that volunteering wasn't as easy as it sounded.

"No charity wants me," I told my dad. "I guess promoting nightclubs isn't high on the list of skills they're looking for."

"Have faith, son," he said. "Something will turn up."

Still, the rejections continued pouring in, one after another. Maybe it didn't help that my newfound integrity had compelled me to be more honest than I had been in the doctor's office a year earlier.

Do you smoke? *Yes.* Drink? *Uh-huh.*

I was frustrated by the rejections. But they only hardened my resolve. I had a one-track mind, and I *would* find an opportunity to be useful. Something *will* turn up, I thought.

With just a month left on my apartment lease, I borrowed money from my parents to pay the final $3,500 due to my landlord. I didn't want to go back to New York, because what if the bouncer was still looking for me? So I asked a good friend named Aubrey to help me wrap up the details of my old life. Aubrey arranged for the piano rental company to pick up the baby grand, and then he and his girlfriend packed all my stuff into a U-Haul and drove it to my parents' place.

When they arrived, Dad and I spent hours going through boxes and making separate piles for things I'd keep or sell.

To keep: Not much. Business papers, some clothes, photos, items of sentimental value from my travels.

To sell: Anything of value. Computers, cell phones, musical equipment, my video camera, office supplies, a major collection of CDs and DVDs. The proceeds would fund the next few weeks in France and support me on the humanitarian mission I hoped to find.

My apartment building in New York was next to a video store where, over the years, I'd bought at least $7,000 worth of DVDs—all the movies I'd missed seeing as a Christian kid. I filled an old steamer trunk with 201 DVDs and sold the whole thing on eBay for $1,000. I sold my folks an office chair for $20, and a three-hole punch for $2. My room was filled with packages ready to be sent out, things I'd sold online.

At one point in the purge, my father and I came across my porn collection. I'm sure Aubrey had just taken out the drawer next to my bed and emptied the contents into a box. Porn DVDs didn't exactly belong in my "keep" pile, and probably not the "sell" pile, either. So Dad and I created a "total destruction" pile. We sat together in the living room, breaking into little pieces DVDs with titles I can't print here. It was like that scene in *Office Space* where the guys take a baseball bat to an office printer—except Dad and I laughed the whole time we were doing it, this time shielding our eyes. There was a profound finality to it. I made a silent vow to be done with that stuff forever, and it was a promise I kept. I haven't looked at a pornographic image since.

When I called Tex to ask about staying at his place, he was living in Las Vegas, and in the process of opening a restaurant/nightclub with a famous chef. I told him I was leaving nightlife and waiting to hear about a volunteering gig abroad. He said he was happy to hear from me. Deep down, he'd always known this day would come.

"Unless you're a very special type, the nightlife business consumes and destroys you," he said. "Too much booze. Too many girls. The most you can last is about fifteen years. By then, you're in AA, NA, SA, and Everything-Else-A."

"Well, I'd love to take some time in France to recharge and figure out what's next," I said. "Is anyone using the house?"

"It's yours, mate, stay as long as you want," Tex said. "The key is in the usual place—the rusted saucepan in the corner of the woodshed, covered by leaves."

Staying in Tex's place would give me time to get clean, eat healthier, and hopefully quit smoking and drinking. Maybe I could find work as a waiter, or volunteer locally until a reputable charity took me on.

A week later, I threw my two bags into the family station wagon and drove with my folks to the train station in Raritan, New Jersey. The three of us stood there on the platform for a moment with a sense of expectation and quiet wonder. Mom and Dad's prayers had finally been answered, and something new was happening. Somehow, we felt like a family again.

Two weeks later, at the end of September, I finally got a break on the volunteering front. I was riding my bike through a remote village in the Pyrenees. This place was a cell phone dead zone, so I almost crashed from the shock of hearing my phone ring. Someone from an international organization called Mercy Ships was on the line.

Mercy Ships was founded in 1978, when I was three years old. Since 1987, it's been sailing hospital ships to impoverished regions, bringing the best volunteer doctors to perform surgeries on people who can't afford or access medical care. The organization had passed me over once before, but a position had unexpectedly opened up in the communications department, and the next ship was leaving for West Africa in four weeks.

"We're considering you for a volunteer photographer job," the woman on the line said. Her name was Tianna and she worked as Mercy Ships' communications manager.

"Yes. That sounds amazing," I said.

This was a coveted job—it came with two expensive Nikon D1X cameras, an arsenal of good lenses, and a small office. If they picked me, I'd spend eight straight months living in a floating hospital, taking photos of the doctors as they operated on patients, and documenting the charity's work in some of the most remote villages in the world.

"It's one of the more difficult roles on the ship," the woman said. "You're out in the field representing the organization, often by yourself."

I could hear the subtext loud and clear: *We don't want a loose cannon out there wrecking our good name.* What Tianna hadn't told me was that she'd Googled my name and found a blog I'd written about partying across Europe, complete with a photo of me flipping the bird at the camera.

Shortly after the call, Tianna emailed.

> Scott, it was great talking with you on the phone today . . .
> We'd like to keep talking, but we do have a request. Would
> you be willing to jump over here to Germany in the next
> week to just see the ship for yourself and get a feel for
> the place? With your independent background (being self-
> employed, the NY scene, etc.), this environment might feel
> like the twilight zone!

She said that the team just wanted to meet me in person, but we both knew that this assignment represented a huge life adjustment for me. A lot of people go on foreign volunteer assignments because they're running away from something. They're emotionally adrift, and they hope that this kind of work might provide a fix, but instead, they end up becoming a distraction for the crew. They don't do their work, they need babysitting, and are often sent home unceremoniously.

If Scott Harrison couldn't handle living on a ship with 350 strangers, surrounded by human trauma, with no takeout delivery or bottle service (alcohol was forbidden onboard) it would be best to discover that before I set sail. Deep down, though, a part of me felt that I needed to suffer a little bit. Not just as penance for my reckless past, but to see if I could handle it.

The very next day, I got on a series of trains to Bremerhaven, Germany. For a day and a half, the train sped north through the lush French and then German countryside until finally reaching the town where the ship was docked. The *Anastasis*, a 522-foot passenger liner that Mercy Ships had gutted and retrofitted with hospital facilities, was much bigger than I'd imagined. I went onboard, gave my name, and a volunteer led me down a series of tight passageways. I had to turn sideways and press my back against the wall anytime a nurse, ship's hand, or mechanic hurried past to somewhere important. We arrived at the communications office, where I met Tianna and a woman named Brenda, who would be my boss on the ship if I got the job.

"Look," Brenda said, getting right to it. "You're not the typical applicant." By that, she meant I wasn't a good Christian kid looking for a gap-year service project. "This is not a come-and-go-as-you-please kind of ship," she continued. "You're going to have to work under rules and regulations, not just because it's a seagoing vessel, but because it's actually a working hospital. For example, there's a chain of command. There's a curfew. And everyone is required to attend devotionals."

There they were again: rules, curfews, moral codes, boundaries. The old me would have been repelled by this, but the rebellion had ended. I was ready to salute and conform.

Brenda went on to say how hard it could be to share a cabin with strangers, to be stuck occasionally taking cold showers and eating food that tasted as bad as it smelled.

"I'm okay with all that," I said, trying to put her and Tianna at ease. "Honestly, none of that stuff bothers me."

I'd never worked so hard to impress people who weren't buying expensive bottles of booze. After about a half hour, I felt like I was slowly winning them over.

"Scott, as long as you're moving in a forward trajectory, then your past doesn't matter so much to us," Tianna said. "I believe that the spirit of where you are right now is in line with our values, as individuals and as an organization."

I didn't realize it then, but they were showing me the true meaning of mercy. I jokingly promised that I wouldn't throw any wild parties, and they gave me the job.

I left Germany with an orientation packet explaining the ship's dress code (modest apparel, please), what to pack (malaria pills, rain jacket, hiking boots), how to receive mail and make phone calls at sea (not easily), and other logistics. I had three weeks to shop, close up Tex's house, and get myself to Tenerife, the capital of the Canary Islands. Once there, I would board the *Anastasis,* and we'd set sail for Benin, Africa, where Brenda had told me we'd witness unthinkable human suffering. Then, after a four-month stint in Benin, we'd move on to Liberia, a country I'd never even heard of that had just emerged from fourteen years of civil war.

Back at Tex's place, I took a walk in the forest, wondering whether I'd actually be able to do this job I'd talked my way into. Could I be the selfless person they expected me to be? And on a practical level, I still needed to figure out how I was going to afford the $500 a month I'd have to pay Mercy Ships for my room and board.

"Don't worry about being prepared," Brant wrote in an email. "Your feeling of being unprepared is exactly how God can use you best. Be blessed, be strong, head up, chest out, back to the world, and face to the wind."

I shuttered Tex's house and set out on a three-day road trip to Madrid—south through the green-blanketed mountains, and then west to Spain, where I'd catch a plane to Tenerife. My second-to-last night on the road, I stayed in a $70-a-night hotel room in a village on the border between France and Spain. Before I checked in, I'd walked past a casino next door to the hotel. I always loved gambling, and fancied myself pretty good at it, too. *So*, I thought, *one last hurrah?*

After dinner, I strolled inside and sat at an empty blackjack table. I ordered a bottle of Jack Daniel's.

A couple hours later, half the bottle of whiskey and $1,500 was gone. It was three months' worth of ship expenses. I don't remember if I ran out of money or just couldn't take out more from the ATM, but I got up from the table and stumbled out in despair.

Back in my hotel room, I went out on the balcony and sank to my knees.

"God, I'm so, so sorry," I said through tears. "I screwed up again. I am so stupid. How could I have just done that? Please, God. *Please* give me another chance."

A couple days later, I was in the Canary Islands waiting for the Mercy Ship to arrive.

On my last night alone, I smoked my last three packs of Marlboro Reds and guzzled a six-pack of beer in the hotel room, knowing I'd have to give it all up in the morning—cold turkey. I woke up with a splitting headache. Armed with blister packs of Nicorette and a fresh nicotine patch on my arm, I threw my vintage Louis Vuitton duffel over my shoulder and headed to the dock.

The *Anastasis* looked smaller than it had in Germany, now sharing a modern port with giant cruise ships. I walked up the steep gangway and went inside.

"Good morning, and welcome aboard!" a receptionist named Maria said with a smile. She handed me a clipboard with paperwork to fill out. I surrendered my passport, signed a code of conduct, and had my photo taken for an ID badge.

Another volunteer led me through the ship's narrow corridors. We descended two flights of metal stairs—with me ducking to clear the ceilings—and then down another flight and another corridor until we finally reached cabin 2056. It was barely 125 square feet and its single porthole hovered just above the water line. Through dim lighting, I surveyed the cracked linoleum floor and the three twin beds.

My new roommates, two African men, were waiting inside. They worked in the engine room and smelled of hot grease and sweat. Tossing my bag on a bunk, I inspected the bathroom, a tiny stall with cockroaches scurrying out of the sink and shower drains.

This was it. My new, opposite life. There was no going back.

"Welcome home!" my roommates said with wide grins.

II

FOCUS ON THE HOPE

12

A New Day

The *Anastasis* entered the Port of Cotonou, Benin's largest city, in the early-morning hours of November 5. Hundreds of Mercy Ships volunteers emerged from their cabins and crammed together on the decks, leaning over the railings to wave at our cheerful welcoming party down below.

I paced the main deck with a pair of cameras around my neck and found a good vantage point. Through the zoom lens, I could see dozens of people waiting on the concrete seaport: women in long yellow-and-green dresses, men in suits and ties, and a naval officer in a crisp white uniform holding the flag of Benin—its three bands of green, red, and yellow representing hope, courage, and wealth. A brass band played the national anthem, "L'Aube Nouvelle," or "The Dawn of a New Day."

I was finally here. This was everything I'd been waiting for. And in just a few days, I'd get to meet and photograph patients. But warm welcome aside, we had our work cut out for us.

During orientation, I learned that Benin is a French-speaking country of about eight million people who had (and still have) extremely limited access to health care. At the time, there were four doctors for every one hundred thousand people, and the average life expectancy was fifty-one years. (For comparison, currently in the United States the rate is one doctor for every three hundred twenty-five people, and the average life expectancy is seventy-nine years.)

Months before we set sail, a Mercy Ships advance team had coordinated with local hospitals to blanket the city and countryside with flyers. The notices explained our work and showed pictures of tumors, cleft lips and palates, burns, cataracts, and a slew of other medical problems. Word spread: *A hospital ship is coming. These are the things they can fix. It's free of charge.* The organization had been to Benin twice before, building trust and recognition, so the advance team reported that the buzz in town was positive.

Three days after we docked in Cotonou, I woke up before dawn, excited for my first official assignment: screening day. Today we'd set up a makeshift clinic at Les Halles des Arts, an indoor sports stadium in the center of town. My job was to photograph the medical team as they examined people who came for care, and to shoot "before" images of patients scheduled for surgery. Ever since I'd been accepted as a volunteer, I'd been itching to see patients the way a war reporter itches to reach the front lines.

By 6 a.m., I'd donned hospital scrubs, eaten breakfast, and climbed into a convoy of aging white Land Rovers. The vehicles were packed full with folding tables and chairs, lab equipment, food, water, and boxes of medical supplies like gloves, gauze, tongue depressors, and antibiotics. Over breakfast, someone told me that we had 1,500 surgery slots, which represented the maximum number of patients Mercy Ships could provide medical care for in a four-month tour. I remember thinking, *How on earth are we going to find 1,500 people who need surgery?*

Our convoy snaked through Cotonou's potholed city streets. As we approached the city center, I inhaled my first proper whiff of burning trash and rubber tires. It's a smoky, acrid smell, the kind that coats your nostrils and throat. Exhaust-spewing *zémidjans,* or motorbike taxis, swarmed like bees through the cracks in traffic, honking their horns when a car got too close. Many of them didn't even come to a complete stop before picking up or dropping off their passengers. I loved the chaotic energy of the streets. I was high on adrenaline, high on purpose.

My job as lead photographer had a simple mandate: document our work, both on the *Anastasis* and in the field, then process and archive the photos so Mercy Ships could use them for marketing, education, recruitment, and fundraising. I took the job seriously—as if I were on assignment for *National Geographic. I am much more than a volunteer,* I thought. *I am a humanitarian photojournalist on a mission to show the world things they've never seen before! I'll find the poorest, most destitute villages! Live with lepers! Save sick children from death's door! Speak truth to power!*

My mood quickly turned from swagger to shock as our Land Rover pulled into the dusty stadium parking lot. Thousands of people— literally *thousands*—were waiting in a line that wrapped around the building and then back against itself several times over. Women clutched the hands of children with cloudy eyes and cleaved mouths. Men wore million-mile stares. Many had dramatic facial deformities, misshapen bodies, skin that appeared to be melting off their bones, wounds that would seem exaggerated if you saw them in a horror film.

"Are we going to get to them all?" I asked a nurse as we got out of the truck.

"No, but we'll do our best," she replied, unloading her gear. "Some of them have walked for days or weeks to get here. You hear about them selling cattle or even their homes to pay for the taxi ride." Clearly, this wasn't her first screening.

Before going inside to help set up, I wanted to take a photo of the sheer mass of humanity waiting outside the stadium. It was impossible to get it all in frame from street level, so I ducked into a run-down hotel at the edge of the lot and spoke in broken French with the owner.

"J'ai besoin de toit . . . les photos" ("I have to get to your roof to take photos"). I pointed at my camera and showed the owner my ID badge. He threw his hands in the air—the universal sign for "I have no idea what you're saying"—which I took as a green light to charge the stairs. I reached the roof and looked out over the dirt parking lot, where more sick people were arriving. Some of them limped, others were barefoot; several had rags covering their faces. They made their way to a thin blue rope, tied to stanchions, which funneled the crowd into a single orderly line. I snapped away in the early gray light, and then rushed back down through the crowd.

It was oppressively hot inside the stadium, ninety degrees Fahrenheit and rising. All across the pavilion floor, volunteers had arranged tables and chairs into dozens of makeshift medical stations: cleft palates here, tumors there, burns in this corner, orthopedics in the opposite corner, cataracts here by the stairs.

At 6:30 a.m., Dr. Gary Parker, the ship's chief medical officer, waved his hand and gathered everyone around an open space at the center of the stadium.

"There are more than five thousand people outside," he said. "Every single one deserves our attention and kindness. Look them in the eye. Provide them with first-rate health care. Try not to be overwhelmed by the numbers. Focus on the human being in front of you and how you can help them. Let's pray."

We bowed our heads as Dr. Gary asked God for wisdom and compassion.

"Father, please give us the ability to help these patients today," he said. "And for those we cannot help, we pray that you might open another door for them. Give them the comfort they need. Amen."

As I walked to my photo station, the security team flung open the heavy stadium doors. Tension and excitement spread like electricity through the line outside. People in front stood and alerted the others that, finally, the screening was beginning.

When five thousand people show up for free medical care, it's a bit of a mixed bag. Some come to ask, "Can I get some tablets for my heart?" Others want to know, "Can you fix my foot fungus?" Handing out aspirin and antibiotics is easy. But Mercy Ships' real expertise is in maxillofacial conditions (diseases and injuries to the head, neck, face, and jaw), orthopedic problems (bone fractures, clubfeet, bowed legs), and plastic and reconstructive care for burns and major wounds. The organization also provides dental and eye surgeries and corrective surgery for women who develop chronic incontinence during childbirth (a problem that often results in abandonment by their husbands and ostracism by their communities). For these conditions, Mercy Ships provides medical care from talented surgeons, physicians, nurses, and other specialists who volunteer *and* pay room and board just like everyone else on the ship.

By 6:45 a.m., my photography studio was ready: ten square feet in a corner of the stadium, with a couple of white sheets as a backdrop and two wooden stools where the patients could sit. I set up the tripod, got my flashes and battery chargers, and headed over to the maxillofacial (or "Max-Fax") station to pick up my first patients.

Dr. Tony Giles, a surgeon from the United Kingdom, was examining Alfred, a fourteen-year-old boy who had a giant fleshy tumor spilling from his mouth and pushing his jaw down to his chest. His mother explained through a translator that the tumor had started out, four years earlier, as a small bump on Alfred's jaw. Now the size of a volleyball, it consumed everything below his nose and pushed his tongue back against his throat, making it almost impossible for him to talk, eat, or breathe properly. Alfred's teeth looked like white Chiclets crookedly embedded in the pink, oozing mass.

Horrified, I took a couple of quick, blurry candids of the doctor prodding the tumor, all the while reminding myself, *Just breathe. Act normal. You're not disgusted. His name is Alfred. He's a fourteen-year-old boy. You were a fourteen-year-old boy once.*

"Hey, buddy!" I said, touching Alfred's shoulder. "My name's Scott. I'm from America! It's nice to meet you."

His eyes met mine, full of anger and defiance, glaring a hole through my lens. I pointed the camera directly at his face and suppressed a queasy feeling in the pit of my stomach. It felt like I'd been caught staring at a car crash. Like I was magnifying his shame by capturing it on film.

Mercy Ships typically doesn't take patients with late-stage malignant cancers or terminal conditions, so the pathologists bring sophisticated lab equipment to screenings. They can learn within minutes if a tumor is benign or malignant, and determine whether they can admit the patient or not.

Fortunately, Alfred's tumor was benign, and Dr. Giles scheduled him for surgery on the ship. I escorted the boy and his mother to the photo station, where we took his picture for ship records.

"Okay, buddy. I'll see you next week," I said. His mom smiled at me, but Alfred did not. He'd been poked and prodded enough for one day.

Almost all patients, or their parents, sign a release to be photographed. It means they're among the lucky ones—they've received a surgery date. Not all are so lucky. A couple hours after Alfred left, I met a boy named Serafin. He looked to be the same age, and his giant tumor, the way it consumed the lower half of his face, was almost identical to Alfred's. Serafin looked scared when the doctors took a biopsy of his tumor. Honestly, everyone around him looked scared, even the volunteers.

Serafin's lab results were bad. His tumor, unlike Alfred's, was malignant. Cancer. It meant we couldn't help him. Everyone at the station knew this frightened little boy was going to die soon.

Hearing the news, his mother sobbed loudly and embraced him. Serafin remained stone-faced, maybe more to cushion his mother's suffering than anything else. The whole scene bowled me over with grief. I mustered up a smile, touched the boy's shoulder tenderly, and then rushed off to a corner of the stadium. I was a mess: tears, convulsive breaths, snot running down my nose. I was ashamed to be crying. There was a little boy dying right in front of us, and there was nothing we could do. How could I continue to document this kind of pain?

A few minutes later, Dr. Giles appeared at my side. His kind green eyes peered at me through rimless glasses.

"Scott, we're here to help these people, and you have an important role to play," he said in a firm English accent. "Remember, most of these stories will end well. Try to focus on the hope. On the people we *will* help."

He walked away, and I took a deep breath. *Focus on the hope.* Those words got me back on my feet. Hope would get me through the day.

Around noon, I walked outside to see how things were going. The line was moving at a crawl. The tone of the crowd had changed: cheerful conversations turned into sharp bickering as the midday sun started to bear down. There was no shade, and only a few people had umbrellas or hats.

Volunteers moved through the line handing out bread and water to try to ease the tension. Nurses prescreened the patients with smiles and probing questions, gently sending away the ones with conditions we couldn't treat. These nurses seemed to have the hardest, most emotionally demanding jobs.

"You're dealing out great hope or tragic sorrow to every person in line," one nurse told me. "It just kills you to send someone home without help."

Sometimes, a nurse would walk toward the back of the queue, quietly ushering forward people who looked the most desperate. And although it was rare, sometimes a patient would show up choking to death on his own tongue from a massive mouth tumor. These patients were rushed to the ship for an emergency tracheotomy, lest they die in the next twenty-four to forty-eight hours.

I headed back inside, stopping at the kids' play station. A few volunteers were goofing around with hand puppets, getting the kids to laugh. There was music and face painting and balloons and bubbles. Most of the children had never seen bubbles before, and I snapped some photos that ended up being my favorites from the day. Bright, open faces and watchful eyes. I turned the camera around to show the children their portraits on the monitor, and laughed as they giggled and pointed. They gathered around me like I was the Pied Piper.

Some of the kids wore colorful, clean pullover shirts and dresses, their Sunday best, while others were wrapped in dirty and fraying fabrics. The sickest ones were rarely, if ever, touched by their caregivers. I couldn't help but playfully hug them. I wanted these children to know that they were valuable. That they were worthy of direct and purposeful looks without revulsion. Worthy of hugs. Worthy of love.

Back at the photography station, I looked through my lens at another patient—a girl whose cleft lip had turned the groove below her nose into a snarled tangle of flesh, teeth, and gums. She had hard eyes for a ten-year-old.

Worldwide, one in seven hundred babies is born with a cleft lip or palate. In America, cleft-born children get simple corrective surgery at birth and are left with an almost imperceptible scar. However, in some villages, particularly the most remote ones in West Africa, a child born with a cleft is thought to be possessed. There's tremendous social pressure for parents to stop feeding the baby, or to hand it over to the witch doctor so he can kill the infant and destroy the evil spirits before they harm the entire village. Parents are sometimes forced to flee in the middle of the night, worried that a neighbor might snatch their child away.

But I could tell *this* little girl in front of me was loved. She wore carefully woven braids and small gold hoop earrings. Somebody cared enough to make her feel pretty. It reminded me of something Dr. Gary had said during an initiation lecture: "The hopes and dreams in a mother's heart are the same anywhere in the world."

By the end of the day, I'd photographed men with tumors the size of basketballs growing from their heads and necks, and women with eyes so clouded by cataracts that they'd never seen their children's faces. I'd taken shots of kids who'd lost lips, noses, and cheeks to a horrible flesh-eating disease called noma, which is caused by bacteria that live in all our mouths. But noma primarily afflicts children who live in conditions of severe poverty and are malnourished, dehydrated, and drinking bacteria-infested water. I cringed thinking about the many times back home in the clubs when I'd casually order a half-dozen $10 bottles of sparkling water for the table and no one even opened them.

As I studied the patients' faces through my viewfinder, I wondered if the ones with fire in their eyes, like Alfred, fared better than those whose eyes showed only defeat. I prayed for all of them. *Please, God, let them have successful surgeries and quick recoveries. Let them grow up to enjoy all the simple dignities I've taken for granted—clean water, a roof over my head, a doctor when I get sick.*

As we began to pack up, medical specialists combed the line one last time, looking for small children and the worst cases among the adults. Tomorrow morning, we'd come back and do it all over again, until we'd filled all 1,500 surgery slots.

At sundown, I jumped on top of a Land Rover with my wide-angle lens. I wanted to capture a shot of the people we were leaving behind. Shutting the clinic's doors, I came to learn, was the most difficult moment of the day. As security guards placed barricades across the stadium's entry points, a wave of anxiety swept through the once-orderly crowd. Hundreds of men and women surged toward the front, pushing and shouting for our attention.

"We've *got* to go," someone said. The crowd was starting to surround our vehicle. Hands slapped the hood in frustration. Faces pressed up against the windows.

"Scott, we have to go. *Now!*"

I pressed the shutter button one more time before jumping down and sliding into the Rover. *We have important work to do here,* I reminded myself. *Focus on the hope. Focus on those we can help.*

13

Patient Number One

"Scott . . . Go to bed!"

My roommate Tony was yelling. It startled me. What time was it?

I took off my headphones and glanced at the clock. Yikes. It was 2 a.m. For the last five hours, I'd been writing a story in our tiny fifteen-by-fifteen-foot cabin. Poor Tony slept in a bunk bed adjacent to mine, which meant his head was about three feet from all my banging on the keyboard.

My other roommate, Danny, jumped in from the bunk above: "Scott, you have hammers for fingers." Guilty as charged. To this day, I'm still the loudest typist in any room.

"If you're gonna keep this up, can you *please* go to your office?" Tony said.

We'd been on the ship for over a month now, and most nights, I'd work in my photo office, a tiny room on one of the lowest decks. It wasn't much, but it had a single porthole that looked out across the water, and the door locked for privacy—a scarce resource on our floating village. There, I could keep the lights low, play my music loud, and bang on my computer as much as I pleased. But tonight, I hadn't wanted to waste the time it would have taken to walk there and set up.

"I'm sorry, guys. Super important story. I'm really almost done."

There were six writers, photographers, and editors in the communications department, and we met frequently to discuss assignments. Initially, my boss, Brenda, tried to pair me with writers, but I pushed back and asked to shoot and write everything myself. I wanted to be a one-stop shop for life-changing stories, and Alfred, the boy from screening day, would be my first major assignment.

I closed my computer for the night and set the alarm for 6 a.m. Alfred was having surgery today. I knew it would be a long and brutal battle between Dr. Gary's scalpel and Alfred's giant tumor, and I was going to be there to document it.

In the morning, I went to see Alfred and his father, Bessan, in the ship's ward, a cramped unit with forty-two beds, low ceilings, and bright fluorescent lighting. A nurse was sitting by Alfred's bedside, giving the standard instructions.

"Try not to be frightened when you wake up and discover that you can't speak yet," she warned Alfred. "This is normal. You can make hand signals, and we'll give you paper to write on, but speaking properly again will take time."

"Hey, buddy!" I said to Alfred, holding my hand up high. "You're going to do awesome!"

Alfred weakly slapped my palm. He looked frail, and thinner than I'd remembered. The skin on his arms was stretched so tight that I could see the outline of his joints and bones. Dr. Gary later told me that Alfred had been slowly starving. To eat, he would shove food over the tumor and into his mouth, but he barely had any teeth left with which to chew. At fourteen years old, he weighed only forty-four pounds, and that was if you included the five-pound tumor.

Through a translator, Alfred's father told me their story. He said they lived in a mud hut in Tokpa-Daho, a small fishing village on Benin's Lake Ahémé. They were fervent practitioners of voodoo, the religion of their ancestors and community. At first, Alfred's parents believed that his growing tumor was the result of a curse, so they hired witch doctors to free him from it. These men cut holes in Alfred's face with knives and spread pastes into the wounds. They danced, sacrificed chickens, and begged the ancestors for healing. But the tumor refused to obey.

The family took him to two hospitals and consulted more witch doctors, but none of the treatments had any effect. It was then that a visiting pastor heard about Alfred's condition and told them about our ship. They have tumor specialists, he said, and they might be able to help.

Bessan initially refused. "Nothing worked before. Why would these doctors be any different?" he asked. But Alfred's mother pleaded with him until he relented. They scraped together the $10 taxi fare, and she took Alfred to the screening in November, where I first met them.

As I pulled a set of clean blue OR scrubs over my clothes and washed from fingertips to elbows, I thought about how many times I'd done this routine growing up, putting on scrubs in the garage, getting pure for Mom.

For the next ten minutes, the OR nurses put Alfred's face through a similar routine, washing his neck and chest with a reddish-brown antibacterial solution until the skin was as clean as possible. I hovered with my camera, documenting every step. Alfred lay quietly on the operating table, hooked up to monitors that recorded his heart rate, pulse rate, and the oxygenation of his blood. The anesthesiologist placed an IV in the boy's hand and chatted with him until his eyes closed and his face went slack.

With their patient ready for surgery, the medical team (three nurses, an anesthesiologist, and an assistant) huddled up with Dr. Gary to discuss the operation. To this day, Dr. Gary has never lost a Mercy Ships patient on the operating table, but he knows that with every massive tumor surgery, the risk is always there. In Alfred's case, he could bleed out. Facial tumors often have such a rich blood supply that the patient can lose as much as twice his body's blood volume during the operation. Crew members were standing by to donate blood, and Alfred would need at least three units (about three pints) throughout his surgical procedure.

Dr. Gary said a brief prayer. "God, please show Alfred your love and protection through this surgery. Please guide us so that we may do our best work in your service. Amen."

And then he picked up a scalpel.

The last surgery I'd witnessed was a minor one. I was nine, swimming at the beach in Ocean City, New Jersey, when something bit my hand. I woke up in the middle of the night to find that my thumb had swollen to the size of a cherry. It hurt like crazy. My parents came to my bedside, took a look at it, and prayed.

"Let's have faith that God will heal it," Dad said. "God has the power to heal all wounds."

"Amen," Mom said.

"Amen," I repeated.

The next morning, I woke up whimpering and begged Dad to take me to the doctor. Instead we piled into the station wagon and drove to church. It was a muggy Sunday, and we sat on the lawn in the overflow section, singing hymns and praying hard. Years earlier, I'd been hospitalized with a severe ear infection. The doctors scheduled me for surgery, but my parents prayed all night for a miracle. Amazingly, by morning I had healed, and my surgery was canceled.

This time, though, it seemed that God didn't have time to look into my thumb problem. By the end of the service, it was still throbbing, and a bubble of milky pus was now growing on top.

"Can we go to the doctor now?" I asked Dad.

"Okay," he said. He looked a bit defeated. I could tell he'd wanted God to get the glory, not a physician.

We drove to the urgent care clinic, and a doctor gave me a shot in my thumb that stung like bees before it numbed my skin. Then he stuck a small needle right into the pus bag, lancing it. Liquid exploded out in a violent gush. It was awful, but the pain ended immediately.

Years later, my parents would speak regretfully of this incident, saying they had been young and naïve in their newfound faith. Today, they don't believe any less in the power of prayer, but they've come to appreciate that God does things in His own way.

Dr. Gary cut into Alfred's face. He sliced through skin, tissue, and muscle, moving his scalpel around the tumor and down to the jawbone. His hands were strong, swift, and precise. He'd done thousands of surgeries—each time, praying for God to guide him.

Dr. Gary was the Obi-Wan Kenobi of Mercy Ships. People talked about him in hushed tones of awe and admiration. He was tall, grayhaired, clean-shaven, and handsome. His voice had the texture of cashmere. He wasn't chatty, but if you did manage to get his attention and engage him in conversation, he made you feel like you were the only person in the room. I knew right away that I wanted to learn from him. He was faith incarnate, quietly looking after widows and orphans, as the verse in James said.

Before joining Mercy Ships in the 1980s, Dr. Gary was a wellrespected surgical resident at UCLA. He could've stayed in Los Angeles and gotten fabulously rich working at a prestigious hospital or reconstructing the faces of beautiful people in Beverly Hills. But instead, in 1982, he went to do five years of maxillofacial surgical training at Glan Clwyd Hospital in North Wales. Then, in January 1987, he signed on for Mercy Ships' maiden voyage from Los Angeles to Mexico. The plan was to spend three months on the ship, and then move on. That was thirty years ago. He just never left. He even met his wife, Susan, onboard, and they raised two children on the ship.

After three hours of dissecting, removing tissue, and finally getting to the intersection of Alfred's normal jawbone and the tumor, Dr. Gary made a final cut, digging a centimeter and a half into healthy bone to be sure he got it all—clean margins. He then broke the giant mass loose and placed it on a stainless-steel surgical tray. Alfred was liberated! A scrub nurse took the tumor to a sterile table in the back, where she weighed it and eventually sent it off to be incinerated.

With the tumor now gone, Dr. Gary put down his scalpel and spent the next few hours stitching muscle, connective tissue, and skin back together, while the nurses vacuumed away blood and bone matter. He talked throughout the procedure, to make sure everyone was on the same page.

"Why do you leave so much extra skin?" I asked as he sewed up Alfred's lower jaw. An inch-long flap of loose skin hung down from his face, stretched out by the offending tumor.

"Facial skin has memory," Dr. Gary said. "Alfred's skin will contract and tighten to its original place, just like a mother's belly eventually contracts after childbirth."

As the anesthesiologist gently turned off the gas, mixing in pure oxygen and other medicines that would help Alfred's brain awaken, Dr. Gary watched Alfred closely, waiting to see a special moment that almost always happens with tumor patients. It's a moment, he told me, that they won't remember, because they're still straddling the dream state between waking and unconsciousness.

For Alfred, it came a few minutes later, when he briefly opened his eyes and reached toward his mouth, only to find an empty space. Dr. Gary smiled. A nurse gently wheeled Alfred to the recovery ward, where he rested his hand on his bandaged chin, took a deep sigh, and closed his eyes again. His tormentor was gone.

14

Ship Time

When you're packed into a tight space with the same group of people, sharing three meals a day, and going through the same intense experiences together, relationships accelerate at warp speed. Friendships that might take years to develop on land happen within weeks on a ship. At one point, someone told me that more than three hundred couples had gotten married after volunteering together on the Mercy Ship.

Don't get me wrong. It wasn't all rainbows and roses. Dating was far from my mind at the time, especially since I shared a tiny cabin with two guys and a squadron of cockroaches that scurried into hiding every time we flipped on the lights. When roaches crawled up from the shower drain, we'd stamp and yell, "I got one!" and then make a new hash mark on a piece of paper Tony had tacked to our bathroom door, each tick representing a successful kill.

I met Tony and Danny a few weeks into my assignment with the ship. At first, I'd been put in an even smaller cabin with two African shipmates who didn't speak English. We smiled a lot at each other, but it was lonely. Then Tony and Danny, who had a free bed, invited me to bunk with them—although they weren't so sure about me in the beginning. They were all-American, khaki-wearing, yes-sir-no-ma'am

Christian boys, and I was only a few months removed from nightlife. They'd heard rumors that I'd shown up hungover my first day on the ship, and it probably didn't help that I left my designer shirts and jeans in piles all over the cabin floor, or that I name-dropped constantly.

We'd be watching a movie, and I'd say, "See that guy? I saw [*insert name of famous celebrity who shall remain anonymous*] in our club once. He was drugged up out of his mind, and we had to carry him out."

"Cool," they'd reply without skipping a beat. "That must have been right after you broke up with Jennifer Aniston." Tony and Danny always gave it right back to me.

Tony was twenty-three, a premed and philosophy graduate, who grew up in small-town Indiana. He wore a lot of hats during his three years on the *Anastasis*: deckhand, helmsman, forklift operator, and water engineer. As if those roles weren't enough, he was also in charge of patient transport. When patients came out of the operating room, there were no elevators to take them to the recovery unit, one flight below. Tony was one of two strong guys who would carry them on stretchers to a series of pulleys and ropes, and then lower them down to the recovery ward. He made sure that nobody ever got dropped.

Danny was nineteen, from Florida, and taking a break from college to figure out who he wanted to be. When he applied to Mercy Ships, he said he'd do any job, an offer he soon regretted. They stuck him in the kitchen, where he sliced oranges and made mashed potatoes for 350 people every day. Danny, I soon found out, was a budding videographer whose talents were going to waste.

When I'd first arrived in Benin, I bought an old Suzuki 550cc motorcycle from a deck hand for a few hundred bucks, purchasing the freedom to come and go as I pleased without having to sign out a ship vehicle. On Danny's days off, I'd take him with me, and he'd ride on the back of my bike filming local color. We explored the countryside, shooting hundreds of photos and videos: women walking home from the market with their shopping baskets balanced on their heads, farmers tending to cassava crops, barefoot children playing soccer in wide-open fields.

I like to think that Danny found himself on the back of that Suzuki.

Years later, he started his own video production company, and I reached out to my old friend when I needed help shooting and editing.

As my roommates and I grew closer, they came to embrace my eccentricities. One day, Danny mentioned that he liked the style of my designer cargo pants, so I found a tailor in Benin and brought him back to the ship. He showed us fabric samples and took measurements. A couple weeks later, Danny, Tony, and I had new pants and dress shirts. We were the sharpest guys on the ship.

I knew some people thought I was crazy. *Really? Custom-made pants, Scott?* But in my former life, going to a great tailor in London or New York City cost at least a thousand bucks. Here in West Africa? Less than $50, all in.

Always pushing boundaries, soon I was studying the crew manual to find ways to work in a little fun for me and my friends—without breaking ship rules, of course. For example, alcohol, tobacco, and gambling were forbidden on the ship, but the rulebook said you could drink beer or wine in moderation off-ship, provided you were *also* eating a meal in a proper restaurant. So, my roommates and I started an epic poker game, Texas Hold 'Em, in a private room at a local restaurant. Tony went to the carpentry shop and painted pieces of scrap wood red, white, and blue and then sawed them into little square chips.

The buy-in was about $5 and Tony would always sweat it out. "I *gotta* win this hand," he'd say, rubbing his last pennies together. We laughed hard and bluffed even harder.

Finding the fun in work has always been important to me, whether it's tying a balloon to a mop, making people wear pajamas to a fancy club, or treating my roommates to the Savile Row experience in Africa.

Pretty soon, a friend of Tony's named Lafe started hanging out with us. He was a lanky, soft-spoken guy from Colorado. The four of us would scout the flea markets of Benin for cool clothes—vintage American jeans ($1), screen-printed T-shirts of teams that had lost the big game (GREEN BAY PACKERS, 1998 SUPER BOWL CHAMPIONS) (ten cents), and once, a pair of vintage Pumas that smelled like urine and took months to air out ($3).

Lafe ran the Mercy Ships team that helped build wells in the villages. Occasionally, I'd join him in the field to take photos. The earliest pictures I have of Lafe show him working with a group of African teenagers who are shoveling a hole ten feet deep and wide. At the time, wells didn't mean much to me. I didn't understand how life-changing clean water could be or why a bunch of people would put in hours of backbreaking work to dig a giant hole in the ground. So I snapped some pictures to pad out the Mercy Ships archives, and then spent the rest of my time photographing a little boy chasing a bicycle tire with a stick.

It was only much later, when Lafe showed me the actual dirty water people were forced to drink, that I'd get the significance of clean water. Eventually, I'd even come to appreciate why a village would work day and night just to find it.

15

Homesick

DECEMBER 2004

Even though I was surrounded by hundreds of other people, the holidays got lonely. A week before Christmas, I woke up and went down to my photo office, walking past cabin doors decorated with miniature Christmas lights, popcorn strings, big red bows, and fake green wreaths. In a week, we'd put our shoes outside our cabin doors, like the Dutch do, and our friends would fill them with gifts. Ship traditions like these felt interesting and new, but I missed the familiar ones from back home. For me, Christmas meant cozy sweaters and snow on city sidewalks, but Christmas in Benin was red dust and ninety-degree heat served with a side of oppressive humidity. I was homesick.

I flipped on the light in my office, switched on my PowerBook, and started a pot of coffee. Though my day was just starting in Benin, it was about 2:30 a.m. in New York. Six months earlier, I would've been sitting in a nightclub booth, listening to Jay-Z's "99 Problems" and chasing vodka with Red Bull. Now I was halfway across the world gearing up to document the eye surgeries of seven blind children who were coming from an orphanage five hundred miles away. This, I thought to myself, was a problem actually worth chasing.

Later that morning, I went to the dock to watch the children's arrival. Seven boys, ranging in age from seven to fifteen, staggered out of a minibus looking shell-shocked and terrified. They had driven for fourteen hours, and three of them had thrown up on the way. It was their first time in a car. Their caregiver, a tall, blonde Dutch missionary named Marjan, had worked hard to get them to the ship, hoping that a simple surgery might bring each of them perfect 20/20 vision.

Starting with the youngest, the boys were brought one by one into a small exam room. I sat on a crate of medical supplies in a corner and snapped photos, while the doctor stood across the room next to an eye chart.

"Cover your left eye and read the top line, please," she said to the first child. The boy just stared ahead blankly, shaking his head. He couldn't see the letters at all. The doctor brought the chart closer. He shook his head. Still nothing. She shone a light in his eyes for a moment and then sent the boy out.

The next child was brought in. Same results. And then another. After a while, I put down my camera. The doctors exchanged worried looks and shook their heads. These orphans could barely see anything, just flashes of a moving hand. Not even the big letter *A* at the top of the vision chart.

Cataracts, it turned out, weren't the problem. The children's blindness had been caused by blunt-force injuries that happened long ago—maybe a blow to the head as infants. Whatever they'd endured, the sheer force had detached their retinas, causing blindness. And treatment for a detached retina has to happen immediately after the injury. Despite all our Western technology and the eye surgeons' expertise, there was nothing we could do to help these kids see again.

The doctors brought Marjan in to give her the terrible news.

"None of them?" she asked. "Not a single one?"

I rubbed my wet eyes with the bottom of my shirt.

Marjan bit her lip as she called the seven children back in, huddled them close, and explained what the doctors had told her. I held one of the boys by the shoulders, squeezing him tight. Not one of them cried.

Marjan forced a cheerful smile as she told them, "The good news is we get to spend the afternoon in Cotonou! We'll have a nice lunch, and ice cream for dessert!"

I was in awe of the strength it took for her to assume a happy face. People like Marjan, I thought, have to be stoic to survive work like this. Sometimes there's no hope at all. Just heartbreak.

Candy canes and mistletoe were starting to disappear throughout the ship. Routines fell back into place as the crew returned from their holiday vacations.

One morning in early January 2005, I went looking for my boss, Brenda. Back then, we didn't text, so people just tracked each other down in the corridors or cabins to talk face-to-face. When I first joined the ship, I was always getting lost, trying to navigate five or six different decks. Over time, though, I'd found my bearings, devising special shortcuts to the main deck, the dining hall, and the Comms office—just about anywhere I needed to go.

That morning, I found Brenda in her cabin ironing a shirt with her door open.

"Brenda, I'm going to jump down to Cape Town this weekend," I said. "Do you think they'd let me sign out one of the Land Rovers overnight?"

She stopped ironing and gave me a funny look.

"My ex-girlfriend is going to be there for a modeling shoot," I explained. She'd be in South Africa only a few days, but I wanted the comfort of seeing someone familiar. I longed for the feeling of home, however slight or fleeting.

"Scott," Brenda said. "You can't just drive to Cape Town from here. Like, you actually *cannot* drive through the Congo. It's dangerous."

Normally when someone tells me I can't do something . . . well, you know where this conversation was headed.

"Okay. Forget driving," I said. "I'll just fly."

"Yes, but the flights alone will be, like, twelve hours," she said. "You'd have to turn right back around. Have you looked at a map? Do you have any idea how big Africa is?"

She had me there, and it was embarrassing. Until Mercy Ships, Africa had been a distant place in my imagination, a place forever at war, a place where little children shooed flies from their eyes. As a kid in church, I'd listen to visiting missionaries and think to myself, *Man, I am never going to that place.* Africa was hot, dirty, poor.

But in my short time in Benin, I'd learned that Africa was something else entirely. It was yellow mangoes and red dirt, wide skies that stretched farther than I'd ever seen. It was lost kingdoms and French jazz. Strong women who walked ten miles with jugs of water on their heads and sleeping babies tied to their backs. Men who worked hard in the hot sun, throwing hundred-pound sacks of rice onto trucks all day in order to feed their families.

And, as I learned from Brenda, Africa was also *much* bigger than I'd thought. Certainly too big to drive across in a single weekend. Maybe it was time to accept that my old life was gone. For now at least, the ship was my home.

"Right," I said. "Okay, never mind. I'll just tell her I can't make it."

A couple weeks later, I went down to the ward to check on Alfred. I felt so connected to this brave kid. Recovering in a strange place with other sick kids, away from your mom and siblings—it had to be lonely. But Alfred was taking it like a champ.

It had been three months since Dr. Gary removed his tumor. Since then, ship doctors had grafted bone from Alfred's ribs and hip to a titanium plate, forming a new lower jaw that would replace the bone he'd lost in the surgery. Dentists created new teeth to perfectly match Alfred's bite. He bounced back from both surgeries and never complained.

As Alfred healed, I watched him learn how to speak and eat again the way a parent might watch their child's first steps. Whenever I dropped by for a visit, his eyes would light up. I got permission to take him off the ward to see my photo office, and I showed him the pictures I'd taken, documenting his transformation. Alfred was mesmerized. He'd never seen a computer screen before.

Looking at those photos together, I thought about the witch doctors who'd carved into Alfred's face, leaving him even more deformed and full of rage. Now, he often grinned mischievously, and I knew his healing wasn't just a physical one but an emotional and spiritual one, too.

By late January, Alfred was ready to go home. He'd eaten enough rice and beans, pork, and vegetable stews to pack twenty needed pounds onto his thin frame. He still had some swelling in his jaw, but Dr. Gary said it would continue to go down as his body got used to his handsome new face.

Most patients leave the ship with enough cab fare to get home, but I offered to drive Alfred myself. He sat shotgun next to me in the Land Rover. The two nurses who'd cared for him on the ship's ward sat in the backseat with his father.

The road to his village cut straight north for about two hours. We passed giant ferns and banana trees. I saw countless women walking to and from market.

As we got closer to Alfred's small fishing village, I had an idea. He was almost fifteen. It was about time he learned to drive. I pulled over, pointed to the steering wheel and stick shift, and said in my limited French, "Tu le fais!" You do it.

Alfred's eyes grew wide with excitement as we got back on the road and he steered the Rover, shifting us into high gear. The nurses giggled nervously (certainly this was a violation of some Mercy Ships rule) and Alfred's father smiled, taking in his son's delight.

"Pas trois—cinq!" I scolded, placing my hand on top of his and guiding it from third to fifth gear. He looked up at me and grinned. That hard look in his eyes was gone.

As we turned onto a dirt path and toward Alfred's town, dozens of people came out to cheer his arrival. When we parked, Alfred jumped out of the car and was immediately surrounded. His neighbors stared at his new face with awe and wonder. I snapped photographs of him as he floated through this adoring crowd, and was struck by how seamless his homecoming had been. His cursed past, forgotten.

Back in my office later that night, I banged out Alfred's story in a burst of energy. I couldn't wait to share his happy ending with the whole world. Unfortunately, it wasn't that easy. Mercy Ships media moved slower than the *Anastasis* arrived in port. Stories and images went up the chain of command and then on to headquarters in Texas. If approved, they would eventually be published in direct-mail news-letters, press releases, and brochures—but the whole process could take months. An entire year might pass before Alfred's story saw the light of day.

Thankfully, I had my own channels. Before setting sail, I'd cre-ated a personal blog, onamercyship.com, and I'd converted my fifteen-thousand-strong Brantly&Scott Inc. email list into a Mercy Ships newsletter. My club friends were going to receive weekly dispatches from the field whether they liked it or not. Including this one: "Alfred is 14 and suffocating to death on his own face . . . Here are the pic-tures . . . Click on the link to see how his amazing story ends."

I couldn't wait to see how people would respond. I wondered if they would see in Alfred what I saw: *Look at this kid! He's like Muhammad Ali giving the thumbs-up—king of the world! And here he is, coming home to a party. To a new life!*

Both of us have new lives, I thought to myself as I clicked the Send button.

That day, Alfred's story traveled across the world to my family, friends, and thousands of people I knew from the clubs. I got more than a few "unsubscribe" requests, which I guess I should've expected. I mean, imagine sitting at your desk on Wall Street or Madison Avenue, thinking about where to have lunch, when some reformed Christian party boy kills your appetite with a full-on visual assault of human suf-fering. My old girlfriend wrote back—and I could almost hear her cute Danish accent: *Scott, that's gross. Send me a preeety picture of Ahfreeka.*

A few of my friends joked in emails that perhaps my new life was just a ploy to get girls. I could just imagine the conversations they were having about me: *Scott's a do-gooder humanitarian now? Please. What a stunt! Who does he think he's fooling?*

My email list shrank at first, but I kept sending out stories, and in the months to come, it started growing. During the four months the *Anastasis* spent docked in Cotonou, there was so much to write home about: 429 adults and children received surgery for facial deformities, hundreds more had received eye surgeries, and more than 2,000 people had visited the off-ship dental clinics. Mercy Ships volunteers had also built crucial infrastructure in Benin: a rural maternity clinic, fourteen latrines, and three freshwater wells. In March, we'd leave Cotonou and sail up the coast for a four-month tour in Liberia, where there would be even more stories to share.

My parents forwarded my emails to everybody in church, leading prayer vigils and fundraising campaigns for the neediest cases. Strangers wrote to me, sharing their own experiences in Africa and the joy of doing charitable work abroad. Others sounded envious, like they'd begun to imagine what a completely different life might look like.

"Wow. Wish I could trade places with you right now!" one woman said.

"Thanks," another wrote. "You've reminded me that there's more to life than getting past the velvet rope."

"Everyone here wonders what's going on with me, because I have tears streaming down my face," a friend wrote from her desk at Chanel. "I just read Marthaline's story. How can I give her money? How can I give my time?"

Reading their comments only strengthened my conviction that I'd made the right decision to volunteer. In fact, maybe I was actually good at this gig. What if my photos and stories could inspire people just like me, people who'd never thought much about charity before, to give *their* time, talent, and money to help the poor?

16

"Actions, Not Words"

It was a three-day sail from Benin to Liberia. On our last night at sea, I watched a documentary about Liberia's vicious war. I saw villages reduced to rubble and ash, children toting AK-47s, mothers sobbing over rows of mutilated bodies. I heard heavy mortar fire and sirens. When I closed my eyes to sleep, the scenes kept playing in my mind.

In the middle of the night, I woke up in a sweat. It was hot and dark in my cabin, and my roommates were stirring. *Why am I still hearing sirens?* I wondered. I stumbled out of bed and quickly realized it wasn't sirens at all; it was the ship's fire bell going off—a terrible, industrial tone, like the sound of a nuclear power plant's alarm. At first, I thought this must be a drill. But then—no. Nobody holds a drill at 1 a.m. Our ship really was on fire.

Here's what's supposed to happen when the fire bell goes off: You grab your "go-bag" of food, water, ID, personal mementos, sunscreen— basically anything you'd want if you were stuck in a lifeboat for a long time. Then you head to your assigned station on the promenade deck and await further instructions from the captain.

I didn't have a go-bag ready. I was lucky to get a pair of pants over my legs, throw a life jacket over my shoulder, and jump into flip-flops. Up on deck, hundreds of my crewmates nervously milled about in pajamas. A haze had enveloped the ship as thick black clouds billowed from the smokestacks. I saw Danny.

"Where's the fire?" I asked.

"In the engine room."

That was bad news. The engine room of the *Anastasis* was located in the very heart of the ship, and most days it was covered from top to bottom in oil and grease. Danny said that Tony had gone down to fight the blaze with the other four guys on his fire team. They said it felt like Dante's inferno down there.

The station masters shouted out names for roll call, making sure no one was missing. Looking around, I saw parents clutching their kids. I saw fear in the eyes of nurses and doctors who'd shown ironclad calm in the operating room. And that's when I knew—we all might die tonight. All this time, I'd been mentally preparing myself for our mission in war-torn Liberia, a place of horrific human suffering, and yet our ship might go down in flames before we even got there.

I pictured my mother and father getting a late-night phone call and learning that their only child had died at sea. That would kill Mom. I snuck down to my photo office to shoot them a final email. Belowdecks, I heard volunteers knocking on every door, yelling, "Cabin check!" and looking in closets, bathrooms, and even under beds. In a crisis like this, people sometimes hide out of fear, refusing to come out.

"The ship is on fire," I wrote my parents. "We may need to use the lifeboats. Please pray for us." It was a practical request more than anything else. If anyone could pray a fire out, it was Chuck and Joan Harrison.

Back on deck, crew members held one another, crying. Heads were bowed in small circles of anxious appeal. There was nothing to do but wait and pray. We were a full twenty miles off the coast of Ghana. I wondered if we had enough lifeboats for the three hundred adults and fifty children aboard the *Anastasis*.

It seemed an eternity before the inky smoke clouds started to thin and dwindle. Then, finally, the captain's voice came over the loudspeaker. The fire had been contained, he said. *All clear.* I took in a very deep breath. We cheered and hugged one another and wiped away tears. I don't think anybody went back to sleep that night.

The next day, the ship arrived safely in the port of Monrovia, Liberia's capital. The only casualty of our fire was the generator that powered the air-conditioning system. It could have been much worse. And yet, without AC, our floating village quickly turned into a sweltering metal oven. For four weeks, we endured 110-degree temperatures inside our tiny cabins, even with the portholes open. We sweated buckets of water and drank gallons more to stay hydrated.

The ship's galley, where Danny worked, had about twenty small electric fans blowing during the day, so Danny started borrowing them at night and bringing them back to our room. We rigged five of them from the ceiling and bookshelves so that they'd blow into one another while drawing in a breeze from the porthole to create a vortex of cool air. Our wind tunnel was so powerful, Danny could drop a sheet of paper in the middle of the room and it would spin around for a good fifteen seconds before hitting the ground.

Fixing the ship's generator should've been a simple process, a matter of a few days at most. But in Liberia it took four weeks just to get the parts.

When we arrived in March 2005, Liberia was eighteen months removed from a brutal fourteen-year civil war that had left a quarter of a million people slaughtered and a million more displaced. There were still fourteen thousand UN troops roaming the country in white tanks. Our first week in Monrovia, I saw helicopters, barracks, and razor wire everywhere. UN soldiers kept firm grips on their AK-47s as they guarded our ship. You had to show ID at several checkpoints just to get into the port, and the UN enforced a strict 10 p.m. curfew.

I couldn't wait to take my motorcycle out to explore the city. Liberia, which means "Land of the Free," was founded in 1822 by thousands of freed American slaves. The national language is English, and the flag is an exact copy of the American flag, except with one white star instead of fifty. Many Liberians see themselves as kin to Americans.

And yet despite our shared history, as I drove through Monrovia, all I could think was: *This is the craziest place I've ever seen.* All the buildings were riddled with bullet holes. There was no running water, electricity, sewage systems, or mail delivery. If you did see a light on at night, it meant a generator was chugging loudly nearby. Fuel, too, was incredibly scarce. To fill up my bike, Danny and I would roll into one of the many makeshift roadside gas stations—just a rickety table with large glass bottles of brownish-yellow D-grade fuel. The attendant, typically a teenage boy, would stick one end of a green hose in his mouth and the other into a bottle of fuel. He'd then suck on the hose to draw the gasoline up, trying his best to pull the hose out of his mouth and shove it into the tank before the bitter liquid reached his lips.

If the boy got sick from working as a human gas pump for hours on end, he was out of luck. Ninety-five percent of the country's clinics and hospitals had been looted and destroyed during the war, and fewer than thirty-four government doctors were caring for the needs of three million citizens, often graciously accepting chickens or goats as payment.

The patients that Mercy Ships screened in Liberia suffered from many of the same diseases as those we saw in Benin. But here, we also saw evidence of torture and mutilation. Children who'd had hot oil poured on their bodies. Women with noses and ears cut off. There was always an edge in the air, the threat of recent horror never far from anyone's mind.

And yet, the people I met wanted only peace. They wanted to rebuild their lives. You could see it in the way mothers draped blue tarps across the broken windows and bombed-out walls of their homes, just to give their families a sense of security and privacy. Or the way that fathers returned to their looted storefronts to clean, restock, and start over again.

The more I experienced Liberia, the more I turned to Dr. Gary for wisdom. Was I supposed to just take photos? Was that really helping anyone? It was one thing to look through the camera and document suffering, but quite another to actually help people. I wanted to do more.

Like Mother Teresa, who cared for lepers and orphans in the streets of Calcutta, Dr. Gary challenged me, and every other volunteer, to go out and look after the most vulnerable and needy. "Christians have a mandate from the Bible to care for the poor," he said. "We have a responsibility to actively fight injustice in the world." He would quote from Matthew 25, where Jesus says, rather provocatively, that at the end of our lives, God will judge us by whether we fed the hungry, gave water to the thirsty, offered hospitality to the outcast, clothed the unclothed, healed the sick, and visited people in prison. Do these things for them, and you do them for Him.

I found myself praying more and enjoying the new connection I felt with God. Hungry for a deeper faith, I'd sign out weathered books from the ship's library and take my motorcycle out to a desolate enclave called, of all things, Thinkers Beach. I'd read, watch the powerful waves come in, and talk to God (sometimes out loud), truly believing he was listening. *There are so many desperate people here. How can I help them? Show me the way.*

When I got back to the ship, I would try to steal ten or twenty minutes of time with Dr. Gary. I'd hunt him down after a surgery or in the mess hall, and he'd help me process the things I was feeling.

"I really want to help the poor," I said once. "But there's just *so* much need. We're sending patients back to homes that have no roofs. Children are going back to villages with no schools. It's all so overwhelming. I don't even know where to begin. Or if I'm really making a difference."

In his usual calm way, Dr. Gary told me a story about Kwanam, a patient from a few years back, who had large facial tumors that smelled so bad she'd become an outcast in her village. Kwanam gathered the courage to leave home, for the first time ever, and go to a Mercy Ships screening to see if she could get help. As she waited in line, she felt so scared that she almost turned around and left. But then a volunteer who was passing by saw her and stopped. He walked up to her, put a hand on her shoulder, and said, "We're going to try to help you." It was the first time anyone had touched her in ten years. She decided to stay.

"We still don't know who it was, but that person changed Kwanam's life," Dr. Gary said. "Scott, Mercy Ships isn't looking for Mr. or Mrs. Super Christian. We're looking for people who are courageous enough to obey that little voice in their heads telling them to help another human being.

"God isn't asking you to do everything," he continued. "Take care of the two or three things you can, and leave the other eight to Him. Remember: Actions, not words, are what people need from us."

And yet Dr. Gary's words were exactly what I needed. To this day, I can still hear his voice reminding me, "Actions, not words."

17

"They *Drink* This?"

During the four months we toured Liberia, I went all in on action. I remember one night in particular: I was walking down the street in Monrovia with my Comms teammate James when a beggar asked us for coins. James was taken aback when I opened my wallet and emptied it into the guy's hands. There was no way to know how far the money would go or what the man would use it for—it certainly wasn't enough to change his life—but that didn't feel like an excuse for not giving.

Every new encounter with people who were poor or sick or marginalized gave me strength. Some weeks, I'd go out with our physician teams to bring medical gear to an HIV hospice or help set up a dental clinic in a remote village. When I discovered a leprosy clinic in Ganta, a town about six hours from the ship, I went back three or four times to visit the patients, bring them medical supplies, and take photos. Once, I dragged Lafe out there for a sleepover. When it got dark, we rounded everyone up in the front yard, pinned a giant white sheet to the clinic wall, and showed the patients an hour-long slide show of all the photos I'd taken of them. We even blasted William Orbit's version of *Adagio for Strings* from a portable speaker as the images rolled across the screen. It was so over the top, but the patients cheered and laughed.

"Just seeing their portraits like that—larger than life on the side of the building—must have made them feel like 'I matter,'" Lafe said.

One morning in May, shortly before the end of our Liberia tour, I grabbed my camera bag and tracked Lafe down in the port's vehicle lot. Before he could speed off, I jumped shotgun into his idling Land Rover and said matter-of-factly, "I'm going out in the field with you today."

Lafe had been working on a water project in Bomi County, a district of twelve small villages that housed about six hundred people. When we arrived, I saw homes made of mud and sticks, only a handful of which were furnished with corrugated metal roofs. The residents kept their prized possessions inside—a couple plastic tubs for washing clothes, a pot for cooking food, a machete for farmwork and cutting branches.

I followed Lafe to the work site, where a group of men stood around a large hole in the ground. One guy was at the bottom of the hole digging; more were at the top hauling up buckets of rocks and soil on pulleys. Lafe had been teaching them how to build their own well.

"C'mon," Lafe said. "I want to show you something."

We got back in the car and Lafe drove about five minutes up the road, and then pulled over near a small dirt path. We got out and I followed him through tall grass and into a nearby forest. Brown leaves crunched beneath our feet as the canopy grew thicker over our heads. After a few minutes, we walked over a huge system of ropey tree roots that encircled a small pond filled with muddy green water. It smelled of rot and was brimming with water bugs. The surface of the pond was covered in lily pads.

Across from us, at the edge of the pond, a group of women and girls was approaching the water. They carried yellow Jerry Cans (the kind of plastic containers that people back home use for gasoline). Except these women were filling their cans with pond water.

"This is it," Lafe said.

"This is . . . *what*?" I said.

"That village we were just in. This is their water source."

"You've got to be kidding me," I said. "They *drink* this?"

Mosquitos hovered over the surface of the water, and I was pretty sure I saw something big move below it.

Lafe nodded. "Yep. It's all they have."

I couldn't believe it. The water was disgusting. I didn't even want to touch it. And the people here were *drinking* it?

I honestly hadn't understood water poverty before. It had been one thing to hear Lafe talk about people drinking bad water, but seeing it up close made me angry. I decided right then that if I could ever do anything to help these people, if I could help Lafe build more wells, I would do it in a heartbeat.

"Let's go," he said.

As we left, I turned back and saw a young girl bringing a plastic cup of dirty water up to her lips.

By June 2005, my tour with Mercy Ships was ending, but I wasn't ready to leave. My education felt incomplete, and I didn't want to say good-bye to my mentor Dr. Gary. If anything, I wanted to do more to help Mercy Ships' cause. So I put in for another year of service, with a promise to return to the *Anastasis* in October 2005—this time, for a full eight months in Liberia.

Many of the returning crew would take the summer off, but I hated the idea of sitting around just waiting for the next leg to begin. A week before we took leave, I was cleaning out my photo office, archiving the last of my images, when an idea hit me.

Over the last eight months, there had been times when I'd just sit in my office looking at patient "before" and "after" pictures over and over again, reliving those moments of joy and transformation. It gave me an extraordinary feeling, and I wondered if there might be a way for me to share that feeling with everyone.

There wasn't much time, but maybe, with the support of my old club friends in New York, I could do something *more* with these photos and stories.

18

---

mercy.

As my yellow cab crawled through evening traffic on the Manhattan Bridge, New York felt charming and strange all at once. The buildings seemed taller, and the landscape at night reminded me of a giant Lite-Brite screen. Cruising up First Avenue toward Brantly's apartment in Alphabet City, I rolled my window down and inhaled familiar smells: spicy lamb from the halal vendors, cigarette smoke outside a bar, rotting garbage in the alleyways. I was home.

Brantly was now living in a walk-up on Fifth and Avenue A, and had said I could crash on his couch for a couple weeks.

"Bro, how have you been?" I asked, excited to see my old friend.

"Same, same," he said. "Same, same."

Indeed, he had been doing pretty much exactly what he'd been doing when I left—babes, booze, repeat. The club names were the only things that had changed. Milieu had been a short-lived venture, and he seemed weary, more cynical. Or maybe I was just getting a fresh look at how I once felt.

It had been almost a year since I'd escaped nightlife, trading models and bottles for sweaty roommates and operating rooms. I'd returned to New York armed with fifty thousand digital photos and a vision: to produce a major multimedia exhibition that would bring more publicity and donations to Mercy Ships.

Somehow I'd convinced Mercy Ships to approve my idea. It was a huge leap of faith on the organization's part, considering they'd need to underwrite the cost of a show and cross their fingers that I could deliver the results. Honestly, I didn't even have a plan yet for when, where, or how this exhibition was going to happen.

Before getting to work, I went to see my parents. The news from home was that Mom's health had improved. She felt well enough to leave the house with Dad, go to church, and even eat at restaurants. When I got off the train in Raritan, New Jersey, she was there on the platform waiting for me. We hugged, and it was the first time in decades that I could recall not worrying about the odors from my clothes irritating her. She still had bad days now and then, and she still needed to be vigilant about avoiding chemicals, but her illness was lifting, and doctors couldn't explain why. She'd always give credit to God and say that decades of prayers had been answered. I like to think she was right.

By August, with just a couple months left of my hiatus, I was *still* scrambling to find a gallery space when two incredible gifts came through. The first came from Alon Jibli, a former nightlife competitor and a guy who I'd thought never liked me. He'd read all my dispatches from Benin and Liberia and sent me a few supportive emails along the way. After arriving in New York, I looked him up. "I'm back!" I'd emailed. "If you're game, I'd love to sit down with you and tell you more."

We met for coffee at an Italian restaurant in Nolita, and I showed him photos of Alfred, the blind orphans, and other children with terrible deformities made whole again. He started crying right there at the table.

"What do you need?" he said.

"I want to put on an exhibition, and I need a gallery. But I have no money."

Alon introduced me to his friend Shelly, who worked at the Metropolitan Pavilion, a beautiful multi-use space right in the heart of Manhattan's gallery district. "Just show her what you showed me," he said.

I did. Shelly immediately connected me to her boss Alan. Moments into the same presentation, he covered his eyes and waved me away with his hands. "Please. I can't see this anymore. You can have whatever you want."

I knew the images were powerful, but even I was surprised at how strongly people responded. They were opening their hearts and their wallets to the cause.

Shelly and Alan gave me use of the Metropolitan Pavilion for two weeks in September. It was a gorgeous seven-thousand-square-foot space with white poured-resin floors and an adjacent banquet hall—all totally free. It was a donation worth more than $50,000.

The second gift I received was a place to live. An art dealer friend offered up his loft in the Meatpacking District, just blocks from the gallery. It was a giant, airy, quiet place decorated with Andy Warhol prints and a couple of $1,000 chairs. There, I could work without distraction and plan the exhibition. For hours each day, I would sit on the hardwood floor, blasting music and picking over images for the show. Before long, every spare wall was covered in black-and-white printouts of Mercy Ships patients—Alfred's "before" and "after" shots; Papa James, from the leper colony; two blind twin boys, Assan and Alusan, who'd regained their sight.

As a show of faith in me, Mercy Ships flew a guy out from headquarters named Steve. He headed up the organization's TV and video department and was their best creative talent. Steve turned out to be a great thought partner. To save money, he crashed at the loft with me, even sharing a king-size blow-up mattress. After living in 125 square feet of space with two other guys, I thought it was plenty of room, but Steve found the arrangement a bit awkward.

Tianna, the communications director I'd met in Germany, flew in a couple days after Steve to help design the show's flyers, signage, press releases, and other materials. Some nights, I'd invite her and Steve to meet me at a club—not to party but to work. I'd be hanging out in the VIP section with my laptop open, showing people pink, fleshy tumors to the sound of thumping house music. Every once in a while, a club manager or DJ would scold, "Hey, bro, you gotta tone it down. You're killing the vibe." But mostly, people were curious, and eager to help.

Tianna and Steve had never experienced New York nightlife. One evening, they dropped my name at the front door of BED, a new supper club in Chelsea, and then stared in disbelief as a doorman shepherded them inside and up onto a rooftop crowded with—you guessed it— dozens of massive beds. Guests lounged like toddler hedonists among mountains of soft red pillows, wearing complimentary socks after having stored their shoes in cubbies. And in a scene straight out of *Zoolander*, Steve once saw male models doing push-ups in the bathroom.

When the two finally found me, I'd be pitching the CEO of a fashion company or the head of a PR agency or some other VIP who hadn't heard about Mercy Ships yet. If we got hungry, the kitchen would make us lobster tails, salmon, scallops—whatever we wanted—all on the house.

After about a week, plans for the exhibition were beginning to take shape. We would call it *mercy*. The mixed-media gallery show would run from August 29 to September 8, with a gala benefit and auction on September 7. We obviously couldn't sell my photos for charity— nobody wants a framed portrait of a facial tumor hanging over their designer couch—but we could use the images to tell stories, ask for donations, and sell $125 tickets to the closing party.

I'm a narrative thinker by default, so I wanted the exhibition to be more than just a gallery of pictures. Instead, we'd take visitors through a story that mirrored my experience with Mercy Ships. I could see it all clearly in my mind. As you walked in, you'd first encounter a large video loop showing thousands of patients milling around at screening day in Benin. The next room would showcase Liberia, with the sister U.S. and Liberian flags draped side by side amid images of a pock-marked landscape. Then you'd enter a room with hundreds of Mercy Ships flyers (the same kind that inform potential patients about screening day) pasted haphazardly, floor to ceiling. On the opposite wall— pictures of some of the most common diseases the Mercy Ships doctors treat. Next was the "eye room," featuring stories of patients who had regained full sight through a $150 cataract operation. Beyond this, the main attraction would be a giant video installation of a tumor patient named Friday, his portrait morphing ever so slowly from "before" to "after"—a beautiful, reconstructed face.

That was the vision. Actually pulling it off was another thing.

Back at the Meatpacking loft, the only Wi-Fi signal was in the bathroom, where a neighbor's open network came through. We'd crowd together with our laptops open—me on the toilet seat, Steve on the tile floor, Tianna in the tub. None of us had ever put on an exhibition, and there were a million little details to consider, from security and liability insurance to thank-you notes and tax receipts for donors. At one point, we literally Googled, "how high to hang art," and found some advice from the Smithsonian website. Steve and I would have fiery debates over the scale and size of each installation.

"I think we should have ten TVs," he'd say, referring to the wall of TVs in the "eye room."

"No, no, no, no," I'd say. "We need *sixty!*"

"Scott, where are you going to get sixty TVs?"

"I'll figure it out. If I can get them, do we want sixty or not?"

"I think that's overkill."

"How about forty?"

"Okay. We could probably do forty."

In the end, I managed to get nine TVs donated, and we stacked them in three mini towers.

We also designed a special video installation to support Lafe's work digging wells. A beverage distributor from upstate New York donated 1,700 bottles of water with special MERCY. WATER labels. Guests could buy them for $20 apiece, dropping their cash into a large blue translucent jug. The exhibit ended with a bigger ask of $380 per person.

Mercy Ships had agreed to put every penny the exhibition raised toward the cost of surgeries on the *Anastasis*. So we put up a huge black-and-white sign telling guests that one $380 donation—the average cost of a full surgery—could change a life forever. We set up a table with old-school swipe-and-sign credit card machines, where people could give on the spot and receive a tax receipt from Mercy Ships.

As the week of the event approached, the three of us worked around the clock. I was meticulous about design. The mazelike show was supposed to evoke the feeling of a sterile hospital ward, so the walls and floors and curtains between each station had to be pure white. For all the invitations, title cards, and decorative details throughout the gallery, I chose a jet-black background and white text, to show contrast. Black, white. Before, after.

In the month since I'd first met with Alon and Shelly, we'd gone from having nothing to securing a free gallery space, free printing of postcards and flyers, and massively discounted production and framing for the images themselves. A top PR agency provided its services for free. Liquor companies sponsored the closing night party, and restaurateur Jeffrey Chodorow donated all the food. Friends stepped up with items for the auction—a $1,200 Christian Louboutin crocodile handbag, tickets to NYC Fashion Week, dinner for two at Soho House. All in, we received more than $50,000 worth of gifts in kind.

In the countdown to opening day, I was doing media interviews—I even scored a *Wall Street Journal* piece—and promoting the show harder than any party I'd ever worked.

"Are you pulling an all-nighter?" Dr. Gary wrote one evening after receiving an early-morning request from me to put the *mercy.* show in his prayers. "In the midst of all this, Scott, do take care of yourself."

I appreciated his concern, but I'd never felt better. I knew that the bigger the crowd we could pull in, the more money we'd raise—and the more surgeries and lives transformed. So I'd set a target goal of $250,000, and was operating on caffeine and manic energy to get us there.

Almost every day for the last month, I'd emailed Mercy Ships headquarters with urgent requests and breathless declarations:

> I've got a mailing list 50,000 deep in the city—millionaires, celebrities—let's blast out invitations to them, can you get me charity bulk-mail rates ASAP? . . . I need to meet first thing Monday morning with whoever handles the credit card accounts. . . . I'm not going to be happy about the Gala

unless I get at least 800 bodies into the space that night at $125 a head. . . . By the way, September 7th is my 30th birthday. I can't think of anything cooler than showing 25 years of mercy ships to 800 people!

I was a total pain. And I told everyone at Mercy Ships to expect a huge turnout. "Get ready, because everyone in New York will be talking about you guys by the end of the week."

But then, on opening day, Hurricane Katrina made landfall in Louisiana. All attention turned to the tragedy in the South, the most devastating natural disaster in our nation's history. There was no worse time to ask for money. How could I even talk about the suffering of people thousands of miles away while 80 percent of New Orleans was underwater?

On opening day, Mom and Dad came out to ooh and aah at the exhibits, and a few friends and curious passersby dropped in, but the gallery was mostly empty. By evening, we'd raised only a few hundred dollars. I was exhausted and heartbroken.

This exhibition was everything to me. It was a chance to showcase Mercy Ships, and maybe even an opportunity for me to redeem myself, to prove that the last year of my life had been more than just an escape plan. If I couldn't raise real money in the next ten days—even worse, if I ended up *costing* Mercy Ships money with my high-concept art show—I might as well throw in the towel.

This has to succeed, I thought. *I'll just work harder.* I picked up the phone and paced the empty gallery, calling everyone I knew, talking up the show like it was already a runaway success.

"You have to see it. Please come by!"

"Can't do it today? Okay, how about tomorrow?"

"What time can you get here? No problem, we'll stay open late for you."

I was practically harassing people to come, to make a donation, to buy tickets to the gala—which, in all honesty, was really just a standard cocktail party.

Somehow, though, as they always do, New Yorkers came to the rescue. Friends showed up and spread the word among their friends and families. The $20 donations piled up in the big blue water bottles, coming to almost $11,000 on their own. Adrian Grenier, the star of *Entourage,* and supermodel Jessica Stam agreed to cohost the closing gala. That night, at the party, I got up to give a speech and looked out across a room packed with more than four hundred people. I was grateful for every single person there.

"Tonight, you've come to save lives," I said. "Just by being here and buying tickets, you already have. But I want to ask you to keep giving! Sponsor a surgery. Help us build wells. We can't do any of this without you!"

And they *did* keep giving. In the end, Mercy Ships spent about $30,000 to underwrite an event that raised $96,000—all of which went directly to patient surgeries. It wasn't the $250,000 I had been hoping for, but everyone at Mercy Ships seemed pleased with what we'd accomplished.

A few weeks later, I'd head back to meet the *Anastasis* in Liberia. I was burning with excitement for the next tour. I felt like I'd proved my value, gained some credibility with the organization. And it had gotten me thinking maybe this *could* work.

For the first time, I could see a path forward. I could partner with Mercy Ships and create more shows around the world. I could use my unique nightlife experience, my unconventional skills, to serve the poor. Maybe charity really was scalable as a life plan.

19

Better to Beg

LIBERIA, DECEMBER 2005

My mind was racing. I'd been driving all day, taking a patient named Joseph back home. But we'd just made an unexpected detour that was about to change my life. So much had happened in the last few hours, and I was about to do something totally outside the boundaries of Mercy Ships protocol. *I need to call Dr. Gary right now,* I thought.

Running down the list of rules I'd surely broken, I could already hear the reprimands from the medical staff:

You are not a doctor, Scott. You can't diagnose patients!

Why would you promise someone that we'd help him? You don't control the surgery schedule. There's a hierarchy here!

What if the tumor is malignant? You've created false hope!

All true. All rational reasons for why I probably should never have stopped the car and promised a complete stranger that we could fix his face. But none of these excuses mattered to me in the moment.

Earlier that morning, Joseph and I hit the road for a six-hour journey back to his village. Joseph had recently recovered from surgery for a giant neck tumor he'd endured for two decades. Over the years, as it slowly grew ever larger, he prayed daily for God's help. What struck me was the specificity of his prayers: he asked God to bring a hospital to *him*. And when Mercy Ships showed up, that's exactly what had happened.

Joseph and I had gotten pretty close on the ward. On our way to his home, I gave him money for a dowry and wedding so he could properly propose to his girlfriend. We also stopped at a little bodega in a sleepy seaside town called Buchanan, to buy a few bags of rice for his homecoming party.

As I was paying, I saw a man standing near me in the store, touching his own face and shaking his head. I couldn't hear what he was saying, but that gesture was so familiar. I'd seen it time and again when locals spoke of tumor patients they knew. Something inside me screamed, *Go talk to him*.

"Hi, I'm Scott. I'm sorry. Are you trying to say something to me?"

"Fisherman," the man said. "He has very, very large growth. On face. I can't believe how big."

Of all the rice stores in all the towns in all the world . . .

"Can you take me to him?" I asked.

The man shrugged. He didn't know where the guy lived.

"I know!" said a boy standing in the back of the store who looked no older than six. And off we went, me and Joseph and the boy, to chase down the mysterious fisherman. He wasn't at home. He wasn't at his father's house. On a hunch, we drove toward the ocean. And there he was, walking away from the sea and toward our car.

He looked to be about thirty, dressed in sandals, shorts, and a dirty T-shirt. He was strong, healthy, and handsome—except for a massive tumor that filled his mouth and pushed his left cheek and lower jaw out and down into a taut, soccer ball–size mass. It was the biggest tumor I'd ever seen. A classic Mercy Ships operation. But I was a photographer, not a doctor. There'd certainly be a stern lecture if I showed up at the ship with a patient I had screened myself.

Can I really do this? I thought. Then I remembered Dr. Gary telling me that sometimes it's better to beg for forgiveness than to ask for permission.

"Hi," I said, shaking the man's hand. "My name is Scott. I think we may be able to help you. We have a ship, with doctors from the West, and *this*"—I gestured with an open palm toward my own cheek—"this is what we do."

The fisherman nodded and listened intently as I introduced him to Joseph. As they talked, I went to the Land Rover and grabbed a folder of Joseph's "before" photos that showed his tumor. The man looked at them and nodded. Joseph pointed out how normal and strong his neck now was. Still, this man's tumor was much bigger and heavier. I had no idea if he'd get cleared for surgery or recover as well as Joseph had.

"How long has it been growing?" I asked.

"Too long," he said. Thirteen years, and it had started with a toothache. I asked him for his name, and he told me "Harris," although it came out sounding like "Haruth." It was difficult to understand his speech through the tumor.

"We are going to take Joseph home," I said. "And we will stay there for the night. But maybe I can come back tomorrow? Will you come with me to the ship?"

"Yeah," he said, nodding. "Anystemyuredy." *Anytime you're ready.*

We said good-bye and shook hands. Then Joseph and I got back on the road.

Twenty minutes of anxious stalling later, I called the *Anastasis* and asked the operator to page Dr. Gary over the ship's loudspeaker. After what seemed an eternity, his calming voice came on the line. My voice was shaking as I told him about Harris and the promise I'd already made to him.

"Yes. I understand. Of course I'll examine him," he said.

"That's *great!*" I said. What a relief.

"Bring him in tomorrow, and we'll see what we can do."

"Dr. Gary, thank you *so* much."

The next morning, I picked Harris up in Buchanan, and we were on the road by 9 a.m. Harris was one of the funniest and most outgoing patients I'd ever met. We blasted Michael Jackson and Stevie Wonder tunes in the car and he sang along. At one point, I almost drove the Land Rover into a ditch laughing as he shouted the lyrics to "I Just Called to Say I Love You," his voice soaring high above the music. As we got closer to Monrovia, the police checkpoints increased in frequency, and Harris eagerly took in the sights and sounds of his chaotic capital.

Some patients are scared to board the ship. Many have never seen a staircase before, and others have heard in their villages that white people will eat you. A group of us once spent a full day trying to convince a sixty-two-year-old Fulani woman from Guinea to descend the steps to the hospital ward. She was certain it was the path to hell, and that she'd never go home. We showed her before-and-after photos, we had other patients come out in hospital gowns to tell her all was safe down below. Nothing worked. She just wouldn't budge. Finally, I asked a nurse to sit with her on the dock while I drove through Monrovia at night looking for Fula speakers. After an hour, I found a couple who agreed to come talk to her in her own dialect. Another hour of negotiating later, and she finally relented and entered the ward.

Harris, though? He had no reservations. He bounded up the gangway toward the ship, exclaiming a loud "O!"—a kind of Liberian greeting—at the things he found interesting. Dr. Gary examined him immediately and ordered a round of X-rays and blood tests. The results weren't good.

Harris wasn't strong enough for an operation. An open bleeding sore on the tumor caused his hemoglobin count to dip to one-fourth a healthy person's. Still, Dr. Gary promised Harris we'd get him ready for surgery. It would take at least two weeks of blood transfusions, iron supplements, and solid meals to prepare him for the operating table.

Christmas break was around the corner, so instead of taking leave to go chase adventure or join my friends on safari, I decided to stick around with Harris. We spent a lot of time together, checking out photos in my office and watching movies on my laptop. (He especially loved *Shrek*.) His tumor soon became almost invisible to me, and I began to understand his muffled speech. He was always cracking me up. One time I caught him peeing off the ship's bow with pride, his gown flowing behind him in the wind. On Christmas Day, he wore a fuzzy Santa hat as he tore through the gifts the volunteers had bought him: a radio, a Leatherman pocketknife, a model car.

The night before his operation, he asked if I could save his tumor for him.

"I want to punch it like *this*," he said, violently smacking the palm of his hand with his fist. I was pretty sure the protocol for disposing of medical waste wouldn't allow Harris to keep his tumor for a boxing match, but I promised to do my best.

Harris's surgery took eight long hours—twice as long as Joseph's. I watched the procedure with both curiosity and concern, taking pictures and asking questions.

I've never minded the gore of surgery. Once, when I was a junior in high school, I skipped class, drove to the local hospital, and asked the county pathologist if I could scrub in and watch him perform an autopsy.

"I want to be a doctor someday," I said. "So I can help my sick mother."

Really, I just didn't feel like going to school that day and had wondered if I could talk my way into an autopsy.

"Sure, kid," he said.

So, while my friends were solving boring trigonometry problems and staring blankly out the window, I was watching a physician cut into the body of a middle-aged white man who'd died of a heart attack. The medical examiner was so eccentric that he handed me organs to weigh as he told me dark tales about his work.

"This body's in great condition," he said, as he put the man's broken heart in my gloved hands to place on a scale. It wasn't gross or scary or sad. It was amazing. And I learned an important lesson that day. Sometimes, when you want something, all you need to do is ask.

When Dr. Gary finally detached Harris's tumor from his face, a nurse dropped it in a plastic bin to be weighed. Six pounds, four ounces—ten times the weight of a human heart.

As I suspected, the medical staff was not going to allow Harris to beat up his own tumor, but they agreed to let me take it to the incinerator, supervised by a nurse. One of my roommates came with me, and we videotaped ourselves trash-talking that tumor and pretending to punch it through the medical waste bag.

"This is for you, Harris!" we shouted over the din of the incinerator before tossing it into the flames, reducing it to smoke and ash.

Back in recovery, Harris came to as the anesthesia wore off. I handed him a mirror, and he held it tightly in his left hand, observing himself as he ran his right hand over the contours of his chin and jaw. His face had a completely different shape. His eyes widened for a moment; he nodded, and then fell back asleep.

Three months later, when it was time for Harris to leave the ship, I threw a party for him at a restaurant in his hometown. I paid for dinner for fifty of his friends and drinks for the entire village of two hundred fifty. Harris gave speeches from a second-floor balcony to a rapt audience like he was the mayor of Buchanan. It was the best $190 I'd ever spent.

Dr. Gary and I talked about Harris a lot after he left, about how special he was, how meaningful our meeting had been for me. I learned that Harris's tumor had grown so large that he would have died in the next month or two if not for the surgery. If I had turned my back on Harris that day out of fear of disobeying ship protocol, he would likely have suffered a slow death by starvation or suffocation. That was a life-changing realization for me. A reminder to trust that voice in my head, to never stop fighting to help others.

"Scott, people in Liberia constantly hear the word *no*," Dr. Gary said. "'No, you don't have enough money.' 'No, there are not enough doctors.' 'No, there is no electricity, no water.' 'No, we can't help you.'

"But God sent Harris to you," he continued, "and you said yes."

Harris was a big yes for me. But I shuddered to think of times in my life when I had turned my back on people in need. How many times had I seen a homeless man begging on the streets of New York and avoided making eye contact with him? Or watched a woman struggling with heavy bags up the subway stairs and breezed past her? Or been approached in public by a charity volunteer and barked back, "Late" or "Too busy."

After meeting Harris, my default answer became yes.

Yes, I'll give you my lunch.

Yes, I'll pay for your schoolbooks.

Yes, we will find a way to do this!

The problem was, now I expected everyone else to say yes, too.

20

Africa Time

LIBERIA, JANUARY–MARCH 2006

Ever since the success of the *mercy.* exhibition, I'd obsessed about scaling the show and taking it on the road, putting on even bigger exhibits in train stations, public squares, and famous galleries across Europe. If Americans could give nearly $100,000 to Africa in the aftermath of a disastrous hurricane, who's to say we couldn't raise $1 million or more in some of the world's biggest cities?

My tour with the *Anastasis* was ending in April, and I wanted to start building the exhibition strategy now, in January. But I kept bumping up against Mercy Ships corporate. I'd constantly hear, "This isn't how we do things, Scott . . . This needs approval . . . You don't have the authority . . ."

In retrospect, it was naïve to think that the people at Mercy Ships headquarters would just say, *Yeah kid, whatever you wanna do. Here's a corporate credit card. Go nuts!* But for as long as I can remember, no matter what I was pursuing, I've always strived for bigger, better, more—and faster. Mercy Ships wanted to approve exhibition locations, photos, signage, sponsorship partners. They wanted hard budgets and airtight contracts drawn up by lawyers. Everything was moving at the pace of an ocean liner when I wanted to drive this thing like a speedboat.

I started to wonder if this was how all large organizations worked. I'd only ever known the speed of club life. But maybe charities operated on "Africa Time," a concept Dr. Gary explained to me one day

As Westerners, he said, we have a linear view of time—past, present, future. We are constantly planning for what's next—often obsessively, like I was. But to many people in Africa, time is nebulous, like a cloud. You are here, dealing with the now. Your past exists in the living memory of the oldest person in your village. Your future is unknowable. And so you take each day as it comes.

Dr. Gary called Africa Time one of the greatest gifts his patients had given him. Instead of fixating on things like *Do I have enough money in my pension plan? For my child's college fund? How can I upgrade my job title, my house, my life?*, he'd learned over the years to place a greater value on the moment.

"To be grateful for the day, to be happy that I've got some friends to sit with under the tree and enjoy a mango in the afternoon heat? That's been very helpful for me," he said.

I admired his patience and serenity, but I just couldn't get the hang of it. I wanted to go fast-fast-fast. Do more-more-more. Africa Time was infuriating to me. Not just the metaphorical version I was experiencing with the Mercy Ships corporate office but also literal Africa Time in Liberia. I was constantly waiting for buses that never arrived on time, shops that didn't open at their posted hours, and government officials who didn't turn up for meetings. It felt like everyone and everything were conspiring to slow me down.

Of course, my problems weren't real problems. For example, when Lafe dealt with Africa Time, people's lives were on the line. During the eight months of my second tour, I made four or five trips with him to the villages where he worked. He'd help a small community build a well, and then schedule a weekly class to teach twenty of the residents about waterborne diseases, hygiene, and sanitation, so they could bring that knowledge back to their community. Except it was nearly impossible to get his students all together in one spot at the same time. He'd show up to teach, and there'd be five people. So he'd send two students off to gather the others, and forty-five minutes later, *maybe* he'd have half a class.

Once, Lafe saw a woman carrying a forty-pound Jerry Can on her back to a faraway river, even though Mercy Ships had recently dug a well in her village. He investigated and found that the well hadn't been properly maintained. It's not uncommon in countries like Liberia to find a $5,000 well broken and abandoned simply for lack of a fifty-cent O-ring.

The point being: Africa Time forced me to live in the moment, or at least to *try*. But it also taught me that our work needed to be culturally sensitive and locally led. We had to build relationships with the village elders, find common understanding, and involve them in each project. We had to provide training and education, and get full community buy-in. If we wanted these solutions to last, the people we served needed to see the connection between the present problem (delayed maintenance of a well) and future consequences (sick kids and women with crippled spines).

In most villages, this was harder to pull off when we partnered with the men. The women and girls didn't need to be sold on the value of clean water—they were the ones who carried it for miles every day, and used it to do the cooking and cleaning. So it was astonishing to see what we could accomplish when we partnered with the women instead—especially women like Mama Victoria Thomas, or Mama Vic, as everyone called her.

At the end of January 2006, my roommate Tony took me to meet Mama Vic at the orphanage she ran about an hour outside Monrovia. She looked to be about thirty-five years old, with tight braids, a big gap-toothed smile, and a wide lap for all the orphans to sit on. Tony had met her during our last tour in Liberia, and by now the whole ship knew her story.

In 1990, Mama Vic was married with five children when her husband, a security guard for Liberia's president, was killed in a rebel coup. As civil war broke out across the country, she began to take in the wandering orphans whose parents had been slaughtered in the fighting.

In Dr. Gary's words, Mama Vic said yes to every child. At one point, she was caring for 150 kids, somehow managing to feed, clothe, and protect them. This often meant saying no to herself. Once, when her brother gave her $500 to go toward the schooling of her five biological children, Mama Vic used it to buy food for the orphans instead. Later, she sold all her belongings and pooled the money with her savings to purchase the land where her orphanage was located.

Tony had first heard about Mama Vic from a local aid worker in Monrovia—how she was looking after sixty children and several widows in a six-room shelter made of sticks, mud, and a Red Cross tarp. During rainy season, the roof would cave in and the kids would have to huddle together on the dirt floor, shivering and wet, as the walls disintegrated further with each new downpour. When the rains ended, the children would help rebuild their home, collecting mud in a wheelbarrow and making bricks for the foundation. They prayed for a day when they could afford cement, a day when they could build an orphanage that wouldn't wash away every year.

When Tony visited the orphanage during our last tour, a small boy walked over to his vehicle and started picking out the lettering above the grill. "L-A-N-D . . . Land," he said, and then walked away. Tony was shocked. In a country where schools had been closed for more than a decade, Mama Vic was teaching her children to read. Inside the orphanage, Tony took one look at the crumbling mud rooms and instantly saw his challenge: to raise enough money to build the twelve-room complex these kids really needed—and to do it all before the rainy season hit in two months.

A project of this scale in Liberia would normally take two years and cost tens of thousands of dollars, but word spread quickly on the ship and in the community. "Who's got $40 for Mama Vic?" "Who's got $20?" we'd ask. We wrote home to our churches and schools; we bagged sand from the beaches to make cement. A local construction team donated more than $20,000 in building materials and labor. The Lebanese business community in Monrovia donated a stack of roofing sheets worth $2,600.

For the next two months, a crew of Mercy Ships volunteers and skilled local laborers worked day and night putting up cement walls and installing proper doors and windows. They built a metal roof, wired the building for electricity, and bought bunk beds with mattresses. When all was said and done, Mama Vic's orphanage had undergone an epic transformation—*Extreme Home Makeover: Liberia Edition.*

As soon as we returned to Liberia for our second tour, Tony visited Mama Vic to see what else he could do for her. Her son Willy had already used leftover funds and materials to build a six-room schoolhouse on the orphanage property. So Tony made plans to add a small office and a covered porch and, most important, to dig a well and a latrine. Lafe would be the technical supervisor on the water projects, and I'd be there with my camera to document phase two of the orphanage's transformation.

The closest public well was a mile and a half away, and we knew that the daily walk was brutal for these kids. After a hot trek there, they would get teased by the older local boys, shoved to the back of the line, beaten up and picked on—simply because they were orphans and easy to victimize. It took forever for them to come back home with a single Jerry Can of water.

I wrote about their situation to my aunt Jayne and uncle Benedict, my favorite and most interesting relatives. Jayne was a former soap opera actress, and Benedict a real estate magnate. Over the years, they'd taken me in at their beautiful red mill farmhouse and gardens in Connecticut whenever I needed a quiet place to recharge. I never *asked* them for money. I'd just talk enthusiastically about the things I'd seen: "Aunt Jayne, Mama Vic has done amazing work with these kids, and they're learning to read! But they're getting bullied whenever they go collect water. They really need their own well."

"Oh! Maybe I can help," Jayne would say. "Maybe I can do that, build them a well."

Jayne sent me the money, and I convinced the owner of a local construction company to give us a discount on the culvert pipes and parts we needed. The only task left was the digging.

There are many different ways to find clean water when there is none. One of the cheapest solutions—costing about $2,500 at the time in Liberia—is to hand-dig a well. It starts with six men and thirty days of hard work digging, pick-axing, and sometimes even dynamiting through dirt and heavy rocks until you reach groundwater. Next, you line that deep hole, the walls of your well, with concrete culvert pipes, so it won't collapse. The final step is installing a hand pump, which can deliver about five gallons of clean water, or one Jerry Can, every ninety seconds.

Thankfully, the soft red dirt of Liberia didn't need blasting. The laborers on Mama Vic's land dug straight down and found the water table just thirty feet below the surface.

Throughout the construction process, the older boys in Mama Vic's care earned a small sum working alongside the hired laborers. Those boys worked *extra* hard, eager to prove their worth to the men from the surrounding communities—men who used to ostracize them. Making the orphanage a site of income and employment had changed the way people saw the children who lived there. It helped to repair some of those fractured relationships. Everyone felt invested in Mama Vic's future success.

The day in early April 2006 when clean water flowed right in front of the orphanage was a miracle to these kids. From the toddlers all the way up to the eighteen-year-olds, they jumped up and down, their eyes wide with delight as they pumped the handle and watched clean liquid gush from the spout. It was so cool.

And just like that, I'd funded my first well.

As my second tour with Mercy Ships wound down, I spent most weekends at Thinkers Beach, swimming, reading, camping, and thinking about the future. One day in late March, I invited Mercy Ships' chief officer, Craig Rogers, to join me.

"Yes, mate, let's go and do that," he said in his thick Australian accent.

We ate fresh fish that night at Thinkers Café, a simple concrete structure with a grill, some plastic chairs and tables, and a bare lightbulb. The place was owned by a hardworking Liberian guy who dreamed of building a huge resort someday. He'd taken great pains to salvage the beachfront property so squatters wouldn't take it over.

We shared our table with two physicians who were volunteering at Monrovia's only working hospital. One was American, the other British. I'd seen them around before, and I learned that both doctors had been working in Africa for many years. They understood the diseases of poverty as well as anyone on the *Anastasis*. They also knew how expensive it was to keep a hospital ship afloat.

"Getting spare parts, buying fuel, keeping the ship running?" the American said. "For the same amount of money, you guys could build an entire hospital. In fact, for that kind of money, you could do several each year."

"But how would you staff them?" Craig said.

"He's right," I added. "Not many people are up for living and working in the bush."

We had a lively conversation about the effectiveness of the nongovernmental organizations, or NGOs, we'd seen working in the region. There were so many, focused on things from HIV/AIDS care to building libraries in schools. I enjoyed picking the doctors' brains.

"In your experience, from all you've seen, what's working the best?" I asked. "Where are people doing the most good?"

"Look," the Brit said. "What your team is doing is meaningful. I'm not saying it's not. But with all the illness overwhelming the hospitals here, you could probably reduce the load by half just by giving everyone in the country clean water."

I was intrigued but skeptical. "You know, I've actually seen what people are drinking in the villages," I said, thinking of my time with Lafe. "The water is disgusting. But does it really cause half of all Liberia's sickness?"

"Yes," the doctor said. He ticked off a list of bacteria-induced problems and waterborne diseases. Cholera, diarrhea, dysentery, hepatitis A, typhoid, polio, and even that flesh-eating surgical nemesis noma—

all of them were directly related to poor water quality. Not to mention the two hundred million people every year who contract schistosomiasis, also known as bilharzia and snail fever. It's a horrible disease people get from bathing, walking, or washing in water infested with parasitic worms.

"All these diseases are largely preventable," the British doctor continued. "Most of them would just go away with good water and sanitation. And *then* you could focus on the other crucial issues around poverty."

Later that night, Craig and I settled into our sleeping bags around a crackling campfire on the beach. But I couldn't sleep. All I could think about was water. If it was really true—if half of all illnesses could be traced to bad water, then what could I do to help solve *that* problem?

I'd gotten so much satisfaction from helping my friends build a single well. Just like the surgeries on the ship, it felt so tangible—except, instead of healing just one patient, we were protecting the health of dozens of children.

Maybe, like Dr. Gary had said, the only way to solve a problem as big as the global water crisis was to embrace Africa Time and focus on the present.

One village at a time. One well at a time.

21

No Strings Attached

APRIL 2006

I was thirty-five thousand feet in the air, on a plane somewhere over the Atlantic. Outside my window, the sun was slowly setting under a blanket of cumulous clouds, turning the sky orange, yellow, and pink.

A couple weeks earlier, I'd officially wrapped up my time with Mercy Ships by throwing a huge party at a sushi restaurant inside Monrovia's Royal Grand Hotel. I invited patients, ward translators, day workers, my UN buddies, friends from the U.S. embassy, and my shipmates. I even hired some teenagers from the ship to work the door.

When Dr. Gary Parker and his wife, Susan, showed up, my heart—and if I'm honest, my head, too—swelled with pride. "You know what?" Susan said to someone later that night. "This is what the kingdom of God looks like. It looks like Scott throwing a party and inviting everyone."

Now, that evening seemed like ages ago. I'd flown through London on my way home, for a quick stop at the Apple flagship store there to give a lecture about Mercy Ships. And now I couldn't stop thinking about $14 cocktails. The night before, I'd gone to dinner with two friends at a bustling brasserie in Notting Hill. I almost choked when the $336 bill came. Thankfully, my buddies smiled and grabbed it with a wink, before whisking me away to another bar for $14 margaritas.

I know London has never been cheap, especially for Americans, but after spending so much time in Liberia, I'd forgotten just how expensive things in the Western world really are. Our dinner bill in London would have practically paid for Alfred's entire surgical care; our margarita bill could have bought a couple of new roofs to cover leaky homes.

This might be what I'll miss the most, I thought, as I watched the sky outside my window turn from misty gray to black. I'm going to miss buying a $22 bag of rice that feeds a family of four for a month. I'll miss paying a Monrovia landlord $120 (a *year's* rent) so that a mother and her two previously blind children could live in a home and not a refugee camp. I'll miss spending $55 to put a boy through school.

On the ship, I used to hear the term *culture shock* all the time. Volunteers would spend eight months in a country like Liberia, and then come home and start judging everyone around them: *How could you spend so much on a pair of shoes, a dinner, a watch, a car?* We'd talk about "reentry" like we were returning through Earth's atmosphere from Mars. I never wanted to be someone who judged or finger-wagged, but my recent sticker shock did make me wonder if there was a nonjudgmental way to invite people to use their money for good.

I'd be turning thirty-one in a few months. If you'd asked me a few years earlier what I'd be doing on my thirty-first birthday, the answer certainly wouldn't have been "Oh you know, just trying to save the world." But now, as cliché and naïve and idealistic as it sounds, that's exactly what I wanted to do. I loved the feeling I got when my own small acts visibly changed lives. It was a high that outdid any other I'd ever known, and I wanted everyone to experience it with me.

The hard part was deciding where to focus my energies. It had become increasingly clear that Mercy Ships and I just weren't meant to be. We couldn't come to an agreement over what our partnership would look like. We struggled to find common ground over things as simple as reimbursement for a donors' lunch and as big as who owned the copyright to the tens of thousands of images I'd taken during my tours.

Lately, Dr. Gary was constantly in my thoughts. I was inspired by his ability to stick with a single cause for so long. I felt ready to give my life to something bigger than myself, something that would help thousands, maybe even millions, of people. But I didn't want to start over. I didn't want to find another charity to join or butt heads with another bureaucracy.

"God has big plans for you," Dr. Gary wrote to me after my tour had ended. "He's invested great gifts and skills and put his heart in you. He'll do great things through you . . . But there will be more tests. Stay strong."

His words were like a blessing from afar, affirming my decision to go it alone. And the tests he wrote about would come sooner than I expected.

In late April 2006, I came home to New York completely broke, only to discover that it was worse than that. I was also badly in debt. Brantly and I met at his new place in SoHo one night to catch up. After talking about the new clubs he was working at, he let slip that he'd never dissolved our nightlife business.

"You didn't disband the company?" I said incredulously.

"Nope," he said.

"Did we ever pay taxes?"

"Nah, I don't think so." He pointed to a box on the floor filled with letters from the IRS. Brantly never opened the mail, because he felt like it was always bad news. "It's probably all in there if you want to sort through it."

Tearing through the stack of unopened notices, I discovered that we'd never filed returns, made estimated payments, or kept current with tax payments for Brantly&Scott Inc. Now we were both on the hook for about forty grand in back taxes, late fees, and penalties.

I was furious. Brantly didn't seem to be interested in coming up with the money for the IRS. In fact, he seemed indifferent to most things in his life at that point.

"Sorry about that," he said with a shrug. "You can live here for free if you want, while you're figuring it all out."

I was planning to start a world-changing charity. How was I supposed to do that in a two-bedroom SoHo loft with bill collectors at the door and Brantly's friends coming by to snort drugs off the coffee table? How could I ask people to give me money for a cause when I owed $40,000 in back taxes?

I took him up on his offer. After all, a free place in New York City was worth something, and I had nowhere else to live. At first, I slept in a small bed on a raised loft at the back of the apartment. Later, when Brantly needed that space, I took my pillows and a few blankets to the walk-in closet and slept on the floor beneath a rack of shirts and sweaters.

In July 2006, I opened a bank account and deposited $1,100—all I had in the world—for my new charity. I also hired a personal accountant to dissolve Brantly&Scott Inc., file our tax returns, and set up a payment plan with the IRS. Now I just had to figure out what this new charity would actually do.

During all those hours I'd spent on Thinkers Beach in Liberia, I'd given a lot of consideration to the *act* of charity. The word *charity* is derived from the Latin *caritas*, which means love. I once heard it defined as "helping your neighbor in need and not getting anything in return." That sounded so beautiful and simple to me. Regardless of one's religion or politics, regardless of race or geography, we all could use a little more *caritas*. More action motivated by love, with no strings attached.

Dr. Gary had kept in touch over email, and I shared my next steps with him:

> I'm starting my own charity . . . I opened a bank account . . . I'm going to Uganda at the end of July to visit refugee camps . . . Should I focus on access to surgeries, malaria nets, health clinics, education, justice, shelter, water?

I think he could tell that my head was spinning with ideas. I wanted to do it all. But Dr. Gary provided a much-needed voice of reason.

"Scott, rather than five or ten different issues, perhaps God wants you to focus on one intensely," he counseled. "Pick that one issue carefully."

Focus on one intensely. What if I did just that? Picked one issue to start with? And once I got a handle on it, added new things to tackle from there?

I thought back to the conversation with Craig and the doctors on Thinkers Beach. To the women in Bomi County who were drinking the unthinkable. To my time with Lafe, watching him train locals on well construction and sustainability. I thought about the first well I'd been personally involved in, at Mama Vic's orphanage. And I wondered, *What if I chose water?*

I thought of what water had meant to me growing up—or rather, how *little* it had meant. It was just always there whenever I needed it: coming out of taps and showerheads, clean and never-ending. But the more I learned, the more I realized that those doctors weren't exaggerating when they said that dirty water and lack of sanitation caused half of all illnesses in the developing world. The real number was 52 percent. For years, dirty water was the number one cause of disease and death worldwide. It killed more people than all the wars, terrorism, and violence in the world combined.

But unlike cancer, malaria, and other problems that have sent thousands of smart people searching frantically for a cure—dirty water already *has a cure*. It's a completely solvable problem. Very often, clean water is already there, even in the poorest of villages, flowing like liquid gold in aquifers just beneath people's feet.

I was no hydrogeologist, but I knew from all those trips with Lafe to well sites that many countries already had amazing local organizations working to create solutions—from the most basic hand-dug wells like Mama Vic's to deep-drilled wells, rainwater-harvesting systems, and biosand filters that could be built for as little as $60. If you weren't married to a single kind of intervention, there were countless ways to eradicate dirty water and improve the lives of millions of people.

"We know that the single most powerful thing we can do for the whole human race is to get everyone safe drinking water," Dr. Gary had said once in a speech. "That will affect more lives than anything else."

I loved that he'd said "will." Not "would," not "could," but "will."

I had no seed money or personal savings to draw on, but I was willing to work day and night and do whatever it would take to get this thing off the ground. I wanted to start helping as many people as possible, as quickly as I could.

But first, I was going to need some help myself.

22

Nonprofits for Dummies

NEW YORK CITY, JULY 2006

Lani Fortier got things done. We'd met through mutual friends during my second Liberia tour. In addition to assisting doctors and working in the kitchen, Lani helped repair an orphanage just outside Monrovia and played for the Liberian women's soccer team in her free time. We actually didn't know each other that well until the day she stepped up to save my going-away bash.

On the day of the party, all of Monrovia suddenly went on lockdown when word got out that ousted Liberian warlord Charles Taylor was being flown to Monrovia's airport to be arrested and charged with war crimes. UN and local officials feared his presence could reignite tension and cause riots, so no one was allowed on the streets after dark.

Lani first helped me work with the United Nations and the U.S. embassy to get special clearance for the party, and then coordinated the ship's vehicles to move all one hundred guests in staggered time slots, with a security escort, safely to and from the hotel. I was impressed with Lani's hustle, so I told her about my idea to take the *mercy.* exhibition to the biggest cities across Europe.

"What about coming to work with me when you finish your tour?" I asked.

"Sure," she said, "Why not. I mean, what could be more fun than running around Europe for a year?"

Lani grew up in New Hampshire, studied at the University of Connecticut, and had planned to attend medical school after graduation. But during her stint with Mercy Ships, she discovered that she enjoyed haggling with businessmen over the price of mud bricks and bunk beds as she worked to improve the orphanage. She felt drawn to humanitarian aid work, and her interest in practicing medicine soon faded.

By June 2006, I'd emailed Lani to tell her the big news. The European *mercy.* tour was off, but I was starting my own charity. And I really did need her help.

"Can you just come to New York instead? It's the greatest city in the world. I promise it will be interesting."

"Okay," Lani said, thinking to herself, *I'm twenty-four, I've been living on a ship in battle-scarred Liberia. I've got no set plans. How bad could New York be?*

She gave away most of her clothes and belongings in Africa, packed a small suitcase, and by the end of July was working fifteen-hour days with me at Brantly's place. At night, she crashed on a friend's couch in a small West Village apartment, rent free. We had no cash, but plenty of energy and way too much confidence for two people with zero experience running a charity.

It felt like we were building a start-up. On a typical day, I'd say, "Lani, I need to go to Uganda and chase down some stories. Do you think you could loan us the money to buy a good camera?"

"Sure," she'd say, handing me her credit card.

"Lani, I want to build a huge water exhibition across New York City. Ten parks in ten days. Who do you think I need to meet to get the permits?"

"I have no idea," she'd respond while simultaneously dialing the Parks Department and the Chamber of Commerce. When she finally did find the one guy who granted permits for that kind of thing, I found out where he worked and cornered him in his office. When he wouldn't give a firm yes on the spot, I sent him a stream of twenty follow-up emails and took him out to lunch until he finally gave in.

I was on a mission, with no bureaucracy or approval process to slow me down. And Lani indulged my audacity. Maybe she felt energized by it, or maybe she knew that if my heart was really set on something, it was just easier to get on board.

I liked Lani: she was irreverent and really didn't care what people thought of her. That included me. She'd tag along to my meetings dressed in flip-flops and cargo pants, and call me "Harrison" in a flippant, irritated tone. She'd sit with me across from exhibition builders, bottled-water distributors, and potential sponsors, listening to me boast, "Yes, we're doing a *huge* water exhibit in *ten* major parks across the city. We're going to raise $100,000 in the next two months, and we'll use all the money to build wells with the NGOs we've partnered with in Africa." All the while, she'd quietly think to herself, *Wow. This all sounds great, but none of that is happening yet!*

Running to the next meeting, she'd berate me, "What are you talking about, Harrison? We're gonna do *what*? You're way overcommitting. You've gotta rein it in!"

But I think she knew that there was no reining it in.

In the beginning, we spent most of our money on photo/video gear and trips to Africa—and most of our time creating videos and writing stories. Conventional wisdom says that you don't start a charity by prioritizing content, but I believed we needed compelling stories about real people who were drinking bad water. Without them, there would be nothing to talk about, nothing to inspire donors to care or give.

To find those stories, we needed to find the best local partners: experienced NGOs who could connect our fledgling nonprofit to the people we wanted to serve. I didn't know how to pick them, so I emailed Trent Stamp, the president of Charity Navigator, one of the largest and most respected evaluators of nonprofits. Trent came to Brantly's apartment to hear my pitch, and he helped us choose our first four partners: Healing Hands International in Ethiopia, Concern Worldwide in Uganda,

Water for People in Malawi, and Living Water International in the
Central African Republic, which partnered with a local group called
Water for Good. They were some of the top-rated charitable organiza-
tions building clean-water projects in Africa.

In those early days, Lani and I would basically promise our partners: "We're going to raise money for you. You don't need to do anything. But we need to talk about your work and put your name on our
brochures. Can we use your brand and your trademarks, please?" Getting permission required lots of phone calls and in-person meetings to
show everyone we were really serious. I'm not sure that I would have
let two young humanitarians with no experience put our name all over
their fundraising materials, but in the end, nobody turned us down.

At the same time that I was promising our new partners money that
we had yet to raise, I was also forming an official 501(c)(3) nonprofit
organization. All summer, I'd been reading *Nonprofit Kit for Dummies*
and asking to look at the bylaws of other organizations for ideas. Bylaws are an organization's mission statement, its reason for existing in
the world—and they eventually have to be approved by the IRS in
order for the organization to become tax-exempt, which is how people
get a tax break when they donate to you. I sweated over the wording of
our bylaws, creating multiple drafts with Lani and a group of business
leaders I knew from church who'd agreed to be my founding board
members.

I decided to call the umbrella organization Charity Global Inc.
We'd do business as charity: water first, and then expand to charity:
education, charity: health, charity: shelter—moving from problem to
problem until we saved the whole world. I wanted to be the Richard
Branson of philanthropy. But in the back of my mind, I was terrified
that our 501(c)(3) application wouldn't be taken seriously.

On paper, I was a terrible bet. My story read like satire from *The
Onion*: "Former nightclub promoter, thousands of dollars in debt, starts
charity from friend's cozy drug den." If they really stopped to look, no
one in their right mind at the IRS was ever going to give me charitable
status. Our application needed to be absolutely perfect. So I hired ex-

pensive lawyers who'd taken hundreds of charities through the process. In the fall of 2006, they helped channel my grandiose ideas into an application that felt serious, thoughtful, and legitimate.

"Scott, just be prepared. This process could take up to two years before you get an answer from the IRS," the lawyer said. Two *years*? Had I heard him right?

"And we'll probably have to go through several rounds of clarifying questions," he added. That was devastating news. It meant we wouldn't be able to give donors any tax benefits until then. But what else could we do? We pressed on, hoping for a speedier review.

I went back to Africa in August—this time to Northern Uganda. My mission was to meet with local residents and NGOs and photograph the worst water I could find. By the end of my trip, I'd found it—along with a greater sense of urgency for our work.

On the morning of August 4, I jumped in the back of a blue Toyota Land Cruiser that smelled like dirt and sweat, where I was joined by two local aid workers. We raced through Uganda's wild Northwest, followed closely by a military truck carrying heavily armed soldiers. Security measures were extremely tight because the notorious cannibal warlord Joseph Kony was still on the loose, and rebels from his Lord's Resistance Army had recently been seen in the area.

After eight hours of driving, we finally reached Bobi, the largest internally displaced persons camp in Northern Uganda. Bobi was overflowing with orphans, widows, and broken families who'd fled their villages ten years earlier. They'd been running from Kony's guerrillas, who had snatched scores of children from their homes and forced them to become killing machines. An astonishing 31,638 people were now registered at Bobi. Their one-room dirt-floor homes, just round mud-and-grass huts, were packed so tightly together in some places that there was barely room to walk between them. Cholera, measles, and diarrhea can spread quickly in conditions like these.

But despite all the suffering, overcrowding, and insufficient food, there was a spirit of family and community in the camp. Kids played games of tag and hide-and-seek, running in and out of huts with doors made from flattened tin cans of USAID vegetable oil. Women in faded dresses chatted like old friends as they sat in line for hours with their yellow Jerry Cans next to the only working hand-pumped well.

One well for 31,638 people.

According to UN standards, a single well should serve a maximum of 250 people, which means this camp should've had 125 wells.

"Where's everyone else getting their water from?" I asked.

"This way," a guide motioned. We walked through the camp, then down a hilly slope to a massive water hole surrounded by tall palm trees, where a group of women were collecting stagnant brown water. As we watched them dip their cans into the mud hole, I couldn't help but think that when I flushed the toilet in Brantly's apartment, I was draining half the amount of water that one woman here used to drink, wash, cook, and clean in a whole day. The people of Bobi desperately needed our help. We had to get them clean water *now*.

We weren't even an official charity yet in the eyes of the U.S. government. I had no money and was practically homeless, living off the goodwill of friends. A rational person probably would have thought, *I should focus on getting my own life in order first.*

But none of that mattered to me. A day I spent worrying about myself was a day when more lives at Bobi would be lost. Their needs were more urgent than anything else I could think of.

Still, I *was* broke. So I did the only thing I knew I was really good at.

I threw a party.

23

charity: water

Charity: water's official launch took place in a nightclub, the day after my thirty-first birthday. I had no money or budget, but a good nightclub promoter knows how to work his birthday. It's the one night when you can call in a ton of favors, and everybody comes out because they know you're going to show them a good time. My friends didn't know it yet, but by the end of the night, they'd learn about the global water crisis—and, I hoped, decide to become part of the solution.

A hot new dance club in the Meatpacking District, called Tenjune, gave us the venue for free. Inside, we lined the walls with huge photos of people drinking dirty water in Uganda. A liquor sponsor pitched in enough alcohol to run an open bar for the first hour—a great way to lure people in the door—and celebrities like Mark Ruffalo, Joaquin Phoenix, Lauren Bush, and Terry George (the director of *Hotel Rwanda*) turned up in support. On the night of the event, Lani worked the velvet rope.

"I hate this, Harrison," she said, holding a guest list of RSVPs. "Do you know how hard it is to turn people away?"

"Yes!" I laughed. "I did it for ten years. That's why *you're* doing it!"

To enter, everyone had to drop a $20 donation into a Plexiglas cube at the door. Seven hundred people showed up. A few gave even more than $20—like Brantly's weed dealer friend, who threw $500 in the box and said, "Hey bro. First donation I've ever made to a charity."

The next day, we counted and re-counted the cash, and filled out forms to document the donations. We'd raised $15,000 in one night, all to give the people of Bobi clean water. It was amazing.

"Dude, we're a real charity now!" Lani said. She was right; we were in business.

Being a real charity meant more meetings and even longer hours for both of us, because I was spinning a hundred ideas at a time on no sleep. We created a wonky little website, and began taking donations and selling CHARITY: WATER T-shirts and wristbands. I had this crazy idea to sell custom bottled water (the kind you'd normally buy for $1) for $20, and give all the proceeds to our new NGO partners to build wells. I thought the intentionally outrageous price point would generate awareness and show how far the gap between rich and poor really was.

Bottled water was normally marketed in cheery blues and aqua greens, so we worked with a printer to design all-black labels with white typeface. Our labels read: OVER 1 BILLION PEOPLE WALK AT LEAST 3 HOURS EACH DAY TO COLLECT WATER, and MORE THAN 4,500 CHILDREN DIED TODAY FROM UNSAFE WATER.

I pitched it like this: For $20, you're getting a single 16.9 ounce bottle, but you're providing the equivalent of more than fifty thousand bottles of water in developing nations, given that a well can pump one million liters a year and provide a community with clean, safe drinking water for more than fifteen years. The numbers sounded good, but what I didn't know at the time was that nobody *really* knew how long wells lasted. Years later, I would be forced to reckon with that ugly truth.

Still, the $20 bottles (which we bought for 41 cents apiece) proved to be highly efficient fundraising—a forty-eightfold profit. Later, we started selling them in bulk ($480 for a case of twenty-four), and Lani or a volunteer would deliver water around town, collecting checks and swiping credit cards on our clunky black machines. We had so much water that we were stacking pallets of it up to the ceiling in Brantly's spare bathroom, like a massive Jenga puzzle. One day, Brantly left some incense burning next to the tub and melted half a pallet.

The water was heavy and a pain to move around, but it looked cool, and everyone wanted it. During Fashion Week, we got the staff at Lotus to sell bottles and wear our T-shirts. Celebrities, socialites, and entrepreneurs let us place charity: water at their birthday parties, magazine launches, and posh event spaces—raising $660 here, $2,300 there. We even got the Soho House, the Mercer Hotel, and Claridge's in London to place it in every room. Our name was getting out there. Lani and I had become a glorified bottled water sales team.

Two weeks after my birthday, we kicked off a ten-day, five-park out-door exhibition in Union Square. Lou, a club friend who designed sets for music videos, helped us build an eye-catching display on the cheap: a series of tall black panels on wheels, which told the story of dirty water. We collected scummy green liquid from nearby ponds and rivers and poured it into giant Plexiglas aquariums embedded in the panels. We wanted to show people: *Look at this disgusting water! If your tap were turned off today, this is what you'd have to drink!*

Initially, I had a grand vision for the centerpiece of the exhibition, something that would wow people and draw them in. Lou and Lani listened patiently to my pitch.

"Okay, imagine a giant, gleaming clear cylinder towering over the humanity of New York City. People walking by the park will tilt their heads and say, 'What on earth is *that?*' and they'll *have* to come see it. Then they'll discover it's filled with cold bottles of charity: water—and if they feed the tower a twenty-dollar bill, it drops a bottle in their hands!"

"Sounds great, Scott," Lou said. "But that would cost over $100,000 to build."

In the end, we settled for a piece of a salvaged tin duct as our tower.

We then Velcro-taped hundreds of empty charity: water bottles side by side to hide the ugly metal cylinder, and surrounded that with a Plexiglas bucket, where we stored the actual water bottles that people could buy. The signs and handouts promised that 100 percent of every purchase would go toward building wells with our NGO partners in Uganda, Ethiopia, Malawi, and Central African Republic.

About a hundred family members, friends, and friends of friends came out to volunteer at the exhibit, to speak to New Yorkers and tourists about charity: water's mission. On our first day in Union Square, more than fifteen hundred people showed up, and we sold $3,000 worth of water—enough to rehabilitate one well. On our second day, more than two thousand people came, and we sold another $5,600 of charity: water bottles—enough to hand-dig a new well.

Mom and Dad drove out to help that weekend. I was super busy and constantly moving, but seeing my mother in Union Square, with traffic fumes swirling around her, strangers and their offbeat scents passing by, and her being okay with it all—it was so gratifying. She was present and healthy in a way I'd never experienced.

By our third day, on Sunday afternoon, the forecast called for rain, which threatened to stain and warp the photo panels. I looked up from my phone and asked a young woman who'd been working with us all day to go buy tarps to protect them. She walked off and hurried back with exactly what was needed. We outlasted the rain, and by the end of the day, she was one of the last volunteers standing.

"Hey," I said. "You've been here all day! What's your name? How'd you hear about us?"

She was shy and cute, with big dark-brown eyes, and looked to be in her early twenties. She wore a ponytail and the CHARITY: WATER T-shirt we'd given out to all the volunteers.

"Viktoria," she said. "My neighbor Lou told me what you were doing. I think it's cool."

"Well, thanks for getting those tarps so fast, and for being here all day. If you're free, we'll be back here in the morning!"

I was headed toward the truck to start packing up, but she stopped me.

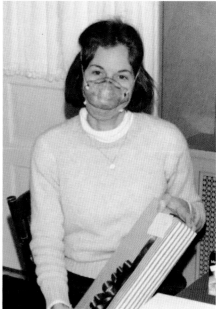

1975: Mom and Dad holding me in front of our home in Philadelphia.

Christmas 1981: Mom in Garni and Pop-Pop's kitchen, wearing her protective mask.

When Mom's immune system shut down, Dad rid our house of chemicals that could trigger her attacks. Here, in 1981, he's ripping out our wall-to-wall carpeting, which contained formaldehyde.

1992: Mom's safe room.

1992: Airing out books on our front lawn.

Airing

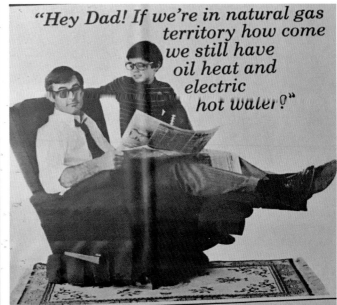

"Hey Dad! If we're in natural gas territory how come we still have oil heat and electric hot water?"

My parents would pay me $1 or $2 for chores like mopping, and I always looked for ways to make them more fun. Here I am at ten, dragging a balloon along for the ride.

The newspaper ad that Dad and I modeled for, not knowing at the time that it was for a gas company.

Sunday River, the band that led me to New York City. (From left to right) Dave Kopp on rhythm guitar; me on piano and keyboard; Bryan Adams on lead vocals; Jim Daly on bass guitar; and Kevin Von Holtermann on drums.

Brantly and me in Crobar's VIP room, where I intentionally flashed my Rolex at the club photographer.

The 522-ft. long *Anastasis*, docked in the port of Cotonou, Benin.

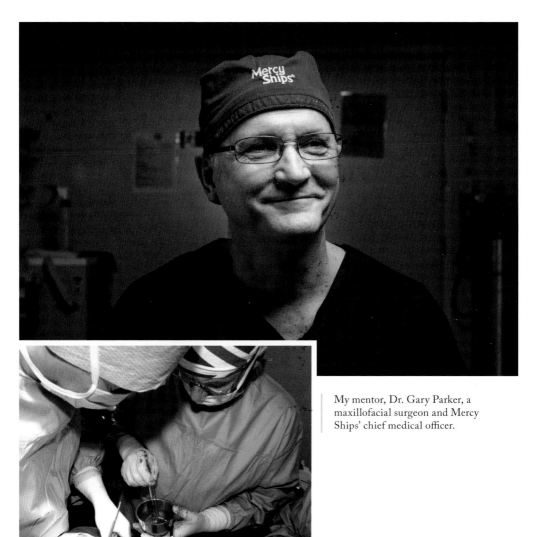

My mentor, Dr. Gary Parker, a maxillofacial surgeon and Mercy Ships' chief medical officer.

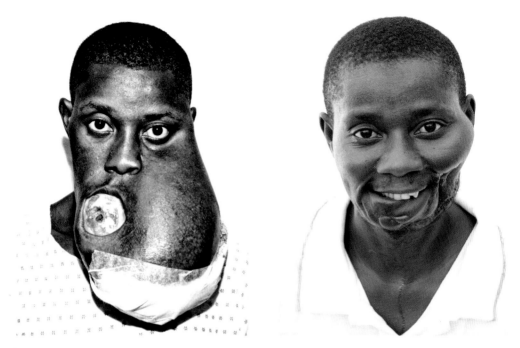

My Liberian friend Harris, before and after his operation with Dr. Gary Parker.

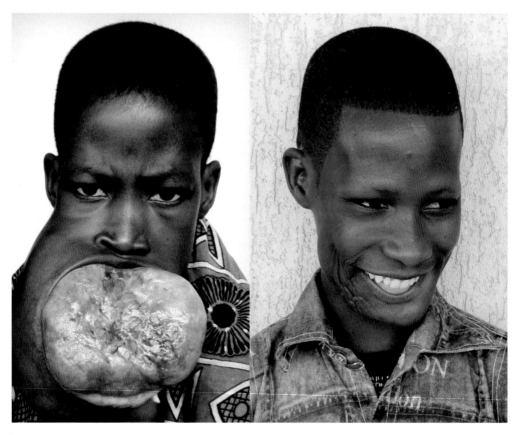

My buddy Alfred at screening day, before his surgery, alongside a more recent photo of Alfred, now a handsome young man.

Celebrating Alfred's successful surgery and homecoming in 2004, at his family's hut in Benin.

When war broke out in Liberia, Mama Victoria Thomas took in dozens of children who'd lost their parents. In 2006, I helped fundraise my very first well for Mama Vic's orphanage.

In 2005, I saw the women of Bomi County, Liberia, drinking from this green swamp and bringing the muddy liquid back to their families. It was then that I began to understand the severity of the global water crisis.

We launched charity: water in 2006 with a fundraiser in a nightclub, the day after my thirty-first birthday. We had no money and zero experience—but I knew how to throw a good party.

Two weeks later, we kicked off a ten-day, five-park exhibition in Union Square that told the story of dirty water and sold enough $20 bottles of water to raise $20,000 to build wells for more than a thousand people.

Viktoria Alexeeva, charity: water's future creative director (and my future wife), volunteering at Union Square on the day we met in 2006. Mom snapped this photo when we weren't looking.

In 2007, I saw this little girl near Mogotio, Kenya, drinking river water and then vomiting over and over again. Back home, I had the water analyzed; it was crawling with bacteria.

In 2007, we left Brantly's apartment and moved into this printing warehouse in SoHo. It had greasy floors and no windows, but it was all ours for next to nothing.

Good branding is key to charity: water's success. In 2007, we created a marketing campaign that showed regular New Yorkers walking for water—just like the 663 million people around the world who must do so every day.

In 2010, we partnered with Jim Hocking, founder of Water for Good, to bring clean water to the Bayaka people living in the Central African Republic. The Bayaka are hunter-gatherers who sleep in grass-and-stick huts. We kicked off their fundraising campaign in the village of Moale. Getting there wasn't easy. Finding water was even harder.

A drilling rig strikes clean water at Abenea School in the Tigray Region of Ethiopia. The yield was so high that more than two thousand students, along with the neighboring community, benefit from this project through a network of distribution stations.

Children in Sikedi, Malawi, celebrate the coming of clean water to their village. Cut off from water by a huge ravine, the community had spent months building a road that would allow the drilling rig to access the village.

My good friends Michael and Xochi Birch (with their daughter, Isabella), the tech entrepreneurs whose generosity saved charity: water when it almost went bankrupt—and whose continued passion for the mission inspires all of us.

Rachel Beckwith's story captured hearts around the world. Her campaign raised over $1.2 million and brought clean water to 37,770 people, changing the lives of many generations of children. Her mother, Samantha, is at right.

When we discovered that 40 percent of all wells at any given time are broken, charity: water began installing sensors to measure water flow and alert mechanics when maintenance is needed. We're leading the water sector in innovation and sustainability, but we're just getting started.

In May of 2000, an Ethiopian woman named Letikiros Hailu was so distraught over spilling a day's worth of water that she hanged herself from this tree. In 2014, I traveled to her village to retrace her footsteps.

Letikiros's mother, Chekolech, outside her home in Meda, where Letikiros was born. Four mornings a week, Letikiros would strap a clay pot, just like this one (left), on her back, walk for hours to the nearest spring, then wait in line to collect about five gallons of water. She'd be home by sunset.

At charity: ball 2016, we matched every guest with a unique person in Adi Etot, Ethiopia, and invited them to learn more about "Someone Like You." The event was held in the Temple of Dendur at New York's Metropolitan Museum of Art.

Our first-ever "live drill" at charity: ball 2016 was an inspired idea—and a technical nightmare. But we had a strong team on the ground in Ethiopia, including Tyler Riewer, who joined us live from Adi Etot.

Viktoria and me with our son, Jackson, and our daughter, Emma, in our neighborhood in New York City.

"Look, I'm sure you probably have tons of people helping," she said. "But I'm a graphic designer, if you ever need *that* kind of help. I can tell from the exhibit that you put a lot of thought into everything."

"Yes!" I said. "You have no idea. We desperately need that kind of help. Can you come to our office next week when the show is finished?"

Out of the corner of my eye, I caught my mother, always the journalist, snapping a photo of us talking.

The following week, Viktoria Alexeeva showed up after work for an interview dressed in heels, her laptop under her arm.

"Oh," she said, looking around at Brantly's apartment in confusion. "Um . . . hi."

I hadn't told her that our "office" at 109 Spring Street was actually a bachelor pad with a sunken living room, a creepy wooden sauna, and a rotating cast of characters who looked like they'd stepped off the set of *Trainspotting.*

When she didn't begin slowly backing out the door, I whipped open my laptop and showed her where it had all begun: the ship, screening day, Alfred's tumor photos, Dr. Gary, Uganda, kids drinking from mud puddles. She was very quiet.

When I stopped talking, she wiped a tear from her eye and asked, "When do you want me to show up?"

"Could you come tomorrow after you finish work?" I said, adding, "I can't pay you."

"Yes," she said. "Tomorrow is fine."

Vik, as everyone called her, was twenty-three and a junior motion graphics artist at a small design agency. She worked on campaigns for big brands like American Express, Nike, and Honda. She didn't know anything about dirty water. She'd never been to Africa, and she didn't come from a family of do-gooders. Like many Americans, her interest in other countries was spurred by a work of fiction, a film. Earlier that year, she'd watched *The Constant Gardener,* a movie about activism and corporate corruption in Kenya, and it made her question whether her talents as an artist could do something more than craft ads for car companies.

Thankfully, we met just as charity: water was bursting into the spotlight. Our ten-day traveling water exhibition raised almost $20,000 in October. We split it four ways, sending it to our partner organizations and helping more than a thousand people get clean water for the first time. Pretty soon, journalists from *USA Today*, CBS News, and Page Six started calling to learn more about our work. We sold out of T-shirts and bracelets. And we started planning a gala because I'd heard that charities raise real money by doing pricey dinners in fancy venues, so I figured we should try our hand at one.

All of this meant that a million random things needed to be designed. Vik came by Brantly's most evenings and weekends to create invitations, brochures, business cards, tax receipts, letterhead, and images for emails. I kept throwing projects at her, and she kept learning new skills to keep up. When I asked her to edit our videos, she taught herself Final Cut Pro and even got her boss's blessing to cut charity: water videos after-hours in the editing suite at her office. When I asked her to add pages to the website, she figured out HTML and JavaScript and learned to code. She was always head down, working hard, ready for more.

After a while, I invited Vik to join me and Lani at church.

"Um, okay," she said.

"Great! Let's meet up for the 11 a.m. service," I said. "We can come back to work at the office afterward." She could have been an atheist for all I knew; it didn't really occur to me to ask. Lani and I had a lot of fun going to church, so inviting Vik to join us was like asking her to go with us for a drink after work.

When I first came back to the States, I church-shopped for a while and found myself drawn to a place called Brooklyn Tabernacle. The rapturous, predominantly black and Latino gospel church met in a former movie theater and was famous for its Grammy-winning choir. On Sundays, there'd be at least eighty people onstage, singing with giant smiles on their faces. The sanctuary held 3,200 exuberant parishioners, and you had to get there thirty minutes early just to get a decent seat. Out in the congregation, the balcony would literally shake and rock from all the dancing. Lani and I were up there every week, clapping and singing next to little old ladies with their hands in the air, shout-ing, "Praise Jesus! Oh! Oh! Oh! He's so good to me!"

Vik's religious upbringing couldn't have been more different from mine. Over a working dinner one night, she told us how she'd grown up in St. Petersburg, Russia, and had come to the States in 1992, when she was just nine years old. She was not a churchgoer. Her childhood encounters with the Russian Orthodox Church were dour and incon-sequential. The priests chanted and swung heavy silver censers. The Brooklyn Tabernacle experience—the exuberant, gospel-singing-at-the-top-of-your-lungs, contagious kind of faith—was completely for-eign to her. I remember, on that first outing, Vik shooting me a startled look when the grandmother next to her went down on blue-stockinged knees and began speaking in tongues.

Ha, I bet she's loving this! I thought to myself. *Who wouldn't?*

Back at the apartment-slash-office, the three of us would sit around the kitchen table late into the night, working nonstop. Vik would crack up when Lani yelled at me over stupid things—the way I banged on the computer keys or talked too loudly on the phone.

"Harrison, take it out on the fire escape, *please,*" she'd yell, sending me climbing out the window to finish my call. Around 8 p.m., I'd start cooking up a big pot of pasta and meat sauce, blasting lounge music from my iPod. My longtime buddy Matt Oliver, who'd attended that basement-video Christian school with me, would come over to hang out. He'd always bring over a few bottles of nice wine. We were work-ing hundred-hour weeks, burning the midnight oil, and building the world's greatest charity. There was no reason we couldn't enjoy our-selves at the same time.

At the end of October, I left again for Africa, this time on a twelve-day trip to Ethiopia to scout potential well sites. I'd been told by our water partners that in this vast country of seventy-six million people, only 24 percent of the population had access to clean, safe drinking water.

It was daunting to think how much money it would really take to make a dent in a problem so big. Still, I wondered: What if Mercy Ships had been put off by the enormous need for medical care when it sent its first ship to Mexico? What if Dr. Gary had been overwhelmed by the thousands of patients waiting to be seen on his first screening day? *Focus on the present,* I thought. *One well at a time.*

During this trip, I photographed children digging in the sand, hoping to find precious water. I saw hunched women walk miles in the heat with jugs of dirty fluid tied to their backs. I toured a health clinic that served a population of 103,000, and learned that 50 percent of its patients were suffering from waterborne diseases. The statistics were real.

I also met a woman who, for as long as she could remember, had walked three hours a day to collect water contaminated with cow feces—that is, until our partners drilled a well that brought freshwater to the center of her town.

"Mai hiwet eyu"—*Water is life*—people would say over and over again in the villages. Water is life.

Returning home in November, I got news from our partners in Uganda that charity: water's very first projects had been completed. The residents of the Bobi IDP camp had celebrated the construction of three new wells, and we'd also rehabilitated three older wells whose hand pumps had broken. It wasn't the 125 wells that Bobi needed, but it was progress.

Now came the fun part. I sent an email to everyone who had attended my thirty-first birthday party, attaching photos and a link to a video of Bobi villagers drinking clean water. "Here are the six wells YOU built in Uganda! You personally helped thousands to get clean water!"

I'm sure some of my friends didn't even remember attending the party. They'd come to a club, thrown twenty bucks in a box, and enjoyed a few drinks. But once they saw what their small donation had accomplished, the response was overwhelming.

"This is really awesome!"

"Wow, thanks so much for following up with me!"

"Do you have any more photos?"

"When's the next fundraiser? Let's do it again!"

We'd proved that giving could be fun. We'd gotten everyone excited about bringing clean water to people a world away. I wondered, *What if it's really this simple?*

24

Three Pillars

Whether you're trying to fund a nonprofit, looking for investors to back your hot new start-up, or asking for a bank loan for your mom-and-pop store, one of the first and most important questions people will ask is "What's your vision?"

Vision isn't about rising sales numbers on a chart. Vision is the bolder quest, the North Star. The thing that drives you to get up every morning and work harder than the day before. Vision, I once read, isn't the thing you're doing now, but the thing you're always going to be doing in the future.

In our early years, nobody had to ask me what our vision was, because I talked about it constantly. As much as we were figuring things out on the fly, my vision for charity: water was crystal clear: I wanted to reinvent charity, to make giving a *joyful* experience, to bring donors back to the true meaning of love through acts of generosity and compassion.

And yet, even back when I was raising money for Mercy Ships, I'd always detected a ton of skepticism around charity. I'd hear it in conversations and random asides.

"Is all this money really going to surgeries?"

"Will it really make a difference?"

"I just don't trust charities."

Americans are known for being generous, but one in three say they have no confidence in charities. For months, I'd been showing people pictures of dirty water, telling them, "Children are dying. This is on fire. It's an emergency—please help me." I had visual proof of human suffering, but what everyone wanted to know was, "How much of my money will actually reach that woman who's giving her kid muddy water?"

Trust was a scarce resource. But it didn't surprise me that people were skeptical. It seemed that every time I turned on the news, there was another scandal. Enron executives clung to claims of innocence even after a court convicted them of lying to their investors, employees, and government regulators. Then there was Tyco's CEO, who stole $150 million from employees and investors and spent it on personal luxuries like $6,000 shower curtains and a $2,200 gold-plated trash can.

The charity landscape was no different. Relief efforts for Hurricane Katrina racked up $2 billion in fraud and waste on mobile homes that were never installed, debris removal that never happened, and relief benefit claims on behalf of children who didn't even exist. It was quite possibly one of the worst times in memory to ask people to trust you.

Dirty water was a billion-person global problem that would require massive resources to solve. If I was ever going to get skeptical people to take the first step, to open their wallets and give charity a try, we'd have to prove to them that charity: water was radically different. We had to prove that every dollar was being put to good use and saving lives. The question was how.

Recently, I'd read about Paul Tudor Jones, a hedge fund billionaire who started the Robin Hood Foundation, which bankrolled poverty-ending programs in New York City. Jones was so wealthy that he and his board promised to pay the charity's overhead forever, freeing up the organization to send 100 percent of all public donations to program work.

To me, that was like dropping the mic. It was such a powerful promise. Take the number one objection that people have about charity—*how much of my money really gets there?*—and obliterate it. I wrote Jones, asking for advice and breathlessly expressing my interest in partnering with him, but didn't hear back.

It didn't matter. We could borrow his idea. I made a vow that every single dollar charity: water raised from the public would be spent creating clean water projects built by local partners in the recipient countries. We called this our 100 percent model, meaning that *all* public donations would go directly to the field. I opened a second bank account, designating one for overhead expenses and one for water projects. I wasn't sure how we'd fund the overhead account, but I knew that the 100 percent model was crucial to our vision of reinventing charity—and reestablishing trust.

To show how serious we were about the 100 percent model, I promised to also refund credit card fees. To this day, when someone uses an American Express card to make a $100 donation, only $96 of it actually comes to us. Amex takes 4 percent. But our overhead account makes up the difference, sending the entire $100 donation to the field.

At the beginning, our lawyers and early donors cautioned us against this model. Actually, "cautioned" might be putting it too politely.

"Scott, in case you didn't notice, you're not Paul Tudor Jones and you're not a billionaire," a friend said.

"This is a surefire way to blow this thing up," another told me.

"How are you going to pay for staff salaries? Office expenses?" a board member asked.

All valid points, but the idea had lodged, and I couldn't see us running things any other way. We'd just have to work extra hard to find private donors and get them excited about funding the boring stuff like payroll, stationery, and toner cartridges.

The second pillar was proof. Not only would we promise that all public donations would go to the field, we'd show everyone exactly where and how their money was used. When someone made a donation, we'd tag it to a specific project, such as a well or a water purification system in a designated region. Then, when the project was complete, we'd send them proof: photos, GPS satellite images, sometimes even videos. And we'd constantly find new and innovative ways to deliver that proof.

For example, we were among the earliest nonprofits to tap into the emerging Google Earth mapping technology. I couldn't believe that Google had built this free place where we could put water-access points on a map and show donors where their money went. We purchased a bunch of $100 handheld GPS devices, sent them to our local partners, and trained them to collect the GPS coordinates for the wells. We then plugged that data manually into Google Earth, and added the photos, donor names, and village information to the coordinates.

The third pillar—and this was key—was that our branding needed to inspire people. When I looked at other charities for inspiration, I always came up empty. It seemed like most of them used tools of shame and guilt to motivate people into giving. It went all the way back to those TV commercials from the 1970s with Sally Struthers, the ones in which starving African children lock hollowed eyes with the camera lens, flies landing on their faces in slow motion, while an American actress pleads tearfully to call the 800 number scrolling at the bottom of your screen.

Even if that kind of plea worked—and it does, because those ads still run today—I wanted to do things differently. I wanted to build an optimistic, imaginative, hopeful organization that people would donate to because they felt empowered and inspired—not because we'd guilted them into it. Imagine if Nike tried marketing its running shoes by saying, "You're fat and lazy. Turn the TV off, stop eating junk food, and go out for a run." But that's not what Nike says. They say, *You can run farther than you ever thought possible. Lost your legs? Doesn't matter. You can finish a marathon. Lost an arm? Still doesn't matter. You can play basketball. You can box.* Nike says, *Greatness is within you.* And it just happens to sell the gear that helps you find that greatness.

Apple was another big inspiration for me. For years, computer companies spent millions on advertisements that boasted technological specs—*2.4 GHz processor! Intel G33 Express Chipset! 3 GB RAM.* But nobody really knew what that stuff meant. So Apple's ad campaigns didn't even show the product. Instead, they said, "Think different," and linked the brand to legendary thinkers like Picasso, Einstein, Bob Dylan, and Amelia Earhart. Apple sold inspiration, and it worked.

Charities *never* did that. Charities shamed you for having money, and then begged you to hand it over. They didn't seem to spend much time thinking about the wants and needs of their donors. Honestly, I think many charities wished they never had to deal with donors. Things would be much easier if they just got large grants and went about their business. But I *loved* our donors. I loved bringing them together at events and connecting them to one another. I loved involving them in redemptive, life-changing work and then showing them the impact of their generosity.

As we worked to build our brand, I obsessed over every detail of the donor's experience. And I expected everyone to follow suit. Once, during preparation for a gala, Vik and I designed beautiful invitations that we worked on for weeks. We got the heavy card stock donated. Vik met with the printer countless times to make sure the invitations were perfect. We had volunteers prepare the envelopes to be mailed out. But when I went to check on their work, half the labels and stamps on the invitations were crooked. I was so angry, I lost it.

"How on earth did this happen?" I yelled at the guy in charge. "We can't mail these beautiful invitations with crooked labels! And look at this stamp! It's at a forty-five-degree angle!"

"Look, they're all volunteers," he said. "You can't expect—"

"Wait a minute," I shouted, interrupting him. "Are you saying that just because you're a volunteer that means you can't put a stamp on straight?"

I forget how the exchange ended. In fact, I think he walked out and never came back to work. I wasn't proud of how I handled the situation, but that didn't stop me from making the volunteers redo every envelope.

"These need to be perfect," I said. "We're not just mailing out party invites. We're inviting people to save lives! Do you *understand*?"

Today, I'm not going to yell at anyone over a crooked stamp (though I will still come by to spot-check them). But back then, on a deeper level, my reaction was about more than just excellence. I was really asking donors to trust me. It might seem like Scott Harrison is just throwing another party. But everything was different now. *I* was different.

Journalist Nicholas Kristof once wrote that "toothpaste is peddled with far more sophistication than the life-saving work of aid groups." I couldn't agree more. Junk food and tobacco companies spend billions of dollars marketing products that make us sick, but the most important causes in the world often have anemic brands and tiny marketing budgets. I mean, think about it. Almost forty-five hundred kids die every single day from dirty water. Forty-five *hundred*. That's like if eleven jumbo jets filled with children crashed to the ground with no survivors—*every single day*. Where is the outrage and shock? The marches on Washington? The celebrity fundraising concerts?

As far as I could tell, nobody cared because nobody really *knew* about the problem. And how can you change the world if you're failing miserably at changing hearts and minds? I wanted to create a new model for charity, one that marketed itself at least as well as a tube of toothpaste.

But first, we needed a full-time designer.

25

True Believers

By the spring of 2007, charity: water was crushing it. More than eight hundred people had attended our first-ever charity: ball, in December. None of us had any idea how to produce a gala, so we just made it up as we went along. On our rookie outing, we raised $250,000 for clean water in one night.

Right before the gala, the attorneys filed our 501(c)(3) application with the government. Exactly fifty-eight days later, I picked up a long voicemail message from our attorney. I could hear the surprise in his voice, like he didn't believe what he was saying.

"Scott, the IRS has approved your application for nonprofit status," he said. "They had no further questions. Congratulations!"

I think I actually screamed, "Yes!" on the sidewalk, startling the people walking nearby. It was finally real—and in record time. We were now a fully tax-deductible 501(c)(3), approved and sanctioned by the U.S. government and the Internal Revenue Service. A tax scofflaw operating from a SoHo drug den had been given the chance to change the world.

But the best part was that by the end of our sixth month, charity: water had raised half a million dollars for water projects. It was amazing when you considered that the water solutions we were funding at the time cost only about $5,000 to build. We'd finished six wells in Uganda and were granting money for our four partners in Africa to build and rehabilitate another sixty-five. We were raising money faster than our African counterparts in the field could break ground.

On the other side of the ledger, though, it was a different story. No matter how hard I worked at it, we were filling the overhead account only in fits and starts—$300 here, $1,500 there. We scraped by every month, with barely enough to pay basic expenses, including about $2,600 a month in salaries for me and Lani.

Meanwhile, our website traffic was growing—which embarrassed me to no end because the page design was primitive at best: black backgrounds with tiny white type, painfully small pictures, a few videos, and a mailing address where people could send checks. I'd designed the whole thing myself after reading a copy of *HTML for Dummies*, and it showed. It was the online equivalent of those crooked postage stamps.

We couldn't build a world-class brand without a top-notch designer. I begged our board members for more overhead money because I wanted to offer Vik a full-time job—hoping she'd even consider it. She was making $48,000 a year at her current gig, with great health care and retirement benefits. There was no way I could match that.

Thankfully, by March, we received an operational gift of $90,000 from the parents of a board member. Lani and I got small, board-approved raises, and I approached Vik with an offer.

"Here's the deal. I think I can pay you $46,000 a year," I told her. "But there are no benefits."

"Yes!" Vik said, smiling. "I can start in two weeks."

We hadn't even talked titles, and I hadn't written a job description. But design was her primary role, and she knew from her seven months volunteering with us that she'd have to pitch in wherever needed. She celebrated by purchasing a pair of black Pumas. They came in handy on days when she'd take a break from designing to deliver cases of water around the city.

We got Lani some help, too. For almost nine months, she'd been playing the role of office manager, bookkeeper, program director, volunteer wrangler, and personal assistant. She'd loyally held down the fort while I scouted for new NGO partners in Africa, dined with donor hopefuls, did media interviews, and tried to find us office space. At the board's suggestion, we hired a part-time accountant to take bookkeeping off her plate, and Lani created an internship program to get some extra hands, but there was always more to do and she was burning out.

Of course, I didn't really notice this because I was terrible at managing people. I'd just never done it before. Performance reviews? Culture building? Soliciting feedback? Honestly, if your paycheck cleared every month, I thought that was enough evidence that I valued your performance.

"Look, Harrison," Lani said in March, shortly after Vik came on board. "I miss Africa. And while I love that you're going back every few months to take videos and do your Anderson Cooper thing, I need to start taking trips, too. And soon."

Vik also wanted in. "Scott, how am I supposed to design with integrity if I've never met the people or seen the places we're serving?" she said. "I'd like to go with Lani."

"Great!" I said. "I'd love for you to do that. But we can't afford to send you to Africa, too."

"That's fine," she said. "I'll find a way."

Somehow, she pulled together a side job, doing animation for a terrible commercial ("Do you want to know who your true love is? Dial 1-888 . . .") that ran late at night on MTV. It netted Vik a quick $2,500—enough for a ticket to Africa, a month's worth of malaria pills, and a few decent meals.

In May, Lani and Vik left for Liberia, the place where I'd first learned about the water crisis. Lani had contacts there from her Mercy Ships tour, so she and Vik spent two weeks visiting proposed well sites, checking in on the orphanage Lani had helped to rehabilitate, and meeting with potential NGO partners for charity: water. The two stayed at an old Catholic health clinic, sleeping on dirty mattresses under torn mosquito nets. Giant tarantulas crawled brazenly up the bathroom wall next to them whenever they used the toilet.

Their first day in Monrovia, they were riding in a taxi through a busy intersection when Vik saw a man lying motionless on the pavement next to a mangled bicycle. He'd been hit by a car, and blood was pouring from his head. Traffic was zooming past and people were walking around his body like he wasn't there. Vik and Lani were horrified.

"We should get out. Maybe he needs help?" they both said.

But their taxi driver waved them off, telling them, "Ah, don't worry about it. He is very dead."

Vik later told me how much it disturbed her to think that this man's life meant nothing to the people rushing by. But fourteen years of war and suffering have a way of skewing your perspective.

Meanwhile, back in New York, I was looking for someone who could help me with an idea for an edgy video I wanted us to make: a public service announcement that could air on TV and online. I knew this was something charities did, but after seeing a bunch of them, I thought we could do better.

One night, I tracked down Terry George, a screenwriter and director who'd been nominated for an Oscar for *Hotel Rwanda* and had just finished making *Reservation Road* with the actress Jennifer Connelly. Terry had come to our party at Tenjune, but we didn't know each other well enough for me to cold-call him. A friend tipped me off that she'd be having dinner with Terry, so I showed up at the restaurant, walked past the hostess, spotted their table, and crashed the conversation.

"Nice to see you again, Scott," Terry said in his Irish brogue.

"You, too," I said, dying to get to the point.

"Terry, hey okay, I've had this crazy idea I wanted to run by you," I said, acting like *Wow, what a coincidence to run into you here.* "I want to make a PSA where we follow a wealthy family as they collect disgusting water from a pond and then serve it to their kids in a nice Tribeca loft."

Terry looked up from his tacos and put his cocktail down. "Interesting idea," he said. "What's your budget?"

"I don't have a budget."

"I *see*. And who do you think you can get to star in it?"

"I have no idea—but *you're* a Hollywood director."

We both laughed out loud. I promised I'd let him finish his dinner in peace and call him the next day.

Some people like to follow up with leads in three days, a week, or some other time frame they've read about in a business book. I mean, you can't seem too desperate, right? But I've always been impulsive, compelled to move *right now*. There are children being born *right now* who will die soon if we can't get them clean water. Some people find my persistence tough to stomach, and I get that. But along the way, I've been lucky to run into enough dreamers—people like Dr. Gary and Vik and Lani—who appreciated my sense of urgency, people who understood the high stakes.

I called Terry the very next day, and he invited me to his Chelsea apartment to give him my pitch.

"Imagine," I said, "if all the taps in New York were turned off, and you and everyone else had to grab a container and walk ten, twenty, or fifty blocks to Central Park every day to collect dirty water from a giant pond."

"Go on," Terry said.

"Now imagine hauling it home, and pouring it into tall, clean glasses. And then serving that green, disgusting water to your kids."

"Interesting," he said.

"Terry, I think it would shock people, and maybe move them to act."

"I like it!" he said. "We could follow a mother and her children on the walk. And cut to two or three other groups of New Yorkers walking, too."

Terry knew dirty water. He'd spent a bunch of time in Rwanda and had seen the problem up close. He also knew that Americans have a hard time wrapping their heads around problems that seem far away.

By the end of our meeting, Terry was in. An award-winning filmmaker was going to make charity: water's first PSA. I was excited.

People always ask how we scored so many wins early on and what my process was for turning a no into a yes. Truthfully, the nos stayed nos most of the time.

No, we don't have the budget.

No, that's not a part of our giving strategy.

No, sorry, but touch base with me next year.

But I simply asked so many people that eventually I gathered enough yeses to get things done.

Basically, it was a numbers game—I felt like I had to outpitch and outwork everyone else because I'm not a naturally strategic thinker. I can't count the number of times I kicked myself for not getting three more introductions or not doing more research before going into a meeting to make the right ask. Just the other day, I backpedaled into a major donor meeting unprepared. I thought to myself afterward, *How is it possible that I just met with a guy worth six billion dollars and I knew so little about him?*

Back then, what I lacked in salesmanship and strategy, I made up for in sheer energy and drive. My meetings were scheduled like clockwork around breakfast (sometimes two breakfasts), lunch, dinner, and drinks. To keep myself from getting distracted, everything was calendared to the minute, even important emails I needed to send. Every once in a while, I'd look at my Sent folder and count them. I was writing more than three hundred emails a day, hunting for new leads and cold-pitching potential donors.

Friends would describe me as passionate—which was a nice way of saying obsessed—and I saw that passion rub off on some of the people I was pitching. I was a true believer. I promised them that if they joined me, we could summon miracles together.

Vik and Lani returned from Liberia in mid-May, newly inspired and more connected than ever to the mission of bringing people clean water. By then, so much work had piled up that I'd brought on another volunteer, a former UNICEF intern named Becky Straw. Becky had processed water and sanitation data for UNICEF while getting her master's degree from Columbia University in social enterprise administration and international social welfare. In other words, she came with lots of academic knowledge under her belt.

When we first met, I told Becky I was wary of her institutional background. "I don't want to hire you," I said. "You're at UNICEF, and I want us to always think outside the box. I hate bureaucracy."

Becky was unfazed. She said she'd gotten her undergrad degree in graphic design and that the minute she'd seen the charity: water website, that was it: she knew she wanted to work with us. (As awful as I thought our website was, apparently it was still more engaging than anything she'd seen during her research on water charities.)

"Nobody's talking about water in such a tangible, beautiful way," she said. In other words, nobody had been doing charity in a way that appealed to a twenty-seven-year-old like her.

"Well, I really can't hire you," I said. "We just don't have any money now."

"Okay, how about this," she said. "I'm applying for jobs, but I have some time. What if I just volunteer for a while? I can help with whatever you need." Still unconvinced, I had her meet with a board member for a second opinion and she got a glowing review. Her persistence paid off, and she was in.

There wasn't enough room for all of us at Brantly's small kitchen table, so Becky sat with her laptop on the carpeted steps of the sunken living room. Like Vik, she stayed late every night, working until someone told her to leave.

At UNICEF, Becky had analyzed water expenditures in different countries, trying to identify trends and bottlenecks for the charity's projects, looking at which policies had and hadn't worked. I'd walk in and throw questions at her: "Tell me more about the water crisis in Ethiopia" and "We're rewriting all the website copy on Malawi. Can you dig up some country-specific facts?" If our pictures and stories were appealing to people's right brains and to their hearts, maybe Becky's facts could hook the analytical left-brain types.

Sometimes we'd all be working late into the night, and Brantly would come home drunk or high and fall asleep on the couch watching French vampire movies as we typed away. Other times, he'd bust through the door with a cadre of models in tow and bellow, "Everybody out. Now!" The four of us would scramble out the door with our laptops, resuming operations at a Starbucks with free Wi-Fi or at a nearby deli called Café Duke. Occasionally, we'd decamp to the kitchen table or to the living room of a board member's apartment.

Thankfully, we had a lot of generous supporters to lean on in those early days. One of them was an eccentric tax accountant named Steve, who worked behind a perpetually messy desk on the Upper East Side. When customers came into his tiny office to discuss their taxes or pick up completed returns, he'd find them savings and then encourage them to donate a portion of their surprise windfall to charity: water. For every $500 you gave, Steve would buy you a case of our water. He collected so much money for us that we eventually loaned him one of our credit card terminals.

Steve called constantly for more water, and one time, Becky answered. When she hung up, she looked a little confused. "Scott," she said. "He wants two cases of water and a pastrami sandwich."

"A what?"

"He said he was hungry."

I sighed. "Okay. Can you pick one up on the way? He's a good donor."

Silence.

"Becky, he's raised tens of thousands of dollars for us. That's a lot of clean water. Please?"

Becky grabbed her jacket and an intern, and they lugged another two heavy cases of water to the uptown train—and picked up a pastrami sandwich on the way.

26

Vik

MAY 2007

Vik had been acting a little sluggish since returning from Liberia. She came in late to work, yawned a lot, and had trouble focusing on tasks. And then one day, she didn't show up at all.

The timing was terrible. Our shoot for the PSA was coming up. We were scrambling to get the filming permits in order, scout locations, organize volunteers, and rent cameras and sound equipment.

It wasn't like Vik to slack off. Lani called her cell phone a bunch of times, but she didn't answer.

"Maybe she's still fighting jet lag?" I guessed.

The next day, Vik dragged herself in late and plopped down on the couch. "Sorry, guys," she said. "I don't know what happened. I passed out in my apartment and slept for twenty-four hours."

I looked up from my laptop and gave her a long, hard stare. She looked pale, weak, sleepy-eyed. Lani and I exchanged worried looks. I knew she was thinking the same thing.

"Vik," I said. "You have malaria."

"No, no, no—I'm fine! *Really*," she said, laughing at us. But thirty minutes later, she was slumped over. "Okay," she mumbled. "I'm not fine."

When malaria hits, it feels like a raging flu. You're nauseous. Your bones ache. Chills, sweats, and fatigue come in waves. You reach the point where lifting a hand feels like an impossible task.

"Vik, you've got to get to a hospital right now," I said. "Did you take your malaria pills?"

"Yes! Wait . . . not all of them. Lani said I didn't need to."

"Oh, man, I'm so sorry," Lani said, sheepishly.

Lani liked to tell doctors that she was immune to the mosquito-borne disease, even as they shook their heads and said that wasn't possible. To her credit, she'd never taken the pills and had never gotten the virus, so who knows? As for Vik, she'd split the difference, taking the pills while in Africa and stopping after she got home. But malaria medication doesn't work that way. It's a prophylactic, which means you have to continue taking it after you leave a malaria-prone region. If you got bitten by an infected mosquito on your last day in-country, your body needs the full regimen to suppress the disease and kill the virus.

I called a board member to get some advice, and she happened to know an infectious-disease specialist at Lenox Hill Hospital.

"Go to Lenox Hill now," I told Vik, sending an intern to accompany her to the hospital. To save money, they took the subway uptown. In retrospect, it probably wasn't a four-star move, sending a malaria-stricken employee to the hospital on the subway. But at the time, it didn't cross my mind that, at the very least, I should have gone out and personally hailed a cab.

Vik ended up testing positive for malaria, and spent four days at Lenox Hill. They gave her quinine, but no one told her that a common side effect of the treatment was temporary deafness. She woke up in the middle of the night with sudden hearing loss. Terrified, she started praying.

On Vik's third day in the hospital, Lani and I went to visit her, bringing her a care package of movies and books. Her parents, who'd escaped communism with no more than $2,000 in their pockets, went to see her every day. They lamented the fact that she'd quit her stable job to work for me. But when Vik recovered, she came right back—just in time to shoot the PSA.

Terry had decided he wanted to direct the video himself, and he even got Jennifer Connelly to star in it. But they both had only a short window of time between film projects to make it happen. It would be a fast-and-furious one-day shoot. Vik and Lani would drive trucks, move people and props to four or five different locations, and assist Terry's crew. I'd handle catering, find seventy extras for the exterior shots, and secure a donor's luxury apartment for the scene where our celebrity actress serves dirty brown water to her children with their lunch. Everything was coming together.

But in mid-June, about a week before the shoot, Vik handed me a piece of paper and broke down sobbing. It was a hospital bill for $40,000.

"I just don't know what to do," she said. "They keep sending me bills, and the numbers keep going up."

I'd never seen her so fragile and scared. Her face was red, like she'd been crying all night. She worried that this debt would hang over her for the rest of her life.

I am an optimist and a problem-solver like my dad, but this really was bad news. I'd lured this talented woman away from a good job with health insurance, given her malaria and, as if that weren't bad enough, a medical bill that exceeded her annual take-home pay.

"Vik," I said, "we'll figure this out. If charity: water has to pay your hospital bill . . ."

"No, I don't want to put that burden on you!" she said. "I know how much you're dealing with already."

"Well, maybe we can go on a long-term payment plan with the hospital. We'll just figure out a way to make it work."

I had no idea how to make it work. We were struggling to raise money for our salaries and operating costs. And our financial position was actually worse than anyone knew. We had exactly $141 in the overhead account, and I was deferring my own salary, hoping some donations that had been pledged would come in soon. My head was spinning. Should I offer to pay the hospital bill myself? I was barely scraping by, and the thought of this overwhelmed me. But Vik was in a dark place, and I needed her to come back. We had so much work left to do.

"Let's pray about this," I said. It was the only thing I could think to do. She closed her eyes. "God," I said. "We could sure use your help right now." We prayed as hard as I'd ever prayed for anything. "Let's give it a few days," I said, giving Vik a hug.

She mustered a smile and then pulled away. "Back to work," she said with a soft laugh as she walked to the kitchen and opened her computer.

A week later, I stood behind the cameras on set in Central Park, watching Jennifer Connelly queue up behind a long line of hip-looking New Yorkers (our extras) who were waiting to step up to the pond one by one to collect the murky water in yellow Jerry Cans.

Somehow everything came together in time. Terry had recruited a decorated cinematographer, and she leaned on Panavision to donate cameras for the day. And the legendary New York restaurant Balthazar (the owner's daughter was one of our interns) catered the shoot. Best of all, Jennifer Connelly agreed to star in the piece for free, with her own children. If we pulled this off, we'd have a $250,000 PSA from an award-winning team on a $5,000 budget.

That was a big "if," though. The shoot started late. Dark clouds threatened to rain us out. The city gave our crew strict instructions not to remove *any* water from Central Park's pond, making it difficult for us to get an important shot. Terry worried that we'd lose light before we got everything we needed.

Meanwhile, Vik and Lani drove a van around town all day like Teamsters, picking up and dropping off crew and running errands in multiple locations. I hardly saw or spoke to them. But then my cell phone rang during an afternoon break.

"You're never going to believe this." It was Vik on the line.

"Try me."

"I was sitting here, parked in the van, when a thought came to me: *Call your old employer.*"

On a whim, she'd called the design agency where she used to work, and was connected with a woman in HR whom she'd never met, in a satellite office across the country. She explained her situation to the woman—the charity trip, the malaria, the hospital bills—and asked if she had any recourse. She hadn't worked at the agency in four months, but maybe there was a health care grace period she didn't know about.

"She was so nice, and she put me on hold."

"Okay . . . And . . . ?"

"Scott, they never canceled my health insurance. Someone screwed up, and they totally forgot."

"Wait, what?"

"I know!" Vik said. "I'm *still* fully covered as if I'm working there! I'm flipping out. I can't believe it. The woman said to send her the paperwork, that they'd process my hospital bill and then cancel my insurance once the claim is closed."

"Are you serious?" I said. This was the best day ever.

"It feels like a total miracle. Like our prayers were really answered . . ."

I wanted to reach through the phone line and give her a hug. I was so happy for her, and for us. "Thank you, God," I heard myself saying aloud.

We don't always get breaks. And believe me, not all my prayers have been met with miraculous solutions. Yet, over time, I've come to embrace the mystery of faith. I think it's my job to work as hard as I possibly can, but also to pray. And when the breakthroughs do come, I try to hold on to them as proof that something much bigger might just be at work.

The rain held off all day. Then, just as we wrapped shooting, the clouds broke, sending a downpour onto the streets of New York. Over the next few weeks, we would edit the PSA, get it up online, and try to get it played on TV. Months later, a nightlife friend would put me in touch with the producers of *American Idol* in Los Angeles, who agreed to run our sixty-second spot during a $1 million time slot the following spring. Our PSA was eventually seen by more than twenty-four million people.

Back in New York, at the end of our shooting day, I finally caught up with Vik.

"You pulled it off!" she said.

"*We* did, you mean," I said.

Vik always has my back, I thought, as we hugged. She never doubted my crazy ideas or rolled her eyes at me. Nobody worked harder than she did. Nobody valued excellence more than she did. And nobody, not even Lani, cared more about the mission. I thought about how much I looked forward to coming to the office each day and being greeted by her warm smile. She was always all in.

This was a good thing, too, because I had a big idea for charity: water's one-year anniversary in September, and I would need Vik's help to make it come alive.

27

Born in September

On my thirty-first birthday, seven hundred people showed up to a party and changed thousands of lives. But with year thirty-two around the corner, I was thinking bigger. Throwing parties in nightclubs didn't scale. You're limited by space and time. But what if I threw a virtual birthday party without walls or a location, a party that brought people together from all over the world to achieve a common goal?

During a brainstorm with the team, we started talking about how our birthdays had become so materialistic.

"They're always all about 'me,'" Becky said. "Like, celebrate *me*! Give *me* presents!"

"Yeah, and who really needs more stuff?" Lani added.

"Totally agree," I said. "Socks, wallets, gift cards—I definitely don't need more of those."

It got us thinking about a radical idea. What if we could change the way Americans thought about birthdays? What if we made birthdays about *giving* instead of receiving?

We called our new campaign Born in September. Basically, we'd ask everyone born in our anniversary month to donate their birthdays, to give others the gift of clean water. If this worked, I believed we could raise ten times more than the year before and create ten times the impact in the field. And it had to work, because we were about to take on our most complicated and expensive water project yet.

I'd recently visited a health clinic in Mogotio, Kenya, where I saw muddy water running out of the faucets. They piped it in from the nearby Molo River, which the clinic's staff used to clean linens, cook meals, and quench patients' thirst. The water was so filthy that all the white bedsheets had turned brown from being washed in it.

The clinic's director walked us down to the river to see the source. Standing nearby was a small girl, maybe three years old. She had big brown eyes, curly black hair, and was dressed in a dirty T-shirt two sizes too big and falling off her shoulder. I watched in horror as she slowly filled a ribbed plastic bottle with the river water and then brought the water up to her lips, drank, and then vomited down the front of her shirt.

When I came home, I brought a sample of that water to a scientist at Rockefeller University, who studied it under a high-powered microscope. He sent me a twenty-four-second black-and-white video of what he saw—tiny vibrating, squiggly bodies. I was horrified. The water was literally alive with parasites and bacteria. *No one should be drinking this,* I thought, *and certainly not a child.*

The staff at Mogotio were proud of their clinic, and for good reason. It had a maternity care ward, an HIV/AIDS counseling center, a lab, and dental services. And yet they lacked the most basic resource for good health: safe water.

Our local partners hired hydrogeologists to figure out how deep they'd have to drill to find freshwater for the clinic. They brought in devices that looked like defibrillator resuscitation paddles, which sent electric currents into the ground to measure the availability and quality of groundwater. Their readings showed that the water was almost a thousand feet down. We'd need an expensive, submersible electric pump capable of bringing water up from the equivalent of one hundred stories underground and sending it to three taps throughout the clinic—all of which our partners would also have to install.

In addition to the hospital, we wanted to bring water to the nearby school district and two other health clinics in the area. A grand total of four water solutions, at a cost of around $40,000 *each*. These four projects in Kenya represented our biggest undertaking yet, and our fundraising effort had to be equally ambitious. Our Born in September campaign needed to deliver.

On August 8, I sent a long email to everyone I knew, asking them to help us raise the first $40,000.

> One month from today on September 7th, charity: water will celebrate its first birthday. And I'll celebrate my 32nd. It all started with a party in New York City, and a refugee camp in Northern Uganda.

I told everybody that we were doing something different this year. I shared the photos and stories of Mogotio, the health clinic with brown sheets, the muddy river water, the sick little girl.

> This year, I'm asking all of you NOT to attend my birthday celebration. NOT to spend money on getting to the party or buying a few drinks.

Instead, I asked everyone to donate $32—my age in dollars—to help us bring clean water to the Mogotio clinic in Kenya. Pretty much everyone I knew had $32 to spare, especially if 100 percent of it went directly to clean water.

> We have three weeks to raise a little over $40,000. If we succeed, I'll be back in Kenya on September 7th with your money, drilling for fresh water at Mogotio . . . It's the best way I can think of celebrating my 32nd birthday, and char- ity: water's 365th day of operation.

We set a bold goal for the September campaign—$150,000 in one month, exactly ten times what we'd raised at the launch party a year ago. It sounded so simple, just move the comma and add a zero. To see if our idea had legs, I asked others who were born in September to join me in giving up *their* birthdays: "Sign up, give us your name, age, and photo, and we'll create a web page just for you," a page where they could ask friends and family to donate their age in dollars. *Who knows,* I thought. *Maybe the idea will spread.*

It did.

In one month, ninety-four people had given up their birthdays. A seven-year-old kid in Texas named Max went door to door asking for $7 and raised $22,000. An eighty-nine-year-old woman named Nona asked her friends to pony up $89, saying she wanted to help people in Africa celebrate as many birthdays as she had. The campaign raised $159,000 in less than four weeks. It was working—which meant a lot more work for us.

Vik, now officially charity: water's creative director, had to hand-code ninety-four custom web pages, with personalized profile photos, mission statements, and PayPal buttons. I'd show up at Brantly's and find her passed out on the couch in broad daylight, exhausted from having worked until 4 a.m. A few hours later, she'd wake up, grab coffee, and start over again.

It was brutal, but at least we wouldn't be working from Brantly's for long. That month, charity: water was moving into its first office—or at least our first real one. It was a 1,560-square-foot unit in a printing warehouse, six blocks west in SoHo. To call it unfinished would be an understatement. Electrical wires dangled from the ceiling, and so much grease had been smeared on the floors over the years that there were places where you couldn't walk without your shoes getting stuck to the ground. And it had a grand total of one window—in a corner by the bathroom, overlooking a cement alleyway. The whole place was dark and grimy, but it was all ours, for a steeply discounted rate.

August would turn out to be the craziest month of 2007, because in the middle of traveling to Kenya, getting the Born in September campaign off the ground, and furnishing a new office, we were also about to lose our best volunteer. Becky Straw had proved all my initial reservations wrong. She was highly creative and committed like the rest of us, but after volunteering for three months, she needed to pay her rent. She'd been doing shoe modeling gigs at $50 an hour, and supplementing that with babysitting money, but it wasn't nearly enough, so she told me one day that she'd gotten a job offer from another nonprofit.

"I'd rather stay, Scott," she said. "What can you do?"

We were stretched thin. I had to borrow money from my parents that month—a $10,000 interest-free loan, to be paid back in $500 monthly installments—just so I could pay rent, taxes, and personal bills.

"Look," I said to Becky. "Lani is leaving us. Can you hang on for a few more weeks, and then I'll have the money to pay you?"

"*Lani's* leaving?"

Yep. Lani, too. She'd been accepted into grad school at Brandeis University and was itching to spread her wings. She couldn't go on being the workhorse and catch-all, schlepping boxes of water on the subway while I flew around Africa looking for new projects and dining with wealthy potential donors—who, by the way, *we really needed* to keep us afloat. Lani promised to come back during breaks in her studies, and help with events and special projects. But her shoes would be big ones to fill. She had a bias for action and a tremendous capacity for getting things done.

"When Lani leaves, we can pay you $42,000 a year," I told Becky. "But no benefits."

"Okay," she said. "Great!"

"On second thought, it's time we try to sort out health insurance," I said, remembering how that went down for Vik. "Can you figure out how that works when you start? I dunno, maybe they give nonprofits a deal?"

Becky took on the title of operations and programs manager, which basically meant she was doing all of Lani's former jobs plus a bunch of new ones.

Meanwhile, I knew we were onto something big with our Born in September campaign, but the long hours it took Vik just wasn't a sustainable model. If we wanted to do this again next year, we'd need to automate the process and significantly upgrade our website.

To thank Vik for all her hard work, I took her with me to Kenya for the live drilling at Mogotio. Well, it was sort of live. We shot video of our partner drilling almost one thousand feet deep to find water. I talked into the camera, explaining what was going on, and we compressed hours of footage into a thirty-second time lapse. We pushed the video out from an internet café over an erratic dial-up connection. *Six hours to go*, the progress bar read. We passed around chocolate birthday cake as we waited. At midnight, after several server time-outs and restarts, I sent everyone to bed. But Vik waited up with me for another few hours before finally calling it a night.

By 3 a.m., after hours of trying and waiting and paying extra to keep the café open, the video finally went out. It was 8 a.m. in New York, and people were headed to work. I passed out, exhausted, as the responses rolled in.

"Wow, you guys really did it!"

"What an amazing video. I can't believe that much goes into it."

"This makes me very, very happy for the people who are getting clean water."

A month later, in October, we came back to Mogotio to film the opening ceremony at the clinic. Our partners had covered the giant cement pump house with clean, white flowing sheets—the exact opposite of the dirty sheets we saw the first time I'd visited. We'd hired a local artist to hand-paint the names of all seven hundred contributing donors in bright blue on the wall. A crowd of about a hundred locals and hospital staff showed up, our cameras rolled, and a worker yanked down the sheets, dramatically revealing the names. Vik and I both tried hard not to cry.

The "donor wall" may have seemed like a disproportionately grand gesture, but we wanted to honor every single person who'd given to this clinic. It didn't matter if they gave $32 or $3. They had all helped to ensure that the children and patients of Mogotio would no longer drink water that was alive.

28

Oblivious

NOVEMBER 2007

By the end of 2007, we'd funded 378 water projects in nine countries. That was a lot to celebrate. Our second annual charity: ball was coming up in December, and we wanted to up our game, making the invitations and exhibits even more beautiful and inspiring. We were pulling all-nighters again, and our grungy HQ was always buzzing with activity. You'd know the time by the sound of the freight elevator gate creaking open, signaling that it was 2 a.m. and the maintenance crew was coming by to empty our trash bins.

One night at around 11:00, I said good-bye to Vik and Becky. "I'm going to call it and grab a bite with Matt."

"I'm going, too," Becky said. "In a bit."

"I'm staying," Vik said.

I felt a pang in my gut. Vik was really amazing. She outworked all of us. She cared so much. And whenever she smiled and waved good-bye, I felt something deeper and more uncomfortable—almost a sense of loss. It had been a very long time since I'd fallen for anyone in a romantic way, and I didn't really know what to do with it.

Walking down Spring Street on my way home, I met up with Matt at the corner deli.

"Bro, I think I like Vik," I said.

"Yeah," Matt said. "I know."

"What?" I asked.

"Uh-huh." Matt just smiled.

Blindingly oblivious again—this time to my own feelings. I'd known this girl for over a year. I always liked being around her. I liked being with her at church, touring museums looking for inspiration on an odd day off, or just walking with her to run errands. I liked sharing the most important things in my life with her. But we worked together. How would that work? What if she didn't feel the same? What if we gave it a shot and discovered that we weren't compatible? I didn't want to lose Vik as a friend, and I certainly didn't want to lose charity: water's creative director.

"I can't," I said to Matt. "Can I?"

"Scott, Vik is a great girl," he said. "She loves God, and seems to want to dedicate her life to serving the poor. She's totally into the same things you are—I mean, what's the *matter* with you?"

"I know. That's what I'm saying. She's amazing."

"Then turn around."

Fifteen minutes later, I stood in our building's lobby, my rising heart rate indicating a possible pending cardiac arrest. I gave our security guard a "yes, we're burning the midnight oil again" look, and then briefly paused at the elevator. I pressed the button, took the lift to the second floor, and then slowly walked into the office. Becky saw me first.

"Oh!" she said. "Crap, I'm still here, aren't I? I said I was going home."

She packed up and headed out. In retrospect, Becky had long ago seen the spark between me and Vik. She was onto us even before *I* was onto us.

I walked toward Vik's desk in the back. She was surprised to see me.

"Did you forget something?"

I sat down in a swivel chair and turned to face her. She looked . . . confused. Now I was starting to lose my nerve. This was too risky.

"What . . . what are you *doing*?" she said.

"Vik." I locked eyes with her. "Have you ever thought . . ."

I had to get the words out, but I was staring at her so intensely, Vik thought I was about to fire her.

"Vik, have you ever thought about   you and me?" I said.

"Um, yes," she said. "A lot."

"Really?" I said, trying not to look surprised, trying not to reveal that something cold and hard inside me was thawing. But I couldn't help myself. I reached over and kissed her, right there in the office. She was smiling when I leaned in, like she'd been thinking the same thing all along.

"I'd like to take you out on a date," I said.

She nodded. She didn't say much. But she didn't have to.

"Wanna get out of here?" I asked.

"Yes."

We put on our jackets, locked up the office, and walked down Spring Street at midnight. She didn't walk two paces ahead, or move her hand away when I went to grab it. She took my hand in hers, like an affirmation. It felt like we were walking six inches off the ground.

On Monday, I had to tell Becky and the board of directors that Vik and I were now dating. I promised that it wouldn't change anything, and for the most part, people were supportive. We were such a small team; there was no official hierarchy or reporting structure. And the work felt lighter when Vik and I were together. There was really nothing else in our lives. It felt like we were partners, a formidable team, a united front.

As we got to know each other better, she shared more of her story with me. I learned that Vik's parents, Elena and Alex, were only seventeen when she was born. It was an accidental pregnancy, and they immediately moved in with Vik's maternal grandparents in a tiny St. Petersburg apartment.

When the Iron Curtain fell and the borders opened, Alex borrowed $2,000 from his brother and flew to New York to establish a new home for the family. Soon after, Vik, Elena, and their Siamese cat, Marty, followed.

"Don't pack anything," Alex told his wife. "They have *everything* here."

Vik, being nine and having never spoken a word of English before, interpreted this to mean that everything was *free* in the Land of the Free. Entering an American supermarket for the first time, a modest Key Food store in Brooklyn, she almost passed out from excitement. In Russia, the shelves were always empty, with long lines for staples like milk and chicken. But here, there were towers of red apples, refrigerated cases brimming with choice cuts of meat, and her favorite: bananas.

Vik and I had radically different upbringings. While my parents rarely drank and banned R-rated movies, Vik's parents dragged her to smoke-filled bars, where she'd sip cranberry juice as they ordered rounds of beer and danced to rock music. Her mother would take shots with Vik's dad and cry about how much she missed Mother Russia. Often, Vik felt like the adult in the family. Sometimes she'd shut their party down and demand to be taken home because it was a school night.

Vik was twelve when her parents divorced. They were freewheeling souls, never really interested in marriage, let alone raising a child. But Luda, Vik's grandmother, stepped in. She'd left behind her life in Russia and moved to America, determined that her only granddaughter would receive the care of a devoted, sane, and sober adult. Every Sunday, she filled their apartment with the smell of sweet Russian pancakes.

Vik had grown up to be shy but fierce. Soft, but strong. I was crazy about her. She wasn't the type of person to throw herself at someone, but she admitted that she had liked me for a long time, since the day she first volunteered at that exhibition in Union Square. She told me her feelings had come in waves, and that she'd pushed them down, not wanting them to get in the way of her work.

"Sometimes it hurt so much," she said, "I didn't know if I could keep working alongside you. But I loved my job and I loved what we were building together." So she'd kept her head down, and prayed that God might show her a way forward.

I'd never dated on the *Anastasis,* and in fact I hadn't had anyone serious in my life since leaving the club scene. With Vik, I didn't want to take anything for granted. I'd had a couple years to reflect on (and be ashamed of) my overly promiscuous past, and I wanted this relationship to be special. Save-yourself-for-marriage kind of special. After a month of dating, I broached the subject.

"Okay, I'll just dive into it . . ." I wrote to Vik in a rambling email that quoted several passages from the Bible, scriptures from Corinthians, Ephesians, 1 Thessalonians. "I think, considering our pasts, we have an incredible opportunity to honor God and set an example for relationships as he created them . . ."

In short, we weren't going to have sex.

When I told friends that Vik and I weren't sleeping together, they looked at me like I had seven heads. I realized how crazy it sounded to most people living in the year 2008, but I wanted to shed the wreckage of my past relationships, the bitter endings, and the reputation I'd developed as a guy who would start a charity just to get girls. That wasn't me—at least, it wasn't me anymore.

"I get it," Vik said after I made a long-winded case for waiting. "I want that, too."

While we never slept together or even spent a night together while dating, it only heightened our desire. I couldn't wait to be next to her. And when we were together, I know the world came into sharper focus for both of us. Vik was even starting to pick up my habit of blind optimism.

One evening in early December, I got back to the office to find her and Becky decorating a beautiful eight-foot-tall Douglas fir Christmas tree. The kind that usually costs $80 at the sidewalk stands that dot the city every winter. Except they'd gotten it for free.

"I just asked!" Vik said. "Like you always do."

Vik, who never liked to ask for anything for herself, had simply walked up to the bearded guys in flannel shirts selling Christmas trees down the street, pitched charity: water, and told them how much we'd love to have a tree to look at while we worked.

And just like that, they gave her a tree, which made our office a little brighter. Surprised, she thanked them for their generous gift. But I think she was the one who gave two lucky guys the gift of watching a beautiful girl smile.

29

———

Running on Empty

MARCH 2008

Hey, guys. Just a quick touch-base. Things are BLAZING . . .

There were fourteen bullet points in my State of the Union email to our board of directors, and it read like an endless litany of good news: new marketing partnerships, new speaking engagements, a round of national press about to drop, and the big reveal that we'd soon pass the $3 million mark for money raised for water projects.

The hits kept coming—which is why I wanted our five board members to grasp the most critical issue, the main reason for my email.

All of this takes money. I know you guys have each pledged $50,000 this year for overhead, give-or-get. $250,000 altogether . . . I'm counting on it. So far, I've only gotten $2,000.

Behind my upbeat tone, the truth was that we had little funding left in the overhead account, a precarious state of affairs that unfortunately had become the norm over the last year and a half.

As charity: water grew, our operating costs constantly increased beyond our capacity. We had a new full-time accountant, which meant a fourth salary on the books. We were doubling down on the next Born in September campaign, which meant we needed to hire web programmers to rebuild our website in a scalable way. Not to mention, Vik, Becky, and I had salaries that were below the norm for a nonprofit in New York, and I wanted to give everyone a small increase. But none of this would be possible unless I found the cash.

As much as I believed in our 100 percent model, it was hard to get people excited to write checks for our salaries and rent. Charity: water was like a sleek, fuel-efficient race car, zooming around the track for the second year with fans cheering us on. If only they knew we were running on empty, about to flame out.

For an organization that was sending millions into the field, we'd been operating efficiently, spending about $100,000 a month in salaries, office rent, paybacks for the credit card fees, insurance, and basic costs. But on several occasions, I quietly deferred my own paycheck to keep us in the black. And once, Becky had to tell everyone else to hold *their* paychecks for a few days before cashing them. It was embarrassing.

Despite these near misses, nobody went looking for a new job. Still, it made me wonder if people had been right to discourage me from the 100 percent model. It was like we'd launched two separate businesses and then had to grow them simultaneously, in perfect balance, from the ground up. Maybe it *was* something that only worked for hedge fund billionaires.

"Dude, just borrow from the water account and write an IOU," friends would tell me. "You've got to pay your office rent, and you've got to pay your people."

But that was *never* going to happen on my watch. I now saw issues of integrity in black and white. Borrowing a single penny from that account to pay ourselves would bring into question everything we stood for. It would topple the most important pillar of our organization and betray our donors' trust.

By June of 2008, I finally let the board of directors know that we were in trouble. We had $881,000 in the water account, but only a few weeks left in operating cash. Unless we found a way forward, we'd need to consider shutting down the charity after the overhead account ran out. It was the most painful idea I could imagine. Going broke with $881,000 in the bank.

I knew the board didn't have the resources to save us, so after sending the email, Vik and I prayed. The get-down-on-your-knees-and-beg kind of praying.

"God, please don't let it end like this. We need a miracle. Money from heaven. Please, God, send us an angel." Honestly, at this point I was praying with very little faith. We'd simply run out of time and runway, and I'd already asked everyone I knew for money. I was out of ideas.

Enter Michael Birch.

Even as I fought to keep charity: water from folding, I'd also been searching for social media partners who could spread the word about our next big Born in September campaign. Back in February, I'd cold-emailed Mark Zuckerberg of Facebook, Tom Anderson of MySpace, and Michael Birch of the UK-based social networking site Bebo. My emails began:

> Hey, I'm a 32-year-old kid from New York who started a water charity about a year and a half ago. I'd traveled around Africa, got sick of seeing people dying of bad water, and decided to do my part . . .

I talked about my personal journey, the founding of charity: water, our passion-filled hundred-hour work weeks, and the first birthday campaign, which raised $159,000. I went on and on, shamelessly . . .

> This year, I have a bigger vision. I just got back from Ethiopia, and there's an incredible need for clean water there . . .
> This year, I want to scale up, and sign up 10,000 people. Our goal is to raise $1.2 million in a month, build 333 wells

and give 166,000 people clean water. We'd love your help.
We think it's a project that might be perfect for ¹/₁₂ of your
community (those born in September) and something that
might also interest the other ¹¹/₁₂ who might want to give
$33. Or $16. Or $1.

I'd been trying to teach our team the anatomy of a pitch—how to
tell your personal story, explain why you care, cite past successes for
credibility, and invite the person you're pitching to help—because why
wouldn't they want to be a part of something this incredible?

Looking back, I find many of my early pitches overly aggressive,
unclear, and all-around cringe-worthy. I'm not sure what I'd do if
someone sent me an email like that today. But deep down, I felt it was
okay to interrupt a CEO's day because I was fighting for the lives of
people who had no voice.

In the end, I got exactly one reply to my cold emails.

Hi, Scott

Ok, you win, I'm inspired!

Congrats on everything you've achieved with this to
date, love the pitch, love the site design, love the photography, and most importantly I love the cause.

There is a lot going on right now so timing may not be
perfect, but would be great to meet up in person next time
I'm in NY and see what we could do together.

Michael

Michael Birch lived in San Francisco with his wife, Xochi. Together, they'd founded Bebo and grown it into the largest social networking site in the United Kingdom. What Michael hadn't mentioned
in his email was that they were in secret talks to sell Bebo. A month
later, AOL purchased the Birches' company for $850 million.

All of a sudden, Michael and Xochi, in their late thirties and expecting their third child, became very wealthy and unemployed. It

was exhilarating but also disorienting. They'd been married since their early twenties, and had always worked.

In June, just as I was coming to terms with the idea of shutting charity: water down, Michael wrote again to say he would be in New York City soon. Could he come hear my pitch in person?

Michael cut a tall, slim frame. His shoulder-length sandy hair, parted down the middle like a Viking's, bounced as he walked through the door of our office. I later learned that Michael was the kind of guy who's happiest wearing nothing more than a loincloth at Burning Man, but I never would've guessed it from his reserved manner. We sat down on the donated couch by our coffee table, and I opened my laptop to start the pitch.

I showed Michael pictures of children drinking dirty water, women knee-deep in mucky rivers polluted with cow dung, and he showed me . . . very little. Michael was guarded and quiet. I'd look up occasionally to see if any of it was registering, but his stoic look never really changed. Was he indifferent? I had no idea. For the life of me, I couldn't read him.

At one point, he peered down at me, steel-blue eyes through black rectangular glasses, and offered only a pointed "I don't really trust charities." Except Michael said it in a dry British accent, so it cut like a knife.

Just lay out the vision, I thought. *Maybe he'll get it.*

"Michael, I know!" I said. "And so many people are just like you. They don't trust charities. And they're not giving. But they should be! Look, this 100 percent model—it's working. It's powerful. People have been telling us that they're making their first-ever donations. We're restoring their faith in giving. But, honestly, we're struggling to figure out the overhead side."

Forty-five minutes later, my time with Michael was up. I had to rush to a sponsorship meeting at Saks Fifth Avenue, and he was headed back to his hotel to check on Xochi, who was fighting a stomach bug. We shared a cab uptown, and I told him how excited we were to be partnering with a luxury retailer. The irony of selling wells in Africa alongside $5,000 handbags made him laugh. I invited him to meet me for coffee the next day.

It was a Saturday, and our second meeting went about the same as the first. We talked a little more about the birthday idea, and how we might be able to scale it online. It turned out that before starting Bebo, Michael and Xochi had started BirthdayAlarm.com, a website that helped people remember birthdays. Michael offered to send an email out to his members promoting our idea. I thought to myself, *Great, but by September we won't even be in business anymore.*

On his way out, Michael asked for our bank details. Cool, I thought. Maybe he'll donate ten grand, build a couple of wells. But that was it. Charity: water was really done.

Three nights later, at 12:30 a.m., I was sitting in bed working, and worrying about charity: water's future, when an email came in:

> Hey, Scott,
>
> The wire should have gone through today for $1M. Let me know if any issues.
>
> Please use this in whatever way you see as most benefiting the charity.
>
> Keep on rocking!
>
> Michael

No way, I thought. *That must be a typo.*

I logged on to Commerce Bank to check our account. And there it was: Deposit pending $1,000,000.

I called Vik from my kitchen, crying, pacing, screaming. "We just got a *million* dollars! One-zero-zero-zero-zero . . ."

I rang Becky and the members of our board, waking everyone up. I didn't care. I had to tell everyone the good news: "It's not over! We're saved!"

When I finally climbed back into bed that night, I suddenly realized just how much stress I'd been carrying over the last year. I'd been trying to shelter Vik and the staff from our impending collapse, trying to keep a positive attitude and believe that something good would happen. But it had been so hard to keep the lights on month after month. It had been wearing me down inside.

And then, in a single moment, Michael and Xochi Birch had changed everything through a radical act of generosity. We went from having only a few weeks of runway left to about thirteen months' worth of fuel. Their gift allowed us to focus on the mission: clean water. And it gave me the head space to be more creative in our pursuit of that mission. Plus, I now had another whole year to figure out how to make this crazy 100 percent model really work.

If that wasn't enough, the Birches came back to us that year and said they wanted to invest in charity: water's technology. They committed to helping us build out our online platform for birthday campaigns, and introduced us to other tech entrepreneurs whose time, ideas, and money could make a difference to our cause. Michael and Xochi would become charity: water's most enduring supporters, and close friends of mine and Vik's.

Before we'd ever met, I remember searching for Michael's picture online and finding a photo of him dressed up for Halloween as Jesus—as a joke, of course. Michael was very open about the fact that he didn't believe in God. At the time, though, I *never* would have imagined that Michael would become charity: water's savior.

And yet he was. The Birches had breathed life into our cause.

Looking back, I'd prayed for an angel, and God—with a profound sense of humor—sent him in the form of a devout atheist.

III

ACTIONS, NOT WORDS

30

Radical Transparency

Jim Hocking turned away from his drilling rig, adjusted his black cowboy hat, and walked toward me with slow, heavy steps. He'd been talking to his drilling team in the local Sango language, so I couldn't understand their conversation. But from the discouraged looks on their faces, I could tell we were in serious trouble.

"Scott, we dug almost three hundred feet, and then the walls of the well caved in," Jim explained. "The sand is clogging up the drill bits, and if we lose them—that's it. We're done."

"So what do you think?" I said. "How worried should we be?"

"It's hard to tell. We've got a little daylight left, and the guys want to keep trying. So that's the plan for now," he said, trying to sound upbeat.

Jim was the founder of Water for Good, our local partner in the Central African Republic (CAR) and the recipient of this year's September fundraising campaign. We'd arrived here two days before in Moale, a small village deep in the heart of CAR's rain forest, to meet with Jim and his team, and to fulfill a promise to bring clean water to every single member of the Bayaka tribe living in CAR. But so far, there was no water—only wet, soupy soil. And that was a big problem.

Three weeks earlier, we'd launched the campaign for CAR, telling everyone (donors, friends, and past supporters) that on our four-year anniversary, September 7, we'd travel to Moale to get real-time video of our two-hundredth project being drilled—this very well. Vik and I had traveled three days and three thousand miles from New York, hoping to deliver on that promise and film crystal-clear water gushing high into the sky and down into the hands of children with smiling faces. Little did we know that Moale would become mission: impossible.

Normally, when you drill a well, you push easily through sand or clay first, and then through rock and gravel. Finally, after tunneling down for as little as fifty feet or as many as a thousand, you hit water. It's like sticking a very deep straw in the ground and suddenly finding a lake to drink from. That's the magic moment, when you know *This is going to work. This village is going to get water.* But so far, in Moale, the magic was eluding us.

For Jim, it was particularly disappointing because this was his third try here. His first had come sixteen years earlier, when he didn't even have a drilling rig—just a team of six guys with shovels and pickaxes. After digging eighty feet down, they ran out of air and had to pump oxygen into the hole so the workers wouldn't suffocate. They went another twenty feet without finding water and gave up. In 2005, Jim came back for a second try—this time with a drilling rig. His team went down to a depth of three hundred feet, and still came up dry.

He knew this was unusual. Groundwater in CAR is typically plentiful, lurking about one hundred fifty feet below the surface. So, by the time we met in 2010, Jim had commissioned a team of experts to study satellite images and maps of Moale. They believed that here, clean water was probably closer to seven hundred feet underground. (Imagine taking an elevator to the seventeenth floor, only going straight *down*.) Determined to try yet again, Jim purchased a new rig that could drill down to eight hundred feet. But he needed money to operate it.

That's where charity: water came in.

"We're in," I'd told Jim over the phone. "In fact, we'll start our anniversary campaign with a video, drilling live from Moale."

"It won't be easy," he'd said. "But I really believe this new rig can find the water. And Scott, this village, the people, they *desperately* need it."

Every year, when the United Nations publishes its "Human Development Index," a study of the overall well-being of residents in 188 countries, CAR consistently brings up the rear. Usually, it ranks 188th—dead last. It was an unforgivably difficult place to work. It took forever for Jim's team to get spare parts—from tires and windshield wipers for the vehicles to O-rings and steel pipes for the wells. And everything cost double what you'd pay elsewhere. Fuel was $10 a gallon, and the compressors and drill rigs slurped it up like liquid gold. Just driving around was a challenge. Less than 7 percent of the country's roads are paved. Months earlier, Jim's crew almost lost a truck and a driver when a wooden bridge crumbled beneath their caravan.

For me, though, working in CAR was the perfect mix of risk and reward. You could argue that I'd picked a poor horse to bet on—a two-time loser. But I liked to bet big. So, before we got here, we made online videos about the Bayaka and the challenges they faced. ABC News, *20/20*, and the *Huffington Post* picked up the story, reaching an audience of millions. In the past three weeks, our donors had raised more than $290,000 for CAR. Tomorrow morning, thousands of people would go to our website expecting to see their money at work in Moale—which, we hoped, would inspire them to continue giving for other projects. We had a lot riding on this well.

As daylight dwindled, Vik and I stood in the rain at the edge of a muddy forest clearing, watching Jim's rig battle the earth. I glanced over at our cameraman, Paul Pryor, huddled under a tarp, trying to keep his gear dry.

For the last two years, I'd spent less time writing and shooting pictures in the field and more time developing the business side of charity:

water. I missed getting my hands dirty, but it was nice to focus on the big picture while Paul worried about schlepping giant camera bags through the airport. Like me, Paul would do anything to get the shot. He'd climb the highest tree for the best angle. Or jump on the back of a Land Rover, wrap his legs around the spare tire, and shoot B-roll of the lush jungle path, holding on for dear life while the truck bounced across uneven terrain.

Video had proved to be an amazing tool for bringing donors into the field with us (if only virtually), and a huge part in the success we'd had on social media. Earlier that year, we broke one million followers on Twitter, and on this trip alone we were planning to upload twenty videos to Facebook. Some were funny—like the night we raided Jim's cooler and found only Spam and pickled anchovies. Others gave short history lessons on the border wars that had taken place between CAR and Congo. We tried to keep things engaging and entertaining, never forgetting that our primary purpose was to help the Bayaka get clean water.

But as the sun set in Moale, that was looking less likely. Jim went to speak with the head of drilling operations, Marcellin Namsené. Jim, like us, believed that the work in CAR had to be led by the locals. Marcellin, his drilling crew, the mechanics, and the drivers were all born and raised in the Central African Republic.

"Why don't you call it a day," Jim said. "Let the crew sleep. We'll try again in the morning."

Marcellin weighed the suggestion for a moment. He was a foot taller than Jim, and his upper body was ripped from a decade of tossing around heavy steel pipes and drilling stems. Today, he wore a bright yellow hard hat and muddy boots, and his face was speckled with dry red dirt.

He looked back at the rig and shook his head forcefully. "No," he said. "We will work here through the night. I'll have the team bring the lights and generator."

"Okay," Jim said. "It's your call."

Jim reminded me a lot of Dr. Gary. The son of American missionaries, he first came to CAR in 1957 with his family, when he was three years old. He learned Sango before he learned English. Jim and his two brothers grew up with no television or video games. But they had pellet rifles, a vast collection of exotic bugs, a large tree house, and forts in their backyard that they'd built from scraps of wood collected at a nearby sawmill. Years later, Jim came to learn how those sawmills contributed to the Bayaka's plight.

Over many bumpy drives and meals together, Jim had educated us on the history of the Bayaka tribe. They were some of the world's last remaining hunter-gatherers, nomads living deep in the rain forest. They slept in small beehive-shaped huts under the forest canopy—a place so thick with towering emerald-colored trees that if you looked up you couldn't even see the sky. It was the Bayaka's perfect home. They knew which roots to eat, what vines were good for making poison arrows to hunt small game, where to find the best wild honey, and how to make herbal medicine. They had little interest in the outside world, even as it increasingly intruded on their way of life.

After attending high school in California, and then Grace College & Seminary in Indiana, Jim returned to CAR in 1977 to follow in his father's footsteps. He quickly discovered that logging and deforestation had pushed the Bayaka to the edge of ruin. As the protective forest canopy disappeared, so, too, did the animals the Bayaka depended on for food. Conservationists laid claim to the remaining forests, where endangered elephants and gorillas roamed, but in the battle between loggers and wildlife activists, the Bayaka were an afterthought. They were forced to create squatter-style settlements on the outskirts of the forest, close enough to villages where they could offer cheap labor and beg for food—but also close enough to catch diseases like tuberculosis and hepatitis B. They lived on a diet of cassava roots, and their children's bellies soon swelled from malnourishment.

Jim had enormous respect for the Bayaka way of life, and I could see why. In all my travels throughout Africa, I'd never met such interesting, hospitable people. The Bayaka rarely reach more than five feet in height. (I'm six foot one, and the tallest of their men came just to my chest.) As part of their tradition and to attract a partner, Bayaka men and women use a hammer and chisel to whittle their top teeth into sharp points, a sign of beauty. They love to sing and dance as they go about their work, and have been recognized worldwide for their melodic harmonizing, documented in albums, movies, and books.

Sadly, these famed people with beautiful voices were marginalized by the taller Central Africans. The locals called them "forest people" and treated them like animals. They exploited the Bayaka for slave labor and sex, and denied them access to the few working wells in the villages. Here in Moale, the Bayaka walked forty minutes each way to collect their water from a muddy brown pond.

Their story ignited a deep sense of injustice in me. I knew that bringing them clean water wasn't going to change their place in society, but I hoped it could at least help them regain some measure of independence, dignity, and health.

After dinner, Vik and I walked back to our tent and shooed away some unwelcome guests—the spiders and caterpillars that had gathered in and around our sleeping bags. It was caterpillar season, and squiggly green spirals crunched under our feet every time we took a step. We lay on top of our bags in the evening heat, saying prayers for Marcellin and his crew and hoping to get some rest after a long day.

Around 4:30 a.m., I woke up to angelic singing. I sat straight up in our tent.

"Do you hear that?" Vik said. Apparently, she wasn't asleep, either.

"Yes," I said. "What is it?"

We grabbed flashlights and our rain jackets, and stumbled through the tall grass toward the voices. Up ahead on the dirt path, we spotted Paul, camera in hand, looking for the source of the mysterious music.

After a few minutes of walking in the dark, we came upon a clearing where hundreds of Bayaka huddled under and spilled out from a large wooden shelter. This was their church. Every single villager—maybe four hundred men, women, and barefoot, sleepy-eyed children—had woken up early to sing in the rain and pray for water. In the distance, we could see the soft glow of floodlights, as Marcellin and his crew continued their work.

Vik gave me a long look, and I knew exactly what she was feeling. These people had such deep faith. They were praying for *our* success.

"Scott, it's so beautiful," she said, holding me close.

Over the last three years, Vik and I had traveled to some of the most remote, forsaken places on earth. She was always game to eat strange food and go for days without a real shower if it meant helping others. She had a depth of compassion that I'd never encountered before. And as I looked at her, I remembered that in a few weeks it would be our one-year wedding anniversary.

We'd gotten married the previous September, before a hundred fifty friends and family. We bootstrapped our whole wedding for $10,000. Aunt Jayne let us hold the wedding on her farm in Connecticut, and paid for flowers when we said we couldn't afford them. Our friends bartended, took photos, and DJ'ed; I negotiated special rates on everything, from the tent and chairs to tableware and wine. When it came time to buy a dress, Vik walked into a David's Bridal outlet and said, "This will do," to one of the first gowns she tried on.

A few hours into the reception, we snuck away to an old but charming bed-and-breakfast in Woodbury, Connecticut. The floorboards creaked and the door handles stuck, but it was the first time we had spent a whole night together, so to us, everything was perfect.

Back in Moale, Vik looked at me with tears streaming down her face and said, "Happy birthday, babe."

Oh yeah, that, too. It was September 7, and I was thirty-five years old today. As we watched the people of Moale serenade the rising sun, I knew there was only one thing I wanted for my birthday.

At 11 a.m., Marcellin gave us an update. It wasn't a good one. After a full night of drilling, the borehole had caved in again. The ground was like quicksand. They couldn't keep the hole open long enough to insert the steel casing, let alone get a pump in there.

"I just want to find water to make these people happy, but I cannot, so my heart is broke," Marcellin said to me in English. "I don't want to take a break . . . Can you see? I'm not even hungry to eat food."

Jim put a hand on Marcellin's shoulder. "You guys did the best you could," he said. "Don't worry. We'll come back."

As painful as it was, we had to admit defeat. The African ground had won again. Jim went to break the news to the Bayaka pastor and the community

"Ngu ayeke pepe," he said in Sango. *There is no water.* "The only consolation I can give you is that I will keep trying."

"Don't worry," the pastor responded in Sango. "It was not God's will to find water today. When you come back, perhaps then He will see it through."

The villagers listened and nodded their heads. Some spoke with gentle voices to Jim and Marcellin. Others shook our hands tenderly as if to comfort *us.* Which made me even more upset. It felt so unfair. We'd brought our heavy equipment in, camped out in their village, and left them with nothing—for a third time.

The people of Moale had been kind to us in the face of great disappointment. But I wasn't so sure that our donors, friends, and followers would show as much grace. We'd promised them a joyful video—and we didn't have it. What were we supposed to tell them?

Sure, we'd move on and build plenty of successful wells throughout the country. But the people of Moale, who had been waiting for sixteen years, would *still* be collecting dirty water.

"We failed today," I said to Vik. "That's the story we have to tell everyone."

"Wait, what?" she said, a little stunned.

"We let this village down. We need to tell the truth and let everyone know what happened here."

She wasn't having it. "Scott, there's no way we can just flat-out say we failed."

Vik's advertising experience had taught her that you never want to appear weak when talking to your customers. It's better to bend the truth, make it palatable, spin a good story.

"Scott, we don't have to send a video," she said. "Maybe we can do an email instead? Keep it upbeat and vague—explain that we had technical problems?"

"But we promised a video," I said. "An email isn't good enough."

"But what if people freak out? What if there's backlash?"

She did have a point. Would our donors start backing out of the campaign because they didn't like bad news? We'd built up everyone's expectations. What if they even asked for their money back?

I had to consider it because I'd spent the last two years trying to repair a relationship with a donor whose expectations I had spectacularly failed. In 2008, a family-owned accessories retailer raised more than $741,000, charity: water committed an additional $500,000 as a match, and we earmarked the entire $1.24 million to clean water projects in Kenya.

But then tribal warfare broke out, causing long delays in well construction. When drilling finally began, we ran into water-quality issues and hardware malfunctions, and the more we shared these problems with the donor, the angrier they became. That was my fault—I'd failed to spell out in the beginning all the ways things could go wrong.

Here in Moale, I knew we had to tell the whole story, even if it made us look bad.

"Our donors need to see what it takes to bring clean water to the most remote places in the world," I said to Vik. "I want them to understand that we don't always succeed, but we'll never stop fighting."

Vik wasn't convinced. She just looked worried.

"Okay," she said. "I really hope you're right."

I found Paul, and we walked over to the drilling rig together. It was 3:11 p.m. Exhausted, I tried my best to strike an encouraging tone.

"Let's do this," I said. Paul started filming.

"As you can probably tell by the scene behind me, we don't have very good news," I began. The drilling rig stood tall and quiet in the background, a symbol of our failure. I tried my best to explain the quicksand and the collapsed borehole, to make sense of a complicated hydrogeology problem for our donors.

"We know there's water here. It's just a matter of time, technology, and determination," I continued. "While we obviously hoped that today would go differently, we talk a lot about transparency at charity: water, and we're committed to showing you the reality of what happens here . . . 95 percent of the wells Jim drills in this country find water, and 5 percent don't and we have to try again. I know many of you will be disappointed. *Know this:* You have not heard the last of Moale. We are determined to fight alongside Jim and make sure this village, as well as every Bayaka living in this country, get clean water."

It took three hours to edit the five-minute video. We spliced in clips of Jim explaining the process, of Marcellin's team working through the night, of the Bayaka watching the drilling with hope in their eyes. It took another four hours to upload the video to our website via a portable satellite unit. We titled it *No Water for Our Birthday in Central African Republic.*

It rained hard that night, and I couldn't sleep. I was eager for morning to come, anxious about what people were saying. (Maybe Vik had been right. What was I doing? I'd turned our failure into a public announcement. What would our donors think of us?) Most of all, I was consumed with grief for the Bayaka, and I hoped that everyone watching would feel the same.

Our failure video, as I called it, became a defining moment in charity: water's history. I knew that the only way we could reestablish the public's trust in charity was if we talked openly about our mistakes, and that video cemented charity: water's commitment to radical transparency.

In the twenty-four hours following the broadcast of *No Water for Our Birthday,* tens of thousands of people watched it and filled our social media feeds with positive comments.

"I think this is even more important than sharing your successes," a donor wrote.

"Even with the best planning, scientific data, and equipment, you can have myriad problems," a field engineer commented. "Thanks for acknowledging the challenges."

"Mistakes are opportunities. It's how you handle them that matters the most," said Ryan Meeks, a pastor from Seattle. "And you guys handled this well."

No Water for Our Birthday would become the most-watched charity:

water video that year. In fact, in September alone, we saw a 23 percent increase in Facebook fans, a 160 percent increase in visitors to the charity: water homepage, and 277,770 views of all our videos. The impact was undeniable—and the September campaign went on to break a fundraising record at the time, finishing at $1.7 million.

Admitting mistakes in a very public way is hard to do. But I respected our donors too much to whitewash our failure in Moale. For many of them, we were their first encounter with a charity of any kind.

We left Moale the next morning with heavy hearts, and promised we'd return for another try. In fact, Jim and Marcellin left behind a pile of expensive steel pipes, as a signal that we really meant it.

I honestly had no idea how we were going to get water out of the unforgiving Moale ground—or when. But I knew that failing the Bayaka a fourth time would be absolutely devastating. We couldn't let it happen.

31

Do Something

In 2011, charity: water turned five. If you only read the press back then, you'd have thought we were a hotshot start-up that was disrupting the traditional philanthropy model. *USA Today* called us a "techno-savvy" charity, and *Inc. Magazine* said we were "reinventing the nonprofit business." Outlets like the *Wall Street Journal, Fast Company,* and CNN wrote about us like we were a Really Big Deal. But in reality? We were hardworking novices who figured it out as we went along. I was a flawed founder who prayed constantly for guidance. And, frankly, we were still hustling to get attention, still struggling to raise money, still putting out fires.

Then, somehow, the White House heard about charity: water—which is how Vik and I got an invitation to the 2011 National Prayer Breakfast. On a very cold morning in February, we found ourselves sitting in the Washington Hilton ballroom about forty feet from the president of the United States, listening to him speak about the challenges of his work.

"Like all of us, my faith journey has had its twists and turns. It hasn't always been a straight line," President Obama said.

No kidding, twists and turns. I thought back to that night seven years ago, when I was a club promoter on the lam, watching this man on TV and feeling so sure that he would become president. Now here he was, halfway through his first term.

"In the wake of failures and disappointments, I've questioned what God had in store for me and been reminded that God's plans for us may not always match our own shortsighted desires," Obama said.

Failures and disappointments. We'd certainly had our share: campaigns that didn't hit targets, broken wells, new hires who were a bad fit. But these experiences had pushed us to recalibrate and get stronger. My faith was stronger than ever, too.

Every Sunday, Vik and I would get together with our church friends for dinner. On the nights when we hosted, thirty or more people would climb the seventy-two steps up to our small one-bedroom apartment in Tribeca. They'd throw their coats on our bed, and we'd all pitch in to buy wine and pasta from a little Italian place nearby. We'd play music and talk for hours about relationships and God and work. It was a rowdier version of those Winston family dinners I'd enjoyed so much as a kid.

On Monday mornings, Vik and I would wake up to sunlight streaming through the tall windows of our apartment. We'd pop into our neighborhood market to buy coffee, and then walk together to the subway station, riding just two stops to the office. Many nights, we'd work side-by-side on the couch until midnight. People talk about finding a work-life balance, but Vik and I had found work-life *integration*. It felt amazing.

Up on the stage, President Obama continued: "It's faith that reminds me that despite being just one very imperfect man, I can still help whomever I can, however I can, wherever I can, for as long as I can, and that somehow God will buttress these efforts."

Listening to the president talk, I thought about how far charity: water had come as an imperfect organization with an even more imperfect founder at the helm. We'd started with three people (me, Vik, and Lani) on Brantly's couch. Now we were thirty employees in a custom-designed SoHo office that a generous donor had given us for only $5,000 a month. (The space was easily worth $25,000.)

As President Obama was speaking, I glanced at Vik and thought about all the hours she'd spent coding birthday campaign web pages, all the cases of water she used to lug around town. (We quit selling water bottles after learning that 38 billion empties got pitched into landfills every year. I didn't want us to be part of that waste, regardless of whom it helped.) Five years after learning to code with a copy of *HTML for Dummies,* Vik had grown into a confident creative director, the architect of a world-class brand. Conferences invited her to speak. Magazines like *Fast Company* wrote profiles hailing her innovative designs.

"I came upon a group recently called charity: water, a group that supports clean water projects overseas," Obama was saying.

Wait, what? I sat up straight in my chair and locked eyes with Vik— *Did he just say . . . ? Did we just get name-checked by the president of the United States?*

"This is a project that was started by a former nightclub promoter named Scott Harrison, who grew weary of living only for himself and feeling like he wasn't following Christ as well as he should," the president said.

Vik squeezed my hand so hard I thought she'd break a knuckle. I completely stopped breathing.

"And because of Scott's good work, charity: water has helped 1.7 million people get access to clean water. And in the next ten years, he plans to make clean water accessible to a hundred million more," Obama went on. "That's the kind of promoting we need more of. That's the kind of faith that moves mountains."

I don't remember the rest of the speech. I was floating outside my body at that point. I felt so many things at once: embarrassed, proud, thrilled, humbled. It wasn't just the shock that someone in the president's inner circle had felt we were important enough to be in his speech. It was the way he'd framed our mission: "the kind of faith that moves mountains."

The president of the United States was affirming the driving force that still gets me up every single morning: faith in action. In other words, not a religion-only, church-only, talk-only, judge-your-neighbor faith, but a faith that takes action. A faith that says we are going to get a hundred million people clean water because a bunch of people around the world got together and decided to *do something* about this enormous problem.

"Do something" is what my dad taught me. Instead of accepting Mom's illness, he did everything in his power to help her get better. It's what Dr. Gary showed me, dedicating his life to helping the poor get world-class medical care. It's what Jim and Marcellin showed me when they kept returning to Moale again and again.

Yet, while faith is a driving force in my personal life, charity: water is not and has never been a religious organization. I believe our job is to get clean water by all means to *all* people in the most effective way. Everyone can participate. Everyone benefits. When I built charity: water, I wanted to invite the whole world to do something life-changing for others. I wanted to replace the old charity model that guilts people into giving with one that brings them excitement and joy.

And, of course, I also wanted it to be fun.

Back in 2009, Vik and I started working on mycharity: water, a social fundraising website, while sitting at the round kitchen table in Michael and Xochi's five-story San Francisco home. It was one of those uneven wooden farm tables where if you push too hard, your pencil pokes through the paper.

We talked for hours, brainstorming what the website could look like. Vik sketched out different scenarios for pages and flows, then handed them to Michael, who went down to his study and actually wrote the code in real time.

When we got back to New York, Michael paid for a software engineer to further develop his code and work with us full time. For the next six months, we hammered out a brand-new platform that let donors build time-limited fundraising campaigns—for a birthday, a holiday, or just because they felt inspired. They could upload photos, write mission statements, set goals, and invite their friends to leave comments and see who else was donating.

We launched mycharity: water in beta in September 2009, and in a matter of months, tens of thousands of people created campaigns. They asked others to give on their behalf—and then *those people* got excited and did the same. In the first four months, mycharity: water raised more than $1.2 million. A year and a half later, that number had climbed to $13 million.

For me, the best part of mycharity: water was that it democratized giving. Every dollar counted. Everyone could participate. Whether you raised $5 or $5,000, you received a report showing exactly where 100 percent of your money went: *Here's the well you funded at this middle school. Here's the satellite image on Google Earth. Here are pictures of the people your $5 helped.*

No matter how small the donation, I wanted everyone to experience the electric feeling that comes from giving. Numerous studies have shown that when people have a choice to give money to someone in need or keep it for themselves, the givers report much higher levels of happiness than the keepers. Researchers call this the "warm glow" of giving, but we didn't need science to know it was true.

In our first five years, 98,000 people created campaigns. People like Jenna Hassan, a donor from Canada who hiked Mount Kilimanjaro with her father in 2011, raising $6,526 from 70 friends. That money helped build a shallow borehole well for 700 people in the village of Siguar, Ethiopia. That same well was also funded in part by a campaign started by Riley Goodfellow, a seven-year-old in Southern California. Riley and her friends called themselves the Beans and Rice Crew, because that's what they ate for twenty-five straight days to raise $5,500 for clean water.

Mycharity: water also gave us a better way to connect with our donors. We started making videos about our amazing campaigners, sending them personal thank-you notes and inviting them to events.

We still honor our donors in unique ways. And to this day, my staff and I regularly open our own wallets and donate to campaigns started by people we've never met. We're constantly inspired by their crazy, creative ideas.

Take Jesse Carey, a podcaster from *Relevant* magazine. Jesse undertook what he called "the ultimate test of human endurance" by listening to the entire Nickelback catalog, on repeat, for a total of 168 hours. He even wore headphones to bed. Jesse's campaign ended up raising $36,390 for eight water projects in Mali.

Brady Phelps, a dad from San Diego, had been putting batter and food coloring into squeeze bottles and making his kids pancakes that looked like their favorite cartoon characters. If you donated $100 to his campaign, Brady would create a pancake of your choosing and post it on his Instagram account, @ThePancakeDad. For $1,000, he'd actually wrap up the pancake and mail it to you. Pancake Dad became an overnight success. *Us Weekly, Business Insider,* and TV news crews picked up the story, and Brady griddled his way to $53,440 in donations. We earmarked it for seven villages in Ethiopia.

"People's lives are going to be changed by these stupid pancakes," Brady told a reporter. "I mean they're *pancakes.* This is a silly, silly thing that I did for my kids because I wanted to make them smile, and now, hopefully, other people are going to be smiling all over the world because they're going to be able to live a life that they wouldn't have been able to if it wasn't for this."

Brady's pancakes, Riley's rice and beans, Jesse's superhuman endurance—*all* these efforts created life-changing results for people across the world. In our first five years, charity: water raised $59 million, and our donors helped us fund almost 6,000 water projects that touched 2.3 million lives in 19 countries.

When you lift 2.3 million people out of water poverty, you give them more than a healthier future. You also give them greater economic opportunities. According to the United Nations, every $1 invested in clean water turns into $4 to $8 in economic returns. When a village in Malawi gets a well, for example, the women have more time to start businesses, repair their homes, and take charge of their futures. When a school in Bangladesh or the Democratic Republic of the Congo gets water and latrines, teenage girls don't have to skip class during the days they're menstruating. These teenage years are critical for girls; when they stay home from school, many of their parents start to depend on the extra help, and will tell them, "You don't need school, anyway. Go collect the water, find the firewood, clean the house."

The massive economic and health benefits of clean water are backed up by data; the facts are undeniable. But I've also seen something that's much harder to quantify: restored dignity, greater gender parity, social progress.

For example, in 2010, we worked with a partner in North and East India to help train and equip twenty-one well mechanics. The need in the area was so great that our partner actively recruited women to become mechanics, a trade that is widely considered men's work. It took the locals a while to get used to the idea.

"In one village," a mechanic in Uttar Pradesh named Sheila Singh told us during our visit in 2011, "the men said, 'You women will break our well even more. Go away!'"

But instead of going away, Sheila and another female mechanic, both wearing yellow charity: water hard hats and blue saris, dropped their heavy tool bags, pulled out their wrenches, and got to work.

"We'll show you how to fix it," Sheila told the men, who stood there, arms crossed and scowling, just watching.

When Sheila and her partner successfully completed the job, a sixty-year-old man was among the first to pat her on the shoulder and say, "Today you have really proved it. You've become your own breadwinner."

My favorite story, though, is about a woman named Helen Apio, a wife and mother of two in Northern Uganda. Helen would wake up every morning before dawn to walk a mile and a half to the nearest water point, only to wait in line with hundreds of other women. She spent hours each day collecting water. Each afternoon, as she returned home lugging a forty-pound Jerry Can on her back, she would ask herself, *How should I use this water today? Should I wash my children's*

*school uniforms? Cook for my family? Garden? Bathe? How much of it can
we drink?*

She had only ten gallons to work with, about as much water as you
or I would use in a five-minute shower. As the woman of the house,
Helen told us, she never used the water for herself. She always put her
family first. But Helen's life changed in 2009, when a well was drilled
in the center of her village.

"Now I have time to eat, and my children can go to school," she
said when our team visited her. "I can even work in my garden, take
a shower, and then come back for more water if I want!" For the first
time, she had enough water to wash *her* clothes and *her* body. Her face
was bright. She wore flowers in her hair.

"Yes," Helen beamed. "Now *I* am beautiful."

It had never occurred to me before that helping Helen feel beautiful
was another benefit of clean water. But over the years, I've heard similar phrases uttered with an equal measure of pride: "Now I am looking
so smart"; "Now we are clean"; "Now we can bathe our children."

As proud as I was to hear President Obama tell my story that day
at the 2011 National Prayer Breakfast, I knew that my personal journey wasn't the headline anymore. It had long ago been eclipsed by the
stories of people like Helen, Sheila, Jim, Marcellin, Brady, and Riley.
Charity: water's story now belonged to the hundreds of thousands of
people around the world who had been inspired to *do something*, people
who believed they could move mountains simply by flipping pancakes.

And yet our success felt like an anomaly.

At a time when the entire philanthropy sector was shrinking, charity: water was expanding. From 2008 to 2010, overall donations for
American nonprofits dropped 10 percent. In comparison, our donations grew 395 percent over the same period. If you plotted our growth
on a chart, the arrow would go up and to the right, year after year. I
mistakenly assumed it would always be that way, even though it really
didn't make any sense.

Especially when you considered that I was the guy in charge.

32

Totally Undisciplined

NEW YORK, 2008–2011

Looking back on our early years, I always thought of charity: water as a start-up. And yet, I'd never even worked in a real office before. I had no clue what a start-up was actually like, much less what a CEO was supposed to do all day—until I met Ross Garber.

Ross was an entrepreneur from Austin, Texas, who had experience running a real tech start-up. At twenty-eight, he'd cofounded an internet software company called Vignette, taking it from zero to three hundred fifty employees in three years. Vignette went public, and in 1999, at the age of thirty-two, Ross handed over the reins to a "professional" CEO and retired. A year later, the company had more than two thousand employees and was worth more than $15 billion.

A mutual friend introduced us over email, and Ross and I got on the phone in late 2008 so he could hear an idea I'd been obsessing over.

"I want to take over the church for a whole day," I said.

"Scott, it's been a really long time since I lived in New York," Ross said. "Which church are you talking about?"

"No, no . . . I mean the 'global church'—I want to raise a billion dollars in one day and have all of the money go toward water projects."

"Go on," Ross said.

"Okay," I said. "It's Sunday morning. Just imagine every single person in every church in the world passing around the basket until it's literally breaking from the weight of the money. Until they raise enough to end the global water crisis for good!"

I went on to describe drilling rigs being deployed across the world. Clean water shooting up in thousands of villages simultaneously. People everywhere becoming their better selves, inspired by a viral giving campaign.

"And the beauty of it is the church would be giving the money to charity: water, a nonreligious organization," I continued. "What a statement that would make! The world's churches care so much about the poor, they're giving a *billion dollars*. With no strings attached. No agenda."

"Okay, okay," Ross said, laughing. "I get it. You think big."

We never did pursue a day of global church giving, although I still dream about it. But from that day forward, Ross became my mentor. Money never passed between us. (Although he did once send me an invoice for his services. The number billed was $1 million—with a balance due of zero.) Ross just felt inspired to help. He knew that the only way I'd get millions of people to care about clean water was if I first learned how to care for my own organization.

Despite our incredible growth, I still micromanaged my staff and obsessed over every detail, from the wording in our emails to the moment-by-moment traffic on our website. The organization had matured exponentially, but my leadership style hadn't.

Case in point: a year earlier, Michael and Xochi Birch's million-dollar gift had allowed us to hire more staff and expand the number of countries and partners we worked with. But we were still burning through about $100,000 a month in overhead. I just hadn't figured out how to sustain the 100 percent model. At least not yet.

In December 2009, shortly after I'd spoken to Ross, I ran an idea by Steve Sadove, the CEO of Saks Fifth Avenue and another mentor of mine.

"Steve," I said. "What if I could get one hundred New Yorkers to give $1,000 a month? Then I could cover my overhead forever!"

"Don't be an idiot," Steve said.

Actually, his response was more gracious, but that's what he should have said. Steve reminded me that if anyone fell behind on payments or decided not to renew for the following year, charity: water would become insolvent on January 1. We'd never survive.

"Scott, ask everyone to sign *three-year* commitments," he said. "That way, you can plan the business. You can plan cash flow."

It seemed so obvious. Why hadn't I thought of it?

"And you need multiple giving levels," he continued. "Tell you what. I'm going to start by giving you $2,000 a month for the next three years."

Just like that, he made himself a founding member of "The Well," a program that pays for charity: water's overhead and administrative costs—all the basic necessities that keep us running. The Well began with a few generous donors, and has since grown to 129 individuals and families from around the globe who give at annual levels ranging from $60,000 to $1 million.

At first, early donors and friends were dismissive of the idea. *No way are you going to convince major donors to pay for your employee health care plan. What would they get out of it?* It was true. In many ways, being a Well member would be the highest, most selfless form of giving. Instead of getting their names on the wing of a hospital or a music hall or even a well that they could show to friends and say, "I did that!" Well members would get reports on rent expenditures, payroll, and credit card payback fees—all so a nine-year-old who raised $109 for her ninth birthday could show *her* friends and family pictures of a well halfway across the world and say, "I did that."

If Steve helped me figure out how to pay charity: water's employees, Ross was the one who taught me how to keep them happy. When we first spoke in December 2009, I told him I really needed a mentor. So he flew in to visit the office and spend a few days talking with charity: water's staff, watching us operate as a team.

"Here's my vision," I told Ross. "I want to raise $2 billion for clean water by 2020!" After listening to my lofty speech, Ross looked around the office and saw that we had one guy in the corner wearing headphones writing all our web code (and he was on the edge of a nervous breakdown from the pressure). We still used QuickBooks for our accounting, even though we'd grown way past its capabilities. Our Water Programs data was buried in spreadsheets, and all our fundraising intelligence was locked away inside my head. Oh, and there was a red velvet rope stretched across my office door, blocking it. Someone on staff had found it in our storage closet and thought it'd be funny to put it there. I didn't consider that it might send the wrong message to any staffer who wanted to talk to me about real issues.

Later that week, on the plane home, Ross wrote me a scathing eleven-page confidential report. He called my "$2 billion by 2020" vision "statistically impossible" and "ridiculous," and listed my blind spots as a leader.

"Charity: water is a shop of 15 people, but a team of exactly one. You," Ross wrote. "You control everything. You even run everything. You are the product design guy. The merchandising guy. The fundraising guy. The message guy. Probably even the check-signing guy . . . Metaphorically, if you're still in the club biz, you can either be the bartender or running the show . . . You can't mix the drinks and run the whole club."

Ross said I needed to start thinking like a CEO, which meant grow up, stop worrying about day-to-day details, and start focusing on big-picture, multi-year goals.

"Whether history records you as a success or failure," Ross warned, "will depend on whether you can shift from living in today to living in tomorrow."

It was some of the best advice I'd ever gotten.

Ross taught me how to zero in, reframe priorities, and get out of my own way. He made me answer tough questions: What is our business model exactly? What are our donation products? How specifically do we plan to scale?

He also paid to bring in an executive coach named Linda Ford to help whip us into shape. Linda specialized in teaching start-up founders and CEOs how to develop their leadership skills to foster a healthy workplace culture. I wasn't sure what that meant, but I was up for whatever these two could do to make us smarter.

Linda, also from Austin, came to our first management team offsite meeting in 2010. She had a warm smile and strong opinions. After a few hours of talking with our small team, she called for a break and took Ross aside into a quiet hallway.

"Why did you bring me here?" she whispered. "These are the least capable people I've ever met in my life—there's no 'there' there!"

Linda saw a bunch of twenty- and thirtysomethings with endless passion but a collective work experience that wouldn't have added up to make one mid-level executive. We'd all started out as volunteers, and I didn't know what an executive team was. The dysfunction in our office, from power dynamics to poor cultural habits, had started at the top.

Sure, I could tell my story to five thousand people in a conference hall, bring the audience to tears, and get them excited about giving money for clean water—but when I got back to the office, I was a terrible manager. Holding employees accountable, making organizational decisions, running meetings, hiring people—I didn't enjoy doing any of these things, and it showed.

So Linda helped us form charity: water's first executive team. We brought on experienced grown-ups, people whom, in the past, I might have dismissed as "bureaucrats," to play key roles in modeling proper work culture for the rest of the staff. In 2010, we hired our first controller, an accountant named Michael Letta, who'd worked at firms like Thomson Reuters and Deloitte before deciding he wanted to do something more meaningful with his skills. Michael got charity: water off QuickBooks and built our first finance team.

We also hired Michael's then-girlfriend (now wife) Lauren Miller, a marketing and publicity consultant. A hardworking leader with a calm presence, Lauren started as an independent contractor, helping us produce the December 2010 charity: ball. We sold out tickets to the gala six days in advance, a first for us, and raised more than *$1 million* in one night. By January 2011, Lauren came on staff as an executive producer—essentially, a get-it-done person.

Over the next four years, Ross and I spoke on the phone constantly and emailed up to twenty times a day. His replies were sometimes brutal, ripping into me for dumb things I'd said ("You're totally undisciplined!") or done ("Stop demanding that everyone read your mind!"), or written to my employees ("Scott, don't send them wet noodle, do-nothing notes like this"). I once shot him a one-line email after we got a commitment from a new Well member because, okay, I get *excited* sometimes. But instead of patting me on the back, Ross chastised me for being the kind of CEO who gets emotionally attached to small victories.

"You're celebrating the present tense. That's what EVERYONE else needs to do. Their job is the NOW. Your job is TOMORROW . . . If you decide you want to be CEO, this is what it has to feel like."

One of Ross's biggest gripes was the way I operated in meetings, something that had always driven the team crazy, too. He called out my bad habits: I was notoriously impatient, prone to distraction, and a fidgety nail-biter. I also talked over people and dismissed underdeveloped ideas that deserved more conversation.

Ross said, "You can't put all of your attention on the content in meetings. You have to reserve at least 10 percent of it to observe what's happening in the room, to watch the body language and pick up on how people are truly feeling."

It was a radical notion for me, the idea that I was responsible for reading the room. And I wasn't even sure why it was important, until Linda sharpened Ross's point: "Everything you do is a clue for other people about how it is and isn't okay to behave," she said. "When you yawn during a presentation, or miss a deadline, or interrupt a speaker, you're telling everyone that that behavior is acceptable."

Until then, I'd been oblivious to how I was being perceived. So, to prove the point, Ross made me stand on a conference room table during a staff meeting and look down at everyone while we had a conversation. It felt ridiculous, totally uncomfortable, but it taught me about the CEO's megaphone effect.

"You know when you say things like 'Hey, we should go and do this,' but you don't *really* mean it? In fact, you've given it no more than five seconds of thought?" Ross said. "Someone is going to go run and waste time doing that thing you didn't even want them to do, because you're the guy with the megaphone. You're standing on top of the table."

Other times, I'd explode into the office on a Friday morning and announce, "I want to wrap every water tower in New York in a charity: water banner," and I'd expect everyone to leap into action. Ross had a shorthand for my impulsive ideas. He'd say, "Scott. Squirrel"—as in "Don't be like a dog chasing after every squirrel you see." Sometimes I'd fight back and say, "No, this is not a squirrel. Doing this one thing is the *whole point*." But most of the time, I'd back off, and my team would breathe a huge sigh of relief.

Ross knew that I was always moving forward at maximum velocity, always reaching for the next rung. Even though he chastised me for getting excited about day-to-day achievements, when it came to the really big wins—the arc-changing partnerships and record-breaking donations—Ross encouraged me to slow down, take a beat, and celebrate.

"Look around. Feel the energy. Inhale deeply. Take a mental picture and put it as deeply into your mind and heart as you can. Just take it all in," he'd said. "At some point in your life, you won't have the chance to live these moments again, and you'll be so glad that you did this. Stop, taste it, really remember it."

The things Ross taught me sound so basic now: Be the leader. Model awareness. Develop your EQ. But at the time, they were completely foreign to me. Today, I'm more patient and professional in meetings, but I still die a little inside when someone pulls out a spreadsheet with numbers in tiny font sizes, or makes me sit through an hour-long Keynote presentation. I'm better about not chasing "squirrels." But still, sometimes I'll get back from a trip to Africa and announce that we're building a library at a school in Ethiopia because—well, they need one. When I'm in the field, surrounded by so much need, I can still hear my early mentors (Dad, Dr. Gary) pushing me to think big and never stop looking for solutions—to keep finding ways to say "yes" in a world that's filled with "nos."

By year five, 2011, those guiding voices had become more important than ever. Charity: water was a healthier organization. We'd doubled our impact in the field year over year, and now worked with twenty partners in nineteen different countries. I was excited to keep the momentum going. But in the summer of that year, I finally woke up to a problem that was more distressing than my conduct in meetings, more alarming than my wet-noodle emails. It was a problem that threatened not just our work in the field but the credibility of the charitable water sector as a whole.

My wake-up call came when we returned to the place where we'd had the most trouble getting to "yes": the village of Moale in the Central African Republic.

33

___

Do Better

Dear Members of The Well: I'm returning to the Central African Republic tonight to fulfill a promise made to the Bayaka, but I wanted to shoot you a personal update before heading into the bush.

I was sitting on the couch, writing our seventy-five Well members about the latest developments—new hires on our Water Programs team, an upcoming campaign to buy a drilling rig for our partners in Ethiopia, and a new event space for this year's charity: ball—when a calendar alert, "Pack," popped up on my computer screen.

I glanced at the clock. It was 7 p.m.

"Babe, do you know what time our car is coming?" I asked Vik. She was working on her computer at the kitchen table.

"Eight. I think," she said. "Oh, soon! We should pack."

Our red-eye flight to London left from JFK in four hours. From there, we'd travel to Paris to meet with a donor, and then fly eight hours south, to the Central African Republic. It had been a year since we said good-bye to the Bayaka in Moale. This time, I'd resolved that we wouldn't leave CAR until the Bayaka had clean water.

I finished my letter and closed my laptop. In the bedroom, I grabbed my Africa clothes (hiking shoes, a rain slicker, lightweight cargo pants) from a pile in the back of the closet and threw them into my bag. My suitcase was always in a state of partial unpacking because I was averaging about sixty-five flights a year, meeting partners, taking donors to project sites, and giving speeches. In my case was a jumble of power cords, converters, gum, Skittles, and four or five of those plastic pouches they give you on overnight flights, with the tiny toothpaste, toothbrush, earplugs, and eye mask. Vik, who thrived on order, was constantly finding those pouches and their contents all over our apartment. It drove her nuts.

"Do you know where my passport is?" she asked.

"I have it. It's in my backpack."

Vik and I are both terrible about keeping track of things. She's always searching for her phone and keys, and I've forgotten laptops in coffee shops and iPads down airplane seat-back pouches. As much as we obsess over details, we also tend to walk around with our heads in the clouds, dreaming about how to top last year's charity: ball or create an innovative new campaign.

I rummaged through the closet and bathroom cabinets, collecting a few additional must-packs: a headlamp (it gets dark at night in the bush), a cassette-to-iPod adapter (to play music on those long drives, as older Land Rovers have only tape decks), Cipro pills (which kill bacterial infections of all kinds), and finally, for the long plane ride, an inflatable neck pillow, long underwear, and three pairs of socks that I would put on as soon as we took off. I get really cold on planes.

While Lord Scott Harrison would have demanded his mimosa in seat 36E, these days I was happy just to get a bottle of water and a blanket. Charity: water has never paid for a first-class or business-class flight. I just couldn't look a Well member in the eye if I knew we were spending their money on luxury travel. In the early days, I always bought the very cheapest ticket, even if it saved us only $25. On long international flights, this often meant ending up in the middle seat. I'd take a sleeping pill, curl my legs up into a ball, and try to pass out. To this day, I have bad knees, a problem I attribute to those years of middle-seat contortions.

Tonight, I wanted to make sure Vik and I got to the airport early enough to beg for an aisle or an emergency exit row, so I could stretch my legs. By 8:15 p.m., after running back upstairs to grab a forgotten power cord from behind the couch, we were finally in the car, headed to see if we could fulfill a promise to the Bayaka. This year, I'd doubled down and invited some good friends to join us on the trip.

"We're in," Michael Birch had said. "Xochi can't wait to experience the country and meet the Bayaka." He and his wife had been traveling with us once a year to visit completed water project sites.

We'd also invited Matt Woll and Ryan Meeks, pastors of EastLake Community Church in Seattle, Washington. Over the last year, their congregation had raised more than $350,000 for CAR, and Matt and Ryan were making a short film of our trip to show their community the difference their giving had made.

No pressure, right?

On Wednesday, July 13, around 4:30 p.m., our plane began its descent to Bangui M'Poko International Airport, in CAR's capital. Out my window, the earth formed a patchwork quilt of tall, leafy trees, silty-black riverbeds, and large swaths of barren dirt fields—the scars of industrial logging.

The moment Vik and I stepped off the plane, we felt the intense heat. *Back on African soil.* We walked across the tarmac toward the airport's arrival hall and saw that our favorite cowboy from Indiana was waiting on the other side of customs.

"There's Jim!" Vik said when she spotted his familiar black hat.

"Great to meet you guys," Jim said, greeting Michael, Xochi, Matt, and Ryan for the first time.

On the long drive out, we talked about the challenge ahead of us. Since our last visit, Jim's team had drilled nearly one hundred wells in nearby villages with the money from the September campaign. And he'd reached out to two new veteran hydrogeologists from a civil engineering firm in the United States.

"They were a tremendous help," he said. "They believe Moale was built on top of a Precambrian layer, which has a lot of heaving sand. It's a difficult type of sand to work through because it just *moves*. It doesn't stay put."

Jim figured that the vibrations from the drill must've been what had caused the borehole to cave in the last time. The hydrogeologists recommended a mud pump, a special piece of equipment for drilling in sandy soil. So Jim had procured the $50,000 unit and arranged for his two experts to meet us in Moale to oversee its use. This was a high-tech, extravagant endeavor for such a remote village, but we were all committed to the Bayaka and willing to do whatever it took.

We reached Moale after dark and set up our tents. In the morning, we listened to the Bayaka's harmonies over a breakfast of crackers, bananas, and cowboy coffee, the kind cooked over a campfire where you end up with sludgy grounds at the bottom of your cup.

The day started with a tour of some nearby completed wells. This put us in high spirits, but I got a queasy feeling when we returned to Moale and learned that Marcellin's team had drilled all day, to no effect. Even with the mud pump, the well walls were still caving in. The next day, the drilling team came up dry again after trying at a new spot with less sand. Another day with no water. I was starting to get the worst feeling of déjà vu.

As the drilling went on, I tried to keep our group busy. We hung out in base camp and played poker with BB-pellet chips. We challenged the Bayaka to a pickup game of soccer, never bothering to keep score because they always won by a healthy margin.

One morning, the Bayaka men showed us how to make slingshots, and we practiced on a hand-painted wooden target they hung from a tree. I was determined to be the best shot out of our group but never quite got the hang of it.

"You've gotta be kidding me!" I yelled after my third straight pellet rocketed off into the woods.

"Really, it's quite simple, Scott," Michael would say with a mischievous smile, as he squinted and scored another bull's-eye like it was child's play. He turned out to be a crack shot.

By nightfall on our fifth evening in Moale, Marcellin's team had drilled down to 240 feet. The mud pump whirred loudly and rhythmically, but the walls of the borehole still wouldn't hold. The ground was winning.

"This is one of the most difficult wells I've ever drilled," Jim said. He was visibly agitated. I was starting to lose hope.

All week, there had been moments when we'd be standing around, watching and saying:

"It's going to work!"

"Oh . . . It's not going to work."

"Yes! It's . . ."

"No."

Then, on our sixth day in Moale, Jim's team finally got the walls to hold, and jammed PVC casing deep enough into the groundwater for drillers to pack gravel around the pipes. This was progress.

"It's looking better," Jim said.

By late afternoon, his team began pouring cement to create a concrete base around the well site. After marking off the opening where they'd install the pump and piping the next day, they left the base to dry overnight. We were so close now. It had taken seventeen years of work to get to this stage. It was the most beautiful six-foot-long block of concrete I'd ever seen.

In the early morning of July 20, we all ventured out to officially open the well. Hundreds of Bayaka stood in the warm rain and thunder, in tight little groups, some huddled under fraying umbrellas, waiting to see what would happen next.

Because this well was so deep, it needed a strong pump and more than 330 feet of plastic tubing to carry the water up. More than fifty men from the village came together to snake a football field's worth of flexible pipe down into the borehole. Marcellin then installed a pump head with a long, curved spigot at the top, and connected it to a round foot pedal at the base of the well.

With everything finally in place, Marcellin sealed the well. Then he demonstrated for the villagers how to jump on the foot pedal while holding the T-bar above it for balance, just like a pogo stick. It took the weight of two large Bayaka teens bouncing up and down on that pedal to bring a gush of clear liquid out of the pipe.

There it finally was: water, from deep underground, in Moale.

Everyone sang and danced. Children rushed in, splashing the cool water on their faces and taking turns bouncing on the foot pedal.

Jim stood to the side, watching quietly, taking in the beauty of the moment.

"You did it Jim," I said. "All those years, you never gave up."

"We all did it," he said, wiping his eyes.

And yet, on the plane ride home the next day, something didn't feel right. The water was so deep, and the well's foot pump seemed so difficult to use.

Vik had the same concerns. "It did feel harder to push than a hand pump," she said. "You have to be really strong to work it."

"And what if it breaks?" I said. "Moale is ten hours from the capital, and that's if the roads aren't washed out or blocked by fallen trees. It's not like you can run down to Home Depot for a replacement part."

Jim was committed to monitoring and fixing the wells we'd funded, and his organization had a team that did maintenance checks and repairs. But Moale was a special case. It was so deep in the jungle that the mechanics could go back only once a year—and only during the dry season, when the roads were passable.

"No matter how hard they work," Vik said, "this project, this promise we made to the Bayaka, it just doesn't seem sustainable."

She was right. Sustainability was the biggest problem facing the charitable water sector. Vik and I had become incredibly sensitive to the issue ever since those troublesome projects of ours in Kenya—a mess we were still trying to fix three years later. We'd been dealing with one fiasco after another: broken pumps, low water yields, high fluoride content.

I'd heard about reports, published a few years back, saying that at any given moment, up to 40 percent of all the wells built in sub-Saharan Africa were completely broken. People threw that figure around like it was the status quo. But I'd never believed it applied to charity: water's work. We'd seen other companies, paid by governments and large NGOs, build a well overnight, leave a few parts for the village, and then move on to the next community. But that kind of "drill-and-leave" method never gives the community a fighting chance. We believed the work had to be led by locals—so that people in the recipient countries were invested in the wells, and got the credit for moving their communities forward.

For projects to be successful, you need to provide sanitation and hygiene training, too. The village needs to form a water committee, made up of elected community members, who will enforce rules and assume responsibility for the care and maintenance of the well site. And in most cases, user families pay a small fee to the committee treasurer—often no more than fifty cents or a dollar a month—which is held in an account for future repairs. That way, if something breaks, the community has the means to fix it.

"Forty percent of the world's wells may be broken," I'd tell donors and journalists. "But that's not true for us, because we're working in a completely different way."

Still, I would meet water sector veterans who would roll their eyes and say it was amazing that 60 percent of the wells worked at all. When you go to the sites, they'd tell me, the electrical grid would often be down, the schools and hospitals without supplies, the cellular network erratic, and the internet nonexistent. In other words, "40 percent are broken" was the industry norm, and everybody just went along with it.

I didn't buy it. What's the point of building a well if it ends up broken and unfixed?

I knew that true sustainability would take much more than picking good local partners, forming committees, and providing education. But after watching how hard Jim's team had worked to finally bring water to the people of Moale, I couldn't stand the thought of their well failing, too. If this community were forced back to using that dirty brown pond, wouldn't it have been better if we hadn't come at all?

"What if we're not doing as well as we think?" I said to Vik just as the captain dimmed the plane's overhead lights.

"What do you mean?" she said, her eyes red and tired.

"Sixty percent functionality might be good enough for everybody else, but it's just not good enough for us and the people we serve," I said. "What if 100 percent became the new norm, and charity: water led that charge?"

"Okay, babe," Vik said as her eyes fluttered shut and she drifted toward sleep. "Good idea . . ."

Maybe it was naïve, but I felt energized by the idea. I had no clue where or how to start, but I knew this was no squirrel. As I closed my eyes to sleep, a vision settled deeper in my mind: somehow, some way, sustainability would be charity: water's new frontier.

Our plane landed at JFK in the late afternoon of July 22. Sleepy-eyed and wobbly, Vik and I rode a long silver escalator down to baggage claim and went outside to catch a yellow cab back to the city.

As our car wound through downtown Manhattan, my cell phone rang. It was Ryan. He'd been with us on the flight back, and we'd said good-bye at JFK, where he was still waiting to board his connecting flight to Seattle. He sounded shaken.

"Scott," he said. "I just got terrible news."

34

Rachel's Gift

On July 20, 2011, on the same day that the mothers of Moale celebrated the well that would bring health to their children, a grief-
stricken mother from EastLake Church was sitting vigil in a Seattle
emergency room, praying for her child's life.

When Ryan called from the airport on July 22, he told me about
Samantha Paul and her daughter Rachel Beckwith.

Rachel, he said, had recently donated her ninth birthday with a
campaign on mycharity: water. She fell just short of her $300 fundrais-
ing goal, but Rachel told her mom she wanted to try again next year,
on her tenth birthday. I knew from the cracking sound in Ryan's voice
that he was about to tell me something awful.

"Rachel was in a terrible car accident two days ago," Ryan said
through tears. "Her doctors don't think she's going to make it."

"Ryan, I'm so sorry," I said. "Is there anything we can do?"

"Can you reopen her campaign?" Ryan asked.

"Yes. Yes, of course."

"She may not get another chance to hit her goal next year, and I
know our community will *crush* her campaign. Maybe we can give her
family some encouragement in the middle of this tragedy."

"Absolutely. I'm almost home. I'll get it reopened."

Vik and I carried our bags up the stairs to our apartment, and I told her what had happened.

"Oh, Scott," she said. "That's awful. I can't even imagine how her parents must feel."

We didn't have children of our own, at least not yet, but we felt an aching sadness for this girl we'd never met.

"She actually told her mother that her two heroes were me and Lady Gaga."

Vik laughed out loud. "*You* and Gaga?"

"I know," I said.

I went to the couch with my laptop and found Rachel's campaign page. Her profile photo was sweet and innocent. She was looking into the camera, a toothy smile, rosy cheeks, dark blue eyes, and a big flower barrette in her brown hair. On her page, she'd written:

> On June 12th 2011, I'm turning 9. I found out that millions of people don't live to see their 5th birthday. And why? Because they didn't have access to clean, safe water so I'm celebrating my birthday like never before. I'm asking everyone I know to donate to my campaign instead of gifts for my birthday.

Tears streamed down my face as I thought to myself: *This little girl totally gets it*. I spent over a decade looking out for no one else but myself before I figured out that giving to others brought the greatest joy. But for her, it had been a no-brainer. I reopened Rachel's campaign, pulled out my credit card, clicked on the Donate button, and made an $80 donation to close the gap on her $300 goal.

I'd never heard the name Rachel Beckwith before that night, but in the days to come, I'd learn so much about her. And looking back, that little girl from Seattle would become one of the most important supporters charity: water ever had.

Rachel, by all accounts, was a happy child with an extraordinary sense of empathy. One year, for Christmas, she told her mom that she wanted to buy gifts for a family in need. So Samantha found a local organization and picked up a list of items requested by one family.

"You obviously don't have to buy everything on the list," they'd told her.

But Rachel was adamant. "Mom," she'd said excitedly. "I want to get every single thing on this list!"

"If we do that, it's going to cut into *your* gifts a lot," Samantha said, mindful of the fact that they weren't exactly wealthy either.

"I don't care," Rachel said. "Let's get them *everything*."

The charity organizers looked surprised when Samantha and Rachel came back with armloads of toys, clothes, jackets, a basketball, Barbies, and more.

Samantha later told me that her child seemed mature beyond her years—perhaps because, for so long, it had been just the two of them. Samantha and Rachel's father had divorced when she was about two, and Rachel only saw him every other weekend. Samantha remarried in 2008, giving Rachel a baby sister, Sienna. But that marriage also ended in divorce. Instead of dwelling on her pain, Samantha got more involved with church and focused all her attention on her girls.

Samantha and Rachel loved spending time together and sharing inside jokes—like when Samantha turned up the radio and said, "Rachel, you've got to hear this new song. It's amazing!" Rachel agreed that it *was* really good, and Samantha said, "Ah, I got you! That was Justin Bieber! You *do* like Justin Bieber!" Rachel would *never* have admitted she was a Bieber fan, even though her mother always suspected it.

In July 2010, when Rachel was eight years old, she saw a video about charity: water in an EastLake Sunday school class. She came home and told her mom about my story and the birthday idea. A year later, as Rachel's ninth birthday approached, Samantha helped her set up a mycharity: water page. They sent out emails, and Rachel's parents, grandparents, and friends donated. When her campaign finished at $220—a worthy number, but a little short of her goal—Rachel wasn't discouraged.

"Oh, well," she said to her mom. "I'm just going to try again next year. I'll start earlier. And I'll tell more people!"

"That's a good idea," Samantha said. She was so proud of her daughter.

On the morning of July 20, the same day we struck water in CAR, Rachel woke up, got dressed, had breakfast, and brushed her teeth as her mother prepared for work and got Sienna ready. That day, the girls would stay at Rachel's father's place while Samantha went to her job at a doctor's office.

"Mom, why don't we just stay home today?" Rachel said.

Samantha thought about how nice it would be to spend the day together, just the two of them. *Maybe I should,* she thought to herself for a second. *Maybe I could just call in.*

But it was Wednesday, she had a lot to do, and it didn't make sense to miss a day of work in the middle of the week.

"No, honey. I just can't today," she said. "I wish I could."

They piled into Samantha's four-door sedan, drove to the I-90 freeway, and joined the morning stop-and-go traffic. Rachel sat behind her mother in a booster seat, and Sienna sat in a car seat next to Rachel.

A little before 8 a.m., Samantha was stopped in traffic when she heard the sound of squealing tires behind her. She glanced in her rearview mirror to see a giant semi-trailer truck barreling straight toward her back bumper.

This could be really bad, she thought, seconds before impact.

Samantha recalls only bits and pieces of the accident: crunching metal, logs rolling across the pavement, waking up confused with a stranger holding her and crying.

Police later determined that the driver of the semi had entered the freeway going about sixty miles per hour. Failing to brake in time, his truck had jackknifed a logging truck, sending logs and metal flying in the air, and then crashed into several more cars. The accident resulted in a fifteen-car pileup.

When emergency medical responders arrived, they saw that the logging truck's rear axle had landed on top of the left side of Samantha's car. Sienna was completely unharmed in her car seat. Samantha's head and face were bleeding. But Rachel, pinned beneath the worst of the damage, was unresponsive. An ambulance rushed them all to Harborview Medical Center, where the most serious high-trauma cases in all of Washington State are handled.

"Is she okay? Is my daughter going to be okay?" Samantha kept asking the nurses in the emergency room. But no one would give her a straight answer, except to say that Rachel had spinal cord injuries and needed surgery. Immediately. While doctors set about putting seventeen staples in Samantha's head to stitch up a nasty gash, Samantha closed her eyes and prayed for her child.

A couple of hours later, they brought Samantha to see Rachel in the children's ICU. Rachel was unconscious, covered in bandages, breathing through tubes, and surrounded by beeping machines. Soon, Rachel's father and other family members arrived. A doctor took Rachel's parents aside to tell them that their little girl had suffered serious brain trauma, and her spine had been broken in several different places. He didn't believe she was going to wake up.

"I know this is a very difficult time for you," the doctor said. Then he explained that they would need to decide whether to turn off the machines that were keeping Rachel alive in a vegetative state.

Rachel's father was hysterical with grief. He punched a wall in the hospital and fractured his wrist. Samantha recalled him saying to her, "I can't make that decision. You have to do it."

As difficult as it must have been, Samantha remained calm.

"I don't even know how to start thinking about this," she told the doctor. "Please help me."

The doctor sat with Samantha, and they quietly talked through her options. He had a daughter, too, he said. And if it were his own daughter in this condition, he would want, first, to know if she'd ever be able to speak or move or think again. He believed that Rachel would not.

That was all Samantha needed to hear. She knew Rachel was gone.

"Okay," she said. "Can we have a couple days to wrap our heads around this, and make sure we're making the correct decision?"

"Yes," the doctor said. "There's no need to rush. I think that's a good idea."

Two days later, I got the call from Ryan to reopen Rachel's campaign. Samantha had spent the last two days by her child's bedside, talking to her quietly and not expecting a response. She held Rachel close, not knowing if any of it made a difference, but wanting to be there all the same.

Although she was totally focused on her daughter, she knew the EastLake community and the local news were talking about the accident and about Rachel's charity: water campaign. Someone had even set up a computer in the hospital room so they could watch the numbers on her page go up and the warm wishes continue to flood in.

Ryan and I were watching, too. Each new donor was a name he knew. His community *was* crushing it—she went from $300 into the thousands, all within the first few hours.

Three days after the accident, on July 23, Rachel's family and friends gathered around her bedside to say good-bye. Her parents stood on each side of her bed, holding her hands, as the hospital staff gently removed the breathing tubes and turned off the machines that were keeping Rachel alive. As Samantha looked into her daughter's face, she started singing Rachel's favorite bedtime song, one that had always helped her go to sleep.

> *You are my sunshine, my only sunshine.*
> *You make me happy when skies are gray.*
> *You'll never know dear, how much I love you.*
> *Please don't take my sunshine away.*

It was only Samantha at first, singing softly, but soon others joined in, until the whole room filled with loving voices. They sang "You Are My Sunshine" to Rachel until she slipped away.

Thousands of people came to Rachel's memorial service at East-Lake. Some had heard about her through church or the news and just wanted to honor her. Others had known her through school. They told

Samantha stories she'd never heard before, about small moments of kindness that Rachel had shown them or their children.

Samantha stayed at her aunt's house for a few days, keeping a computer nearby so she could keep refreshing Rachel's campaign page. It was a welcome distraction, she said, to read the comments from donors.

"Rachel . . . Thank you for making me pause and remember what is important in this world. Rest in peace," wrote a donor named Michael who'd given $25.

"I wish I could give more, but I'm only 8 years old, and this is my week's allowance," wrote a donor named Simon, who gave $5.

Samantha realized that she didn't recognize the donors' names anymore. Neither did Ryan. They were total strangers, moved by Rachel's love for others. When her campaign beat the $47,000 that Justin Bieber had raised for his seventeenth birthday, Samantha smiled and said out loud, "Well, Rachel, you really did it. You just passed Justin Bieber."

But Rachel was just getting started. By the end of the week, she had inspired the largest fundraising campaign in mycharity: water's history: $750,000. And she still had another eight weeks to go.

"Please remember, this isn't about us. This is about her legacy. This is about her spirit of selflessness," I said to our staff during a meeting one week after Rachel's death. Her story had spread to news outlets across the country. Nicholas Kristof wrote about her in his *New York Times* column, and both NBC and ABC nightly news ran segments.

I didn't want anyone to miss the point, and nobody did. Everyone at charity: water was so moved by Rachel's example. One Friday night, the team stayed long after Vik and I had left. They ordered beer and pizza and just hung out together reading the comments from donors that were coming in minute by minute. People were writing directly to Rachel as if she was still alive.

"Rachel, you've done more to make a difference in your 9 years here than most will do in 90—you've inspired millions," wrote a donor named Russell, who gave $90.

Like all of us in the office, people were returning to her campaign like it was fuel. As if it gave them some kind of hope that had been missing from their lives.

"I come here many times a day to be touched by those who also have been touched by this little angel. This is my third donation, with the hopes that I will give more," wrote a woman named Sheryl, who gave $50.

We heard from people in Singapore, Australia, East Africa, and other far-flung regions where Rachel's story had somehow reached them and inspired them to act. People around the world were donating money for clean water all because a little girl from Seattle had believed that everyone around the world deserved life's most basic need.

This was the reinvention of charity I'd dreamed of. This was a *global* movement of compassion, spreading in real time across the planet. It blew my mind. A child was truly changing the world with a single act of selflessness.

A few days later, on August 1, Samantha flew to New York to appear on the morning TV shows. Afterward, we'd planned for her to visit the charity: water offices. I wanted her to meet the staff and personally open the letters for Rachel that had been piling up in the mail room.

As I got dressed for the TV appearance that morning, Vik looked a little worried.

"What's wrong, babe?" I said.

"I'm just nervous about today," she said. "Scott, what do you say to a mom who's just lost her child?"

"I don't know," I said.

"Should I avoid talking about Rachel?"

"Let's just follow her lead, okay? It's going to go fine."

Honestly, I was as anxious as Vik. I'd never met Samantha and had no idea what to expect. In the green room at the TV station that morning, I fidgeted and bit my nails as I waited for her to arrive.

I already knew we'd be sending Rachel's campaign dollars to Ethiopia, where we had incredible local partners. So, what I'd planned to say to Samantha was this: *The only gift I can give you is to show you the true human impact of what your daughter has created. I'd love to bring you to Ethiopia next year, so you can see Rachel's wells for yourself. And see the legacy she's created.*

The speech sounded beautiful in my head. But, of course, when she walked in, weary from a red-eye flight, I marched up to her and blurted out, "Hi, Samantha. I'm Scott. It's so good to meet you—you . . . you have to come to Ethiopia with me!"

"Um, okay," she said, giving me a sideways glance, perhaps wondering if I said this to everyone I met. But then she smiled and laughed.

As we got mic'd up and walked together to the set, Samantha looked tender but stoic. It had been a week since she buried her daughter. If she had been living in her pajamas, crying herself to sleep, and cursing the world, no one would have blamed her. But she didn't look tearstained or sleep-deprived or angry. She walked into the room and took her seat in the chair across from mine with ease and grace, despite the weight of what had to be unbearable pain.

"What a special young lady," the host said, offering his condolences to Samantha.

"I've always been so unbelievably proud of Rachel for all the choices she's made through her life," Samantha said. "I'm just so glad that everyone else can share in the Rachel experience now."

Rachel's campaign closed on September 30, 2011, with 31,997 donations. Tens of thousands of people, most of them strangers, gave a total of $1,265,823 to make her birthday wish come true. And it was up to us to make sure that her wish was flawlessly executed.

Just a few months earlier, all I could think about was conquering sustainability. And then Rachel Beckwith came into our lives. Now all I could think about was how best to honor her legacy. Getting Rachel's wells ready and preparing for Samantha's trip would keep me focused over the next year—a year that would spiral into one of the most difficult and confusing periods of my life.

35

Dirty Brown Laundry

OCTOBER 29, 2011

A month after Rachel's campaign closed, I received a personal email from the corporate donor who'd funded the troublesome Kenya wells. The email began with a story, a reminder of when we met at a conference four years earlier and I showed him pictures of the clinic in Mogotio village, the place where the bed linens turned brown from being washed in dirty water.

In 2008, the donor had raised more than $741,000 from his customers, employees, and friends—an amount that, when combined with our matching funds of $500,000, would bring over $1.2 million in clean-water projects for hospitals and clinics across Kenya. We all had high expectations. But charity: water was just two years old at the time, and the learning curve was steeper than we realized.

For example, we'd underestimated how the 2008 Kenyan crisis—a period of tribal warfare that killed a thousand people and left half a million internally displaced—would slow the permit-approval process to a crawl. Then, in January 2009, our partner's drilling rig crashed, sending workers to the emergency room and causing more delays. By the fall of 2009, construction had resumed, and we invited the donor to Kenya to visit some of their projects. Unfortunately, they saw incomplete wells that had been marked as finished, and one finished well with someone else's name on the plaque. We made a terrible impression.

Since then, we'd been trying to make up for our early stumbles with field visits and financial audits. We even restructured our in-house water team and suspended future work with the partner in Kenya who'd built the wells. By July, we'd proudly reported that all the money the donor had raised had finally been spent, that twenty-three wells had been successfully built in health clinics and schools in Kenya—and we were now ready to send the remaining $419,000 from our portion of the campaign commitment to a new, highly respected drilling partner.

But as I sat there, reading through the donor's latest email, I knew before I reached the end that all our efforts had failed.

On Monday morning, he wrote, a civil suit would be filed against charity: water accusing us of breach of contract, fraud, and negligence. I quickly read to the bottom:

> It is unfortunate that it has to come to this. This lawsuit will
> be public information and people everywhere will be able
> to see your dirty brown laundry.

I had to admit, it was darkly poetic—but it felt like a kick in the gut. I'd misread how bad the situation had gotten. The last time we corresponded, I'd even suggested that the donor come back to Africa with me to see the new wells. But that ship had already sailed. They had no interest in a site visit. They didn't like the fact that several of their wells had been built at schools, as they had wanted to serve only hospitals and health clinics. They didn't agree with our choice for a new drilling partner, and they wanted to approve each future site before a water project was built.

Meanwhile, Kenya was suffering through one of its worst droughts in sixty years. People were literally dying of thirst, and our board of directors, of which I was a member, didn't feel comfortable sitting on the remaining funds. After several failed attempts to get the donor's blessing, we let them know that we were moving on and planned to commit the remaining funds to our new Kenyan partner. That was pretty much the nail in the coffin.

I studied the nine-page complaint. Charity: water, they alleged, had used their money inappropriately, failed to build the wells within the twelve to eighteen months stipulated, and hadn't adequately supervised our Kenya partner. They claimed that I had boasted knowledge and experience that I didn't have, that I had no intention of providing matching funds in a timely manner, and that I had been reckless with the truth.

In hindsight, I should have seen the warning signs of a doomed relationship, like when the donor said they wanted to pay for the wells only *after* they'd been built. Or when we shared our financial audits, and they asked why we'd been paying our local partners for administrative costs if 100 percent of the money was supposed to go toward drilling wells. I hadn't explained that building wells means you also have to contribute to the salaries of the people in-country who do the work—the local drillers and drivers and accountants who have families to provide for, just like the rest of us. You have to cover fuel costs on the ground and provide for the well's maintenance after it's built. It all seemed so obvious to me, but I hadn't communicated any of it to the donor.

To make matters worse, I didn't personally step up and own this problem when the relationship became tense. Avoiding confrontation, I delegated the work to staffers who never should've been handling something this sensitive in the first place.

Honestly, I was just as disappointed with the outcome as they were. It would be like hiring a home builder who delivers the house late and over budget, with broken appliances. It wasn't how I'd hoped things would go, either, but when you're working in places plagued by poverty and unrest, and at the mercy of a government bureaucracy, you don't always get the best service or the speediest results.

Still, I wondered, how had it come to *this*, a lawsuit?

Fortunately, when I started the organization in 2006, I'd purchased directors and officers insurance, not thinking we'd ever really need it. We contacted the insurance company, and they assigned a legal team to handle the suit, at no cost to charity: water.

Of course, by definition, insurance company attorneys are looking out for the insurance company. I realized that we were big enough now to need a part-time general counsel, a quarterback who could coordinate with the other lawyers and get in front of any legal issues we might face as the organization grew. I asked around and found Chris Barton.

Chris was a private-practice attorney with a dozen specialties under his belt: commercial agreements, strategic business planning, HR and employment law, nonprofit organizations, art law. He'd counseled institutions as varied as helicopter companies, fancy art museums, and the Central Intelligence Agency.

Tall, conservatively dressed, and always in dark-rimmed eyeglasses, Chris became a comforting, fatherly presence in our office. He was knowledgeable but not wonky. He spoke plainly and had a warm way about him. And most important, he understood what charity: water was about. He saw that we all lived and breathed only to bring people clean water. Chris had our back. He knew we were doing good work, even if our contracts and processes needed some major improvements.

After a few weeks of reading the complaint and digging into case law, he gave me his professional appraisal. "This complaint reads like a business dispute," he said. "I know you think of charity: water as a start-up, but you're not. You're a nonprofit. And nonprofits are state-regulated, which means they have different protections and different laws. I can't tell you how rare it is for a nonprofit to get sued by a donor if the money actually went to the field."

Chris was right. I'd always thought of us as an innovative start-up, and in the last few years, I'd been treating this donor like a customer I needed to please. As Chris explained to me, that's not how things work for nonprofits.

"Look, charities *can* be sued if they do stuff that is really wrong or illegal, like employment discrimination, or breach of a normal commercial contract. But absent fraud—*real* fraud, like where the charity is taking donor money and buying the CEO a plane—Scott, you guys don't even fly business class. Donors don't get to sue charity: water because the wells took too long to build. The standard can't be 'every single well is perfect.' The standard is you do the best you can, and you do it reasonably."

Shaking my head, I thought, *But I actually want every single well to be perfect.* Still, it was a relief to hear that we couldn't be held liable for failing to deliver perfection.

"Okay," I said. "So where does that leave us?"

"Well, I don't believe this case is ever going to trial. However, it's going to be a huge distraction for you and your team. Your attorneys are pushing for mediation, which is wise. Let's try to reach an agreement with the donor. Otherwise, this could drag on for a very long time."

The case *did* drag on for a very long time. Some nights, I'd wake up in a cold sweat from dreams of a dark figure chasing me. I spent hours worrying about charity: water's reputation, about the harm it would do if word got out about the lawsuit. I could already imagine the headline: "Charity Built on the Premise of 'Radical Transparency' Sued for Fraud."

The work our young team had to do around the lawsuit was even more distracting and time-consuming. Lauren Miller, charity: water's executive producer, and Michael Letta, our controller, spent hundreds of hours collecting emails and financial documents. They created binders of all the correspondence and work over the last three years that had anything to do with the Kenya wells.

Michael and I were both deposed, for eight hours each, in a small, windowless room. It was just like in the movies, where the other side peppers you with questions, trying to catch you in a lie. The problem was, I *wanted* to explain my side. I wanted to tell my story and convince them that we had done our very best. But that's not how a deposition works. A question is asked, and a short, direct answer is given. No more, no less. It was painful to hear charity: water's story being told in fragments and half-truths by an adversary. I wondered, *Is this what they really think of us?*

I couldn't give up on the idea that if I could just sit down with the donor, face-to-face, to explain everything, we could find common ground. If I could just tell our side, this whole thing would blow over and everything would go back to normal.

"Scott, that's a bad idea," Lauren said to me one day in February. We were reviewing the latest report on Rachel's wells in Ethiopia.

"But if they could just see the impact they've made—the school-children drinking clean water and the patients taking medicine with freshwater. Don't you think it would make a difference?"

"No," she said. "Scott, they don't like you. I mean, they *really* don't like you. I'm sorry, but you're just not going to charm your way into their hearts."

She was right. *What's wrong with me?* I thought. *Am I still that kid who wants to be liked by everyone?* I'd worked so hard to prove my worth over the years. I'd worked hard to be a good person and to make people happy. I just couldn't shake my stupid need for approval.

Even worse, I was carrying this baggage into the office every day. My vision of conquering sustainability was put on hold. My creativity flagged. And when our team got together to work on fun ideas—like calling donors to wish them "happy birthday," or tapping comedian Seth Meyers to host our charity: ball that year—I was really proud of them. But I just didn't contribute with the same passion I used to have. Everything felt like work to me. I dreaded coming into the office, and started traveling more. I went from boarding fifty-four airplanes in 2011 to eighty-eight in 2012.

On the road, I gave speeches and told the charity: water story over and over, drinking in the raw energy of the crowd like it was oxygen. I took more and more donors to the field, traveling with the drilling rigs to remote enclaves. I wanted to reignite that feeling of pure joy, like a junkie chasing the rush of his first high. If it was a donor's first field visit, I'd watch their face and look for that spark in their eyes when they saw children drinking from wells that they'd helped build. I needed people to tell me that this work was still meaningful, that it was worth fighting this hard. I needed to see it again and again and again to go on believing.

And then, at the moment I needed it most, I heard a story that shook me to the core.

In February 2012, Vik and I checked into an $8-a-night hotel in Adwa, Ethiopia. Our small group, four or five Well members and friends of charity: water, took up about half the rooms in the hotel. The owner was a short, sturdy Ethiopian man who greeted us upon our arrival. He was a hard worker, the kind of hotelier who also mans the front desk, helps you with your bags, and chops carrots in the kitchen.

We were exhausted. Over the last few days, we'd met women whose spines were curved from carrying heavy Jerry Cans in the hot sun. Others told us stories about wild animals attacking them on their walks for water. Sensory overload had set in, and we were looking forward to a quiet evening of dinner and conversation.

At around 6 p.m., I went to the restaurant to have a beer while I waited for Vik and everyone else to come down. The dining room was tidy and brightly lit, with frilly gold curtains on the windows and a dozen black plastic tables spread out across the linoleum floor. There was a grand-looking oak bar in the corner and a tall mirrored cabinet that held bottles of gin, vodka, and other spirits. It was the fanciest $8-a-night hotel I'd ever seen.

I had just sat down at a table when the owner approached me. He looked to be in his mid-thirties. "You're the water people," he said plainly in English.

"Yes," I said. "You've heard of charity: water?"

"Oh, yes," he replied as he sat down. "I want to tell you a story. Where I come from is very far from here."

I nodded and took a sip of beer. He clearly had something he wanted to say.

"Twelve years ago," he said, "there was a woman in my village. Like the others, she would walk many hours every day for water, carrying a heavy clay pot on her back. But one day, she slipped and fell. Her pot broke, and all the water spilled out. She didn't go back and get a new pot. She didn't go back and get more water."

He was shaking his head now and looking down. I was totally riveted.

"What did she do?" I said.

"She took the rope that she had with her, and she hanged herself from a tree outside the village."

No, I thought. *This can't be true.* I stared at the owner, waiting for an explanation. But he didn't speak. He let his words sink in. I let the silence fill the space between us.

He rose quickly and put a hand on my shoulder. "The work you're doing is important," he said. Then he walked back to the kitchen.

For days, I thought about this woman's story. How old was she? What did her village look like? What sort of life did she lead? I wondered if maybe she was just a legend, a tale people told about the hardships of life in rural Ethiopia, the kind of story that gets passed around like a game of telephone until it bears no resemblance to the original story.

When we returned to New York, I emailed our local partners in Ethiopia. Maybe they could find the village where the hotel owner grew up and then send someone there to check his story out. For years, I'd been talking about how dirty water affected people's lives. But I'd never heard about someone ending her life because of it. The woman's story haunted me, and I had to know if it was true.

———

36

With No One Looking Over Your Shoulder

On April 27, 2012, charity: water's attorneys were scheduled to meet with the opposition in a private mediation—our last chance to find common ground. If this didn't work, we'd go to trial.

Private mediation is a very open, time-consuming, and flexible process with lots of back-and-forth. Our lawyers didn't think my presence would be helpful, but I didn't want to be at the office, either. The time felt sacred and important, so I flew to France and drove to Tex's old forester house in the Pyrenees to clear my head. I'd spend the week praying and hiking in the surrounding mountains while, half a world away, lawyers discussed the fate of my organization.

I'd last been at Tex's place with Vik on our honeymoon in the late fall of 2009, and it was snowy and cold. There was no snow this time, but there was a crisp chill in the air. I parked the rental car in the tall grass, walked to the woodshed, and found the key in its usual place in the rusty saucepan covered with leaves.

That first night, I sat alone on a giant stone windowsill and ate a home-cooked dinner of roast vegetables and chicken. It was still light out, but the clouds were turning dark, and a soft rain began to fall.

The drops sounded like gentle tap dancing on the roof, but they soon progressed into a full-on downpour. Small drips fell from the ceiling, faster and faster, until they made a giant puddle on the floor. I grabbed a big metal pot from the kitchen to catch the stream and then sent Tex an email.

The next day, a local handyman came to investigate the leaky roof. Fallen tree branches had damaged the chimney and broken some tiles. Part of the roof was in danger of collapsing, he said. It would need to be replaced. It seemed like this house was a metaphor for my life. Here I was, trying to find solace, and the house was falling down on top of me. Maybe this was God's way of telling me to get my own house in order.

For the last six years, charity: water's Water Programs team had been led by me and a few junior staff who'd been promoted to director-level positions. We'd worked hard and as smart as we knew how. But now, with charity: water on track to raise $33 million this year, shouldn't we hire people who were *the* best in the world at overseeing projects, distributing funds to our partners in the field, and making sure our policies and processes were top-notch? I knew this was something I'd need to work on when I went home.

The next day, I woke up early, made coffee and scrambled eggs, and went on a long hike. All week, my human interaction was limited to the fix-it man and the handful of villagers I passed picking mushrooms in the mountains. Around noon, I stopped near an overlook to think. The legal mediation would take place in three days. I closed my eyes and silently prayed: *God, please let this go well. Please help our attorneys. This lawsuit is killing me . . .*

I took a deep breath and opened my eyes.

Okay, I thought. *Sorry. Let me try that again.*

"God," I said out loud. "Can you *show* me the lesson here? What am I doing wrong? Am I missing something? Please teach me what I'm supposed to learn from this."

I sat down at the top of a nearby cliff, dangling my feet off the edge, and took out my Bible. Below me, the moss-covered boulders and deep-green forests looked like a giant carpet that had been unfurled and rolled out toward the horizon. I took a photo and sent it to Vik.

"Thanks for being cool with my leaving," I wrote. Thinking about her, and about my parents, about Tex and Dr. Gary—all the people in my life who were rooting for charity: water's success—I knew I couldn't let them down. *I have to stay strong,* I thought. *And if we make it through this lawsuit, I'll do everything in my power to build up the organization even stronger.*

Early on the morning of April 28, I got the phone call I'd been waiting for. Michael Letta had been at the mediation the day before.

"Give it to me," I said. "What happened?"

After praying for four days, I felt certain we'd find a way forward, a mutual settlement that would end this nightmare.

"Scott, I'm sorry," Michael said. "It didn't go well."

Once again, our attorneys couldn't find a peaceful resolution. If anything, Michael said, the talks broke down pretty quickly. The other side seemed even angrier with me and more determined than ever to go to trial.

"Okay," I said. "Please thank everyone for trying. I'm flying home tomorrow. We'll get through this together."

We hung up. I felt totally defeated. All my mountaintop praying, all my high hopes. It had all come to nothing.

But as I packed my bags and began the long journey back home, a new resolve was simmering. I had to stop running from confrontation. If we couldn't apologize our way out of this fight, then we had to face it head-on.

For a year, I'd been weighed down by the same stupid, gnawing fear: *How will this lawsuit be perceived? How will it affect our reputation?* We'd been the cool charity on the block, beloved by the press, by celebrities and sponsors. But I had to accept that we couldn't please everyone. I had to stop worrying about whether everyone *liked* us. What mattered were our core values and our impact in the field.

Back at the office, I had an intense conversation with Vik and the executive team about how we were going to handle negative press:

"Like it or not, something like this is bound to happen again. Should we hire a PR agency? What are our talking points on this thing?"

My head was spinning. Honestly, I don't remember much of what was said. But I kept thinking back to that moment in the Central African Republic when we had to decide whether to tell the world about our failure in Moale.

"Mistakes are opportunities. It's how you handle them that matters the most."

That's what Ryan from EastLake Church said to me after we posted the *No Water for Our Birthday* video. And he was right. This moment was an opportunity for us to again build greater trust with our donors, to show them that we continue to operate with radical transparency. To show them that the work is hard, but we never give up and we live by our values. In fact, charity: water's "ISM" number five states, "We believe character is what you do when no one is looking over your shoulder."

The ISMs comprise a sixteen-page manifesto stating charity: water's eleven core values and practices—We don't objectify the poor . . . We love feedback, even when it hurts . . . We tell the truth: no white lies, please. . . . Every new employee has to read and sign them. Adhering to the ISMs is a condition of employment at charity: water— something we take very seriously.

"We have to tell the truth and get ahead of this lawsuit," I said to the team. "Let's just put it out there. Let's tell people how we failed and what we did about it."

Everyone agreed. It was time to embrace transparency again. We discussed the idea with our board, and ultimately decided that I'd write an open letter about the lawsuit. We'd share it first with Well members, get their feedback, and then post it on our website.

In early May, with the board's blessing and reluctant approval from our attorneys, I sent a draft of the letter in an email to our eighty-nine Well members and a few longtime charity: water friends.

"We've been dealing with a difficult situation for almost a year now," I wrote. "And I wanted you to hear about it first . . ."

It was terrifying to own up to this failure. I was prepared to lose some donors, maybe even some friends, but thankfully, as with our video from the heart of the Central African Republic, that's not what happened.

"Charity does not come with a guarantee," one of our earliest supporters wrote. "When I gave you that check early on, I did it because I believed in you. I had no idea what the results might be, but I knew that you would use it in the best way you knew how."

Daniel Ek, Spotify's CEO, was blunter. "As someone who gets about one personal lawsuit against me per month, my only advice to you is: be as transparent as you legally can be. Which is exactly what you've done," he said. "Don't let it drag you down. You're doing an amazing job."

There were dozens of emails like this. I read them over and over. They gave me strength. We had the most generous, supportive friends of any nonprofit in the world. I was sure of it.

We published the letter online in late May 2012 and waited for judgment to fall upon us. Then . . . nothing really happened. Donors didn't start running the other way. Reporters weren't ringing my cell phone. Nobody called. It seemed like nobody really cared. For so many months, I'd been operating with a dark cloud hanging over my head. But now? I was done worrying. If this case was really going to be played out in front of a judge and jury, so be it. We'd tell our story and hope for the best.

It was time to get back to work, to focus on the people and things that really mattered. And that included a grieving mother in Seattle who needed to see the beauty of what her daughter had accomplished.

On July 22, 2012, Samantha, her parents, Ryan, and a few charity: water staffers and friends met in Ethiopia at Gheralta Lodge, a sprawling complex of stone villas with postcard views of the stunningly beautiful Gheralta Mountains. This would be our home base for the next five days.

Rachel's campaign had raised enough money to build 143 water projects across the northern Tigray Region, reaching a total of 37,770 people. Unlike with our troubles in Kenya, I had total faith in our water partners at the Relief Society of Tigray (REST). Its executive director, Teklewoini "Tek" Assefa, would accompany us as we visited some of Rachel's completed wells.

"Scott, I just want you to know, I'm kind of emotionally void right now," Samantha said to me on our first night in Ethiopia. "If I seem a little out of it, it's not that I'm ungrateful, or that things aren't affecting me. I'm just still having a hard time processing."

"Sam," I said, "I completely understand. Please don't feel like you have to be any certain way for us."

"Thanks," she said. "I'm so glad to be here. Really."

Although I hadn't known it at the time, Samantha was terrified of completely falling apart on the trip. Years later, as our friendship grew, she would tell me and Vik that Rachel's campaign had been a gift in some ways, because it postponed her grieving. But in other ways, it just prolonged the inevitable.

On July 23, exactly a year to the date of Rachel's death, our group awoke before dawn and piled into Land Rovers. For two hours, we drove past rock-strewn mountains and thorny bushes, beneath tall cactuses shaped like Ping-Pong paddles. It was Ethiopia's rainy season, the two-month stretch when the skies pour enough water to nourish farmers' crops of onions, tomatoes, and the grains they grind and bake into *injera*, the flatbread Ethiopians eat with almost every meal.

"You are here at the best time to see Ethiopia," Tek told Sam. "Ten months out of the year, it is a desert. But it's very green and beautiful now."

Around 8:30 a.m., we pulled into a small clearing in the village of Kal Habel. A hundred or so men, women, and children waited for us. They were holding posters that read in English, WELCOME, and THANK YOU RACHEL FAMILY FOR PROVIDING US CLEAR WATER, and WATER IS LIFE.

Tek spoke to a man who appeared to be in charge, and we followed the two of them uphill on a dirt path as children and adults joined us, clapping and chanting. Samantha smiled, quietly taking it all in. At the top of the hill, a priest dressed in a long white robe bowed and waved us into a small stone church.

Inside, it was dark and hardly big enough to fit twenty people at a time. Several priests were chanting in low tones and swinging metal censers. Sam and her parents were ushered to a wood pew at the front. Before them was a tall candlelit altar, where two white candles had been placed next to a framed photo of Rachel. She was smiling at us and giving a double thumbs-up. Samantha bowed her head and locked her hands in prayer as the priests stood over her, chanting ancient Ethiopian hymns.

"They have been praying since midnight," our translator whispered. "They are asking God to keep Rachel's soul in peace."

It was so moving to see these holy men, the most respected members of their community, honoring a little girl who had changed their village forever. When the service was over, we quietly filed out, and Samantha whispered, "I think Rachel was there. I could feel her spirit."

As we traveled from village to village over the next few days, little children greeted us with applause and giggles, and called out Rachel's name in joy. One community had set aside a piece of land and renamed it Rachel's Park, a place for the children to play. In another village, an eleven-year-old boy followed Samantha around, never leaving her side.

"He said he wants to get married," she told us, grinning. "I think he just proposed to me."

On our last day in Tigray, we returned to a community where our visit had been cut short by heavy rain earlier in the trip. Pulling in, we saw women and children doing chores, collecting water from their new well, sweeping around their huts with tightly woven bundles of sticks. They were surprised to see us, and several women ran up to Sam excitedly. They hugged her and spoke hurriedly in Tigrinya, the local dialect.

"They say they are happy you are back, that they really wanted to talk with you," our translator said.

One woman, about thirty years old, spoke with urgency, like she'd been waiting for years to talk with Sam. "We have lost children, too," she said. She put a hand to her face, trying to stay strong as she held back tears. "But your daughter's death. It has brought *our* children life."

To be Ethiopian means to be born with a 9 percent chance of dying before your fifth birthday—a fact that starts to lose meaning when you hear it again and again. Even if I say it a different way—one out of every eleven kids here dies before kindergarten age—it's still just a number, a foreign fact. I think we're all guilty of becoming numb to the world's suffering, maybe even of fooling ourselves into thinking that these mothers *must know* that death is a distinct possibility, like somehow that makes the death of a child easier. But nothing could be further from the truth.

Sam hugged the crying woman and whispered to her, "I know your pain. I feel what you are feeling."

I stood on the sidelines, watching. Nobody was making announcements about wells; no one was praising charity: water or thanking Samantha. None of that mattered. An Ethiopian mother who had lost children was talking with an American mom who had lost a child, too. No translation was needed. They understood each other perfectly.

37

Just Keep Going

NEW YORK, FALL 2012

I came back from Rachel's trip with a deep sense of hope, something I'd lost while dealing with the lawsuit. It was time to put every ounce of my energy into making charity: water stronger. It was time to grow up.

Amazingly, around the same period, charity: water got game-changing news. We'd won a $5 million Google Impact Award, a one-time grant for nonprofits that seek to tackle big global problems. I couldn't believe it. *Five million dollars.* A new executive hire, a woman named Yukari Matsuzawa, who came over from Twitter, had helped us apply for the award. In our application, we'd talked about the hundreds of millions of dollars being spent on water solutions around the world and how 40 percent of those solutions were broken at any given time. If that didn't qualify as a "big global problem," what did?

We'd assumed that there *had* to be technologies out there—sensors of some kind—that could be adapted to our needs and used to monitor the flow rates of wells and other water projects. Now Google had basically wired $5 million into our account and said, "Go figure it out." It was a huge vote of confidence. We immediately found a guy named Robert Lee to manage the project and locate those sensors. Now I needed to hire someone really smart to oversee the overall sustainability initiative and upgrade our Water Programs department.

At the time, charity: water had eight talented twentysomethings in Water Programs. They managed all our grants, audited our partners, and oversaw the accounting—but none of them had ever lived in the countries they were managing. Nor were they fluent in the languages of our recipient countries, which posed a challenge when invoices came in written in French (which is widely spoken in Africa) or Amharic (Ethiopia).

Before I left for Rachel's trip, I'd hired an executive search firm to help us find a leader for Water Programs. It was no small role. We needed someone with years of international NGO expertise—in other words, a bureaucrat, but without all the baggage. Over the years, I'd met people at large nonprofits who were cynical about their work. They complained about restrictive government contracts, which dictated with whom, when, where, and how they spent money. They'd lost their edge, and they sounded miserable.

In the past, I'd mistakenly filled executive-level roles with people like this. They had impressive résumés, having worked for top global NGOs, but then they'd expect to clock out at 5 p.m. every day. I'd also tried the opposite approach, hiring execs from top American for-profit firms. At first, they seemed happy enough to take the pay cut and work for an energetic start-up. But then they'd balk at flying coach, or not want to travel at all.

That wasn't going to work at charity: water. We needed people who understood that we did things differently here. People who'd work hard because they shared our vision. And as Lauren Miller, now an executive, put it, they'd need "humble confidence."

We needed to find more people like Michael Gumbley, whom we hired in September 2012 to lead Financial Compliance and Program Finance under Michael Letta. Gumbley grew up in Australia, studied finance at Georgetown, spoke five languages, and before he came to us, had worked for Action Against Hunger (ACF), a charity: water partner in the Democratic Republic of the Congo.

Five or six months before we hired him, Gumbley stomped into our office and demanded to speak to someone on our Program Finance team. He then berated us about a $1.08 million grant we'd just awarded ACF. "Look," he said, "if we're going to take this million dollars, you need to give me down-to-the-penny, specific parameters on how this money can and cannot be spent . . . or else we just cannot take it." I think he even banged his fist on the table.

As Gumbley explained it, our contracts left too many details to chance, and our timelines and budgets were too simplistic. He wanted more clarity, because if our expectations of ACF weren't clear from the outset, or if we thought ACF had spent the money irresponsibly, they could be at risk of a lawsuit. Of course we knew a thing or two about *that*.

I knew Gumbley would be a strong financial partner for our new Water Programs team lead, if I could just find the right person for that role. I'd spent all summer interviewing prospects, but no one seemed like a fit—that is, until our search firm found Christoph Gorder. The first time we met, he wore a suit and tie, which got him some strange looks as he walked through the office. But he seemed friendly and smart. Christoph and I met a few more times, and then Vik and I invited him and his wife, Alisha, to dinner. By mid-September, when I offered him the job, I think we both felt we'd gotten to know each other pretty well.

Christoph grew up in the Central African Republic, a tall, blond, blue-eyed son of Lutheran missionaries. As much as he probably stood out, he had a calm, easy manner and a knack for fitting in anywhere he went. We discovered that both he and I had attended NYU, and we also both spoke French—except that Christoph had gone on to get his master's (in Spanish and Latin American literatures and cultures), and his French was a hundred times better than mine.

After college, Christoph went to work at Americares, an organization that provides emergency medical care and supplies to disaster zones. During his fourteen years there, he'd handled large-scale projects in more than a dozen countries, like the 2010 earthquake in Haiti, the Southeast Asian tsunami, and Hurricane Katrina. He oversaw 125 employees and was responsible for delivering billions of dollars in medical aid around the world.

Christoph had little direct experience with water, but he knew how to lead a team and empower people to do their jobs well. He seemed to be the whole package: experienced, hardworking, and optimistic. Best of all, we had chemistry.

Lauren would say that I lean too much on chemistry, that I'm prone to writing people off if I don't feel it right away. She's probably right, but when you're spending hours upon hours crammed into Land Rovers and airplane seats next to your coworkers, they'd better be people you like. In October 2012, Christoph joined the charity: water executive team, leading Water Programs, sustainability, and many more projects in a crucial role that eventually came to be called chief global water officer.

Christoph and Michael Gumbley teamed up to formalize our partner protocols, tighten our contracts, revise our policies, and most important, scale the Water Programs and Programs Finance teams. Soon, we had about fifteen experts flying around the world with clipboards, auditing the quality of our projects and making sure the money was spent well. We were vetting our partners with precision, and eventually rolled out a website just for them (partner.charitywater.org), with hard-and-fast guidelines on everything from what we do and do not fund to how to measure impact, collect data, prepare budget templates, and more.

We also got really good at explaining our work to donors, and creating clear expectations. We built a public-facing site (support.charitywater.org) with answers to all sorts of questions, like "How did you calculate the cost of my project?" and "How do you choose your local partners?" And because maintaining the public's trust is a core piece of our mission, we also explained how things can sometimes go wrong.

And we finally made headway on the sustainability initiative. The $5 million Google Award wasn't used just for sensors—although that was the keystone. While Robert Lee was traveling around the world, meeting with hardware and software labs researching the sensors, Christoph's team focused on developing new maintenance programs, like the ones in India that hired female mechanics. In Ethiopia, we funded training for seventeen mechanics who rode motorbikes across a service area of more than thirty-five hundred wells, keeping water flowing for over a million people. We brought mobile banking to Ugandan villages, which allowed water committees to issue payments for repairs online with increased transparency.

And when Robert discovered that the sensors we wanted for our wells literally didn't exist, he met and spoke with labs in twelve different countries (including Mexico, China, and Spain), trying to find sensors in the oil, gas, and irrigation industries that could be adapted for water wells. Unfortunately, nobody was interested in creating what we needed; there just wasn't a market for it. Think about it: Who's going to buy something that tells you when your wells break? Who's going to *pay* for bad news? We would, of course—or at least we tried to. We now knew we'd have to make a sensor ourselves. So Christoph and Robert hired engineers and a design firm to build it.

Meanwhile, just as our processes got more sophisticated, we were fundraising like gangbusters and pumping tens of millions of dollars (and counting) into the field.

"Our growth is crazy," I'd told Christoph in my office during his first month. I took a marker and drew a quick chart for him on my whiteboard:

2012 projected: $33M

2011: $27.1M

2010: $15.8M

2009: $8.6M

2008: $6.3M

2007: $1.8M

Then I drew an arrow up through the years and said, "If this continues, I think we'll raise $100 million by 2016."

"That's a lot of wells," Christoph joked.

But he knew it wasn't just wells. We were actually funding eleven different solutions around the world, choosing them based on what worked best in a given region. In Cambodia, for example, there's plenty of surface water, but it's contaminated, so a more efficient option is to provide families with biosand filters, which purify dirty water through sand, gravel, and a biological film that eats away at harmful bacteria. In Tanzania, which has a short and heavy rainy season, we were funding rainwater harvesting systems that collect drinkable rainfall in sanitary holding tanks, so people can access it during the intense dry season. In places like Rwanda and Nepal, gravity-fed systems were the most cost-efficient way to collect, protect, and then pipe clean water from springs to access points. Plus, we were funding new million-dollar drilling rig packages for REST in Ethiopia, and maintaining hundreds of other wells around the world—including ones built by other organizations.

We were raising so much money that it felt like we might actually get clean water to everyone in my lifetime. Those numbers on the whiteboard *proved* it to me. Each year, as they rose, we got closer to our goal. Each year, they affirmed my worth as a leader.

In hindsight, I had no good way of forecasting our revenue. When I thought about our future, I'd always assumed that we'd grow indefinitely, scaling to $100 million and beyond. In truth, I was setting myself up for a fall.

In early November 2012, our attorney Chris Barton emailed me about a development in the lawsuit. He'd just gotten off a conference call with the opposing attorneys and the federal judge assigned to our case.

"Basically, the judge was angry at both parties for not settling," Chris said. "He read through the lawsuit and couldn't understand why this case was in his court at all."

Trials are expensive for the government, and apparently the judge didn't want to see taxpayer dollars being wasted on ours. So he'd ordered all the parties back to mediation, this time with a court-appointed magistrate in charge.

A new date was set for January 2013, in Los Angeles, where the case had originated. Chris and I would be present along with the insurance attorneys. Before booking our flights, we were told by the court, "Plan on spending the night in L.A." In other words, don't come in and tell the judge you've got a flight to catch, because no one was leaving until this thing was resolved.

The night before mediation, alone in my hotel room in Downtown L.A., I prayed for closure. I'd been living with this pain in my gut for fifteen months, hoping that somehow the donor would see how our organization was maturing and just drop the lawsuit. Even now, after all the exciting progress we'd made at charity: water, I still felt sick about the fact that someone hated me, that they would question my integrity.

I thought of my dad all those years ago, when he forgave the gas company for poisoning Mom. The strength it must have taken to do that, and not become bitter—that's what I needed now: strength, forgiveness, something tangible that would help me to move forward.

On impulse, I opened up my laptop, went to the donor's company website, and bought a leather wallet, a simple black trifold that cost about $55. *Every time I look at that wallet,* I thought to myself, *I will remember the gift this lawsuit gave me.* I'll thank these people for forcing charity: water to operate with a higher level of accountability—for making us stronger and better.

In the morning, Chris and I walked together to the Downtown L.A. federal courthouse, an imposing 1930s-era structure with four grand white columns flanking the entrance. Inside, it looked like the building hadn't been updated since the 1930s.

"I bought us tickets for the L.A. Philharmonic tonight," Chris said. The Walt Disney Concert Hall was just a few blocks from the courthouse, and a twenty-four-year-old piano prodigy was performing selections from Rachmaninoff. It was a kind gesture on his part, an attempt to raise my spirits.

"That sounds great," I said.

We met our court mediator, Judge Jay Gandhi, in his courtroom. He was tall, forty-something, and full of energy. I took his surname as a good omen. He ushered us into a dimly lit conference room with mismatched chairs and desks so haphazardly arranged that it looked like a graveyard for old furniture. The opposing side was sent to another room, down the hall.

For the first half of the day, Judge Gandhi listened to each side's story. He asked questions about our work, about what had gone wrong in Kenya, and what we were ready to offer to settle this. I couldn't get a read on the judge. Did he empathize with us, or did he think we were a bunch of frauds? It was hard to tell. He was so judgelike, so neutral in his delivery. Every hour or so, he'd say, "Okay, I'll be back," and then he'd go to talk with the other side.

In the past, we had agreed on at least one point—that charity: water would be willing to give money to another nonprofit for the purpose of drilling new wells in the donor's name. Call it a do-over of sorts. But we couldn't agree on things like how much money would be given, which charity would get the money, and whether we would pay that charity directly or give the money back to the donor.

I knew the courthouse shut down like clockwork at 5 p.m., so by 4:45, I was worried we were running out of time to reach a resolution.

Just then, the mediator walked in, sat down, and said, "We are going to settle this case."

He placed a piece of paper firmly on the table in front of me. It was a settlement agreement typed out by his clerk, the details of which we'd been negotiating different versions of for the last hour.

"This is where we stand," he said. So far, we'd agreed that charity: water would put money into a trust account to be paid directly to International Medical Corps, a nonprofit that would use the funds to bring clean water to people in need. We'd also agreed to remove any reference to the donor's name from our website.

The final point to decide was the amount of money that charity: water would pay. Until now, we hadn't even discussed it. There was a blank line where the dollar amount would go.

With a flourish, Judge Gandhi pulled out a pen and filled in the line. "If you agree to this number and sign this paper," he said, "they'll dismiss the suit."

I looked down to see what he'd written. It read, "$1 million."

He stood there with a pen in his hand, waiting for my response.

Okay, I thought. *One million. That's a lot of money.* We'd gotten preapproval from the board to negotiate, but how would the sound of "$1 million" go down? I thought of how Michael and Xochi once gave us the same amount to keep charity: water alive, and how every penny of this would go toward providing clean water for people who had none. And wasn't that the whole point? As long as this money went directly to fulfilling our mission, there was no downside for us.

"Yes," I said. "Absolutely."

It was done. I signed and dated the agreement, and put my initials next to the "$1 million" commitment. I felt an immediate sense of peace, like a giant weight had been lifted off my back.

By 4:55 p.m., we were being ushered out of the room. I stopped to shake the mediator's hand.

"I really appreciate your persistence today," I said.

"You guys are doing good work," he said. "Just keep going."

"Thank you," I said, barely getting the words out.

Outside, the sun was setting behind the L.A. skyline, turning the horizon red and gold. I breathed in the cool air like it was oxygen for my soul.

38

All the Sound Bites Are True

Her name, I learned, was Letikiros Hailu, and the story was true. She really had hanged herself from a tree after spilling water. A REST staffer had tracked down the details and discovered that Letikiros came from an isolated village called Meda, located on the northern border of Tigray and Amhara.

Over the last year and a half, I'd shared Letikiros's story at speaking events, but I knew nothing more than what the hotel owner had shared with me. I pictured her as an elderly woman, near the end of her life, who one day decided, *I just can't do it anymore.* People reacted to her story in a visceral way. But sometimes, when you say the same things on a stage over and over again, they start to play like sound bites, and you begin to wonder if what you're saying is actually true.

Lately, I felt like I didn't have the right to talk about Letikiros anymore—not until I went to her village, walked in her footsteps, and saw the tree where they found her body. I needed to experience what her life was like firsthand. So, on a Saturday morning in November 2013, I emailed REST and asked for help coordinating a trip to Meda.

Meda was so off the beaten path that there was actually no way to reach it by car. My contact at REST suggested I postpone the trip until a road was built, but who knew when that would be?

"Even if you are committed to walk the long distance," someone from REST had written back, "we are not sure how long it takes—days or hours."

Okay, so it will be a real journey, I thought. *I'll bring a tent. Food and water. A compass. Whatever it takes.*

"Capturing this story is very important to me," I began my reply. "The hardship is not an issue at all."

I was passionately making my case over email when Vik walked out of the bathroom with something in her hand. "This thing is broken," she said, showing me a pregnancy test wand. It was small and pink, with a digital readout window that read, "Pregnant."

"I'm not pregnant," she said. "Maybe it's expired?"

We'd stopped using birth control a couple of months earlier, without much fanfare or a master plan. Vik was thirty. I was thirty-eight. It seemed like a good time.

"Or . . . maybe you're pregnant," I said.

"No way. I don't believe it," she said. "Could you take one, please, so I can make sure these things aren't broken?"

"Um. Sure, honey."

I went to the bathroom and got a tester from our hulking stash in the cupboard. Earlier that month, I'd realized we had about $500 in tax-free FSA money that we'd lose at the end of the year, so I went on a drugstore shopping spree and bought a ton of pregnancy tests, condoms, and a blood pressure cuff. We had so many pregnancy tests, we were running out of places to store them.

My results, not surprisingly, were "Not Pregnant." I showed the wand to Vik.

"No way," she said. "Take another one!"

We both took another test—I was humoring her at this point—but the results came back the same for both of us.

"Vik, I think we're having a baby!"

"I guess so," she said, stunned. "I just . . . I thought it would take longer."

Neither of us had prepared mentally for this news. I started immediately buying parenting books. Vik searched the internet to learn everything new moms were and weren't supposed to do. The latter list was longer. She was grumpy about not being able to drink wine with dinner, and about having to cut back on the three cups of coffee she usually had with breakfast. At first, I didn't really get how hard it was for her, this sudden change in her lifestyle. Or how, when you're tired all the time, and cravings become insatiable, it can feel like your body is betraying you. I just thought she was being whiny and self-absorbed. We were headed for a blowup.

In January, we went to Hawaii for a vacation and rented a small house with some friends. When we'd planned the trip back in November, Vik had been so excited about the prospect of eating good sushi, soaking in a hot tub, and maybe getting a massage. But now she'd been told that you can't do those things when you're expecting (mistakenly on the massage part, at least). So, the whole trip, she drowned her sorrows in pint after pint of Häagen-Dazs.

"Honey, we're out of coffee ice cream," she'd say. "Will you please get me more?"

"Okay," I'd say, biting my lip and dutifully heading to the market. But one day, I Googled "sugar" and "pregnancy" and totally freaked out. I couldn't take it anymore.

"You have to stop this! You are giving our child diabetes!" I shouted, complaining for the next ten minutes about how cavalier she was being with *my baby's* health. That was it for Vik. She put down the empty ice cream carton and snapped.

"You cannot take this last thing away from me," she said in an almost sinister whisper. "I expect you to be supportive. I can raise this baby on my own if I have to!"

It was one of our worst fights ever. We laugh about it now—the time Vik almost left me for Häagen-Dazs; or, actually, the time Scott forgot he was supposed to be a supportive husband to a newly pregnant wife. But I learned my lesson, and Vik cut back on the sugar. We were about to become a family. Every decision we made, individually and as a couple, affected that sacred bond—including my decision to chase Letikiros's story.

Soon after we had made peace about the ice cream, we had a big talk about the upcoming trip.

"Babe, I need to go to her village," I said. "I need to figure out what happened in Meda, why she killed herself."

"What does REST say?"

"They're not thrilled for me to go. They think it's too far—like I won't be up for the journey. I think they have safety concerns, too."

"Do *you*?"

"Not really, but I haven't been on a trip like this for a long time. I really need it."

She was quiet for a while. Vik knew from her own experiences in the field how important it was for us to be connected with the work. Still, this hadn't come at the best time, with her pregnancy.

"If you really don't want me to go, then I'll wait," I said.

"No. I'm just jealous," she said. "I miss Ethiopia. You have to do it."

We'd been walking for hours in hundred-degree heat when our donkey wobbled a bit on his thin legs. He took a few more steps, breathed heavily, and then collapsed on the ground, taking all my gear down with him.

The poor animal was alive but exhausted. My guide gave him a long drink of bottled water in a bowl, and we decided maybe we all needed a short rest. I sat under the shade of a large rock formation, sore and covered in dust. Looking around, there was no sign of civilization on the horizon: no roads, no huts, no animals, no people, no wells. I wondered, *Are we ever going to get there? Are we lost? Is there even a* there *there?*

Earlier that day, at 5 a.m., I'd met up with Gebremariam, a water technician from REST, in the Ethiopian city of Hawzen.

"Scott, nice to meet you," he said. "Are you ready for the long journey to Meda?"

Gebremariam would be my translator, guide, and company for the entire trip. Teklewoini Assefa, REST's executive director, sent a car and driver to take us about four hours southwest from Hawzen to the Tekezé Dam. Fears of a terrorist attack on the $360 million dam project were so great that the government wouldn't allow anyone to drive near it. But Tek made some calls and got special permission for his driver to pass through a service road inside the dam—with an armed military escort, of course. Tek's handiwork saved us a full day of hiking.

We drove into the dam a little after 9 a.m., and ten minutes later we arrived on the other side, blinded by sunlight and staring at the end of the road. We unpacked the car and sent the driver back to town. As REST had promised, a vendor with a thin camel and the weak-legged donkey were waiting for us. The animals would carry our belongings for the nine-hour hike. After negotiating a price with their owner, Gebremariam and I were off.

For the weeklong journey, I'd brought a solar backpack (to keep my laptop, camera, GPS device, and satellite phone charged), a tent, a sleeping bag, tons of sunscreen, and enough clothes to change every few days. Not knowing what we'd find when we reached Meda, we packed five days' worth of dry food and water, and a small water filter.

It was the toughest walk of my life. The earth, hard and crumbling under my feet, was bleached tan from the constant beating sun. It looked like we were roaming the barren landscape of Luke Skywalker's Tatooine homeland. Ethiopia's Simien Mountains towered in the distance like amber palaces.

We reached Meda just as the sun was setting. As advertised, there was no power or running water. No internet, no post office, no general store where you could buy a Coke or double-A batteries. Just 2,800 people living completely off the grid on a dusty plateau. As we trudged into town, the village elders greeted us, offered us roasted goat and *injera,* and promised to introduce me around the community. At

8:30 p.m., I pitched my tent outside the village chief's house, tucked myself into my sleeping bag, and passed out under a full moon.

The next day, I woke up sharply at 4:45 a.m. to the sounds of rustling outside my tent—Meda's version of rush hour. I looked out to see dozens of people walking about, tending to goats and chickens, laughing and talking. Women were tying yellow Jerry Cans to their backs to begin the daily walk for water. The scene felt disorienting in the moonlight.

When the sun came up, Gebremariam took me to meet a woman named Chekolech. She was Letikiros's mother. Her short dark hair was wrapped into tight braids, and her brown tunic was fraying at the bottom. I could see the faded rings of tattoo ink around her neck, the kind that so many Ethiopian women use to adorn themselves. When Chekolech told me she was fifty-three years old, I was surprised. She looked at least sixty-five.

Gebremariam stood next to me, ready to translate.

"I came to learn about your daughter," I said.

"She was born in this house," Chekolech said. "She lived here with me, her sister, and her husband until she died on May 19, 2000."

"May I ask, how old was she?" I asked.

"Thirteen."

"I'm sorry, thirty?"

"Scott. No, no, no," Gebremariam said. "Only thirteen. Just a little girl."

I was stunned. This wasn't what I'd imagined at all. How could a thirteen-year-old have killed herself over spilled water?

"Please, could you tell me more about Letikiros?"

Chekolech and I spent the morning together talking. I learned that just before she died, Letikiros had been married to a handsome priest's servant named Abebe. Arranged marriages were common in the community. But Chekolech had been abused by Letikiros's father, the result of a poorly arranged marriage. (She later divorced him with the rare support of the male village elders.) So when it was time for her own daughter to marry, Chekolech chose thoughtfully.

Abebe was only a few years older, poor like them, but kind and gentle. Chekolech knew he would take good care of Letikiros. She watched her daughter fall in love easily with the young man. But not much else about Letikiros's life in Meda seemed easy to me.

Chekolech told me that her daughter began walking for water at eight years old. Although most girls quit school once they marry, Letikiros was determined to continue. So, three days a week, she attended class part time. The other four days, she strapped a ten-pound clay pot to her back with a frayed rope and headed out to Arliew Spring, the closest water source.

To make up for the water they missed on Letikiros's school days, the family paid to rent a donkey, which could carry four pots of water on a single trip. But they didn't have enough money to cover the donkeys every week. Also, even when she *could* go to school, just getting there took a tremendous effort. The nearest classroom was a six-hour round-trip on foot. Letikiros quickly fell behind in her lessons, and by thirteen, she'd only completed the equivalent of third grade.

The next morning, with my notebook and camera in hand, I joined the women of the village on their walk to Arliew Spring. It was a treacherous hike up and down a cliff-side footpath strewn with loose, slippery shale. I learned that several women and girls had fallen seven hundred feet to their deaths on this path. Looking down, I had no doubt that this was true.

As we reached the bottom of the ravine, I imagined Letikiros getting in line behind the others here, waiting to collect the water that trickled through the large boulders, which I could see were covered in baboon excrement. This spring trickled enough water to fill about three pots every hour. Chekolech had said that Letikiros would regularly come home around nightfall with about five gallons.

Over the next four days, I fell into the village's routine: early to bed and even earlier to rise. Around noon, when the sun beat down and temperatures reached the mid-nineties, I'd go inside the chief's tiny stone house and take a nap on a goatskin cot. I'd listen to his four children playing while their mother cooked *injera* on the stove.

Chekolech said that on the day Letikiros took her life, she'd walked to Arliew Spring with her best friend, Yeshareg, who still lived in the village. Toward the end of my trip, I went to see her. Happily married now, with three children, she was twenty-seven—the same age Letikiros would have been.

"She was different," Yeshareg said of her friend. "Letikiros always dreamed of a better life for us. She would talk about leaving Meda one day, and helping to bring back health care, water, better education."

Yeshareg remembered meeting her friend on the path to Arliew Spring the morning of that final day. "Neither of us had taken breakfast, because we wanted to get there early," she said. "To get a good spot in line."

She showed me a clay pot in her house. I picked it up by the handle and saw that the surface was badly chipped. The pot bulged at the bottom and felt old and fragile.

"They have the yellow Jerry Cans now," Gebremariam explained. "But this was what Letikiros would have been carrying that day."

Yeshareg recalled that they'd filled their pots at the spring by noon and began walking home together. Around 3 p.m., they reached the fork in the path and parted ways. It was the last time Yeshareg saw Letikiros alive.

Piecing together her story, I imagined Letikiros walking the rest of the way alone. Somewhere along the path, she stumbled. Maybe it was hunger, coupled with the forty pounds she had on her back. Perhaps her legs failed her, or she tripped on a rock. All I knew for sure was that when she went down, her pot smashed against the ground, shattering into tiny pieces. The precious water she'd spent ten hours collecting was gone in an instant, sucked up by the thirsty ground.

Shortly afterward, a village elder was passing by when he saw Letikiros's limp body hanging from the branches, and the pot nearby, broken into pieces. He wailed in grief. People came running. Someone cut her body loose, and another person covered her with a white sheet. They put her body on a board, like a stretcher, to carry her home to her mother.

When Chekolech saw her daughter's body, she was inconsolable. She went into such a frenzy that she threw herself against the jagged stone walls of her house, permanently injuring her back. Abebe wasn't home. He'd been traveling to the market for provisions, a trip that always took a few days. Someone dispatched a messenger to give him the news, and he rushed back to Meda, arriving just after the funeral.

On my last day in Meda, I met the seventy-year-old priest who'd led Letikiros's memorial service. He said she looked so beautiful, a child dressed in white.

"A thousand people came," he said. "Children, adults, everyone."

He walked me to the graveyard, a plot of dry earth behind the church. There were no markings as far as I could tell, but he knew where everyone was buried. He pointed to Letikiros's grave, a simple pile of fifteen or twenty rocks. The broken shards of the clay pot, he said, had been scattered far from the village, where they'd never be seen again.

Another elder took me to the tree where Letikiros had taken her life. It was gray and weathered, like a giant piece of dead driftwood jammed into the rocks. It didn't even look strong enough to hold the weight of a body. But I knew that a thirteen-year-old girl here, where food was scarce, might weigh as little as sixty pounds.

"Why do you think she did it?" I had asked Yeshareg. "Why not go back for water the next day?"

"I think she would have been overcome with shame for her careless-ness," she said. "Her mother was waiting for that water. They needed it. And now she had also broken the pot."

I had to remind myself that although she'd been married at the time, Letikiros was just barely a teenage girl, prone to the same emo-tions and whims that capture so many adolescents' minds. She'd lost five gallons of water and a valuable family possession in one fell swoop. It must have been just too much to bear.

Before leaving Meda, I bought my host family a goat and gave away my flashlights. Gebremariam and I started the long journey back well before dawn, and by evening I'd checked into Gheralta Lodge, show-ered, and fired up my laptop. I wrote Letikiros's story in one long exhale. The staff at REST fact-checked it, and we sent it to charity: water to be posted online.

"I loved your story," Vik said when I called her from Gheralta. "It reminded me of how you used to write when you were with Mercy Ships. You haven't done that in so long."

"Do you really think it's good?" I asked.

"Yes. So good."

"Vik, I've been so preoccupied with the business of charity: water—all the CEO stuff—I think I almost lost the thread . . . why we do this."

"I know, babe," she said.

In some ways, my time in Meda made me feel like I'd been *under-selling* the urgency of our work. Seeing that tree made me so angry—the injustice of it all. Letikiros's story reminded me that the water crisis is a real crisis. And it's urgent.

I know that we're all guilty of becoming numb sometimes. But all the sound bites are true. The awful stories are real. And they're happening right now. There are thirteen-year-old girls around the world just like Letikiros who are fed up and can't take it any longer. There are mothers like Chekolech who live every day with the pain of losing a child, an injury that never heals. There are fathers who will never see their sons and daughters grow up. Their pain felt all the more real to me when I considered that I was about to become a parent myself.

Six months later, on August 18, 2014, Jackson Scott Harrison came into the world. Vik was a champion through eight hours of labor, and I stayed with her in the delivery room, holding her hand and coaching her along, just like my dad did when I was born.

"You're doing great!" I kept saying. "Keep pushing!"

Jackson came out yelling, with big healthy lungs, ten fingers, ten toes, and a perfect Apgar score. He looked like a little, slimy, cone-headed alien. I couldn't wait for us to take him home and just stare at him.

Instead of asking for gifts, we celebrated his birth with a fundraising campaign. I couldn't think of a better way to welcome a child into the world. Vik and I personally donated the first $10,000, and 231 generous donors pitched in to raise $256,000—enough to bring clean water to more than eight thousand people in Niger, West Africa. (Why not Meda, you might ask? Field studies determined that there was simply no reachable groundwater, and the only solution would have been a massive pipe system costing upward of half a million dollars. Our team couldn't justify sending that much money to help one village, plus we didn't believe it would be a sustainable solution. It's one of the hard realities we deal with all the time. The government has been slowly building a road to Meda, and we continue to watch and hope that it might change our options for a solution in Meda one day.)

Over the next few months, as I settled into the rhythm of fatherhood, I thought a lot about what Dr. Gary had once said: the hopes and dreams in a mother's heart are the same anywhere in the world. From the time we met, Vik's and my hopes and dreams had been wrapped up in building charity: water. But now we had a son. It changed my brain chemistry. Jackson became our new everything.

Spending time with him and Vik brought into sharp focus the fact that I'd been drowning for almost three years in reports, spreadsheets, and legal briefs. That just wasn't how I wanted to spend my time and energy anymore. Retracing Letikiros's steps and sharing her story with the world—that was the job I really wanted. Storytelling was the work I'd missed the most. And now, as a new parent, I felt more connected than ever to the mothers and fathers of Meda, Kal Habel, Moale, and all the other places where we tried to bring a better life to future generations. I became obsessed with finding new ways to share those feelings, and the urgency of that need, with our supporters.

39

Chief Water Boy

SUMMER 2015

Growth is good, I've always said. Charity: water grows every single year. And when we get bigger, it's growth that you can feel good about. Instead of putting money in our own pockets or the pockets of shareholders, our kind of growth provides *other* people with the resources they need to live. Growth means our mission is resonating with donors: we are *actually* inspiring people to give and maintaining their trust in us.

In 2014, we had a banner year. Twitter had had an initial public offering the previous November, and a couple of their employees and investors had donated generously. A longtime supporter in Virginia gave us $2.7 million, and a corporate sponsor dropped $5 million in our tank. We were killing it. We raised $43.4 million that year and gave one million people clean water—both records for us. It meant we'd helped one new person every thirty seconds. It was the year when everything went right.

Then, in 2015, everything went wrong. The stock market went sideways, and then tanked. Some of our major donors had to lay off employees and deal with unexpected losses on their investments—which meant they couldn't give us anything at all in 2015.

Market conditions had never hurt our growth before, even with the financial collapse of 2008. But 2015 was different. No matter how much work the fundraising team and I put in, no matter how many calls we made or flights we took, we just couldn't make up the difference. It was the very first year that charity: water didn't grow. Even worse, we shrank. I felt horrible. What had I done wrong?

We'd recently hired a new leader for our fundraising team, a talented woman named Sabrina Pourmand. She came to us from World Vision with proven experience, and she walked right into the fray. I remember Sabrina taking one look at our donor data and saying, basically, *Wait a minute. You raised $44 million last year, and $17 million— almost half of it—came from just five donors?* An impressive feat, but certainly not one we could expect to repeat year after year.

Even worse, when we began to dissect the organization's donation revenue streams (i.e., the different ways we brought in money), we realized we were spending more than 50 percent of our time on the mycharity: water platform. It was our bread and butter, the thing that made us a charity for everyone. The problem was birthday campaigns weren't a "repeatable revenue" stream. Most people donated only one birthday to us. They'd have a great experience, and it would get them thinking about giving to other nonprofits for their next birthday, but they'd move on. And we'd have to keep finding new campaigners to keep the machine rolling.

Why hadn't I thought of this before? It had been as big a blind spot as my idea of getting a hundred New Yorkers to donate $1,000 a month for one year. Steve Sadove had set me straight then, but apparently I hadn't learned my lesson. Every year on January 1, no matter how much money we'd raised for water projects the year before, the ticker rolled back to zero. We'd start all over again. It was exhausting, and there was no easy fix.

By the summer of 2015, it was becoming clear that we weren't going to meet our fundraising goals. Barring a miracle, we would end the year significantly down from 2014. Everyone was trying to stay positive, but I was agonizing over it.

"Scott, it's still early," Sabrina said to me, trying to buoy my spirits. "We still have time. We can get this done."

"Sabrina," I said, "I'm having dreams of my baby drowning." Until that moment, I don't think she realized how hard this thing was hitting me. I felt like I was drowning and taking my baby, charity: water, down with me.

For years, I'd been so confident about our future that I'd told partners like Jim Hocking, "Get ready, because, we're only *starting* with $1.7 million worth of wells in CAR. Next year, it's going to be $3 million, then $5 million!"

So Water for Good began to ramp up for this scenario. They hired people and bought new equipment. Then war broke out in CAR, which didn't help. More important, the new money I'd promised never came. Christoph and his team had some very difficult conversations with Jim and several other partners when we couldn't repeat the size of our 2014 commitment. I had to face the fact that we'd failed them. Or, to be clear, *I'd* failed them.

Looking back, I'd always assumed we'd easily hit $100 million by our tenth year. But now, with year ten just around the corner, I started to wonder if we'd *ever* reach that mark with me at the helm. Even with all of Ross and Linda's mentoring, I still wasn't the CEO charity: water deserved. Come to think of it, I'd never enjoyed the managing, the planning, the day-to-day grind of being CEO—all of which was taking up more and more of my time. I started to wonder what it would look like to put someone else in charge—someone better.

"I think we need a professional CEO," I said to Lauren that summer. "I'll stay on and change my title to something like 'resident storyteller' or 'chief water boy.' I can work with our donors and Well members, make speeches and come up with new ideas, but I don't think I have what it takes to get the organization to the next level."

"I don't know, Scott," she said. "I think you may just need some time off."

"No," I said. "Time off won't fix this problem."

It wasn't the first time someone had suggested I take a break. For years, people had been warning me of burnout. I couldn't count the number of friends who'd told me that the intensity I operated at just wasn't sustainable.

"Scott, you can't keep working like this. You're going to collapse."

"Ninety-eight flights in a single year? In coach? You're crazy."

But every year, I'd proved them wrong, and gleefully reminded them of the fact.

"I'm still here," I'd say. "I made one hundred speeches last year. Haven't burned out yet!" This was my life's calling. I loved the work too much to downshift. Wouldn't you work yourself to death if your job literally saved people's lives?

Despite Lauren's well-meaning suggestion, I wasn't ready to admit that burnout was finally catching up to me. And it wasn't just me. Now that Vik and I had a newborn at home, the work-life integration that we'd previously thrived on had gotten harder for us.

After having Jackson in August 2014, Vik had gone back to work in January 2015. The plan was to spend three days a week in the office while her grandmother watched Jackson. But she soon realized that she couldn't really lead her team part time. And to complicate matters, she'd hired a talented new designer who turned out to be a handful to manage.

"Scott, I feel like I'm failing on all fronts," she said one night. "I can't get this new guy to play nice. I don't think my team respects me. But I don't want to go back full time, because then I feel like I'd be failing Jackson. It's just not working."

"Honey, we're a real mess, aren't we?" I said to Vik, trying to make her laugh. She smiled, but she wasn't in a laughing mood.

Like many sleep-deprived new parents, we felt overwhelmed. But the moment we came home to play with our little boy, we forgot about everything else. We started to imagine our lives differently. What if we became more than just Vik and Scott running charity: water twenty-four hours a day? What if we could reinvent our roles? Maybe we could serve as the organization's full-time innovators and big-picture thinkers. Or, maybe it was time to let charity: water grow without our getting in its way.

By late September, Lauren and I had found recruiters who were ready to start a CEO search as soon as we gave them the green light. We even brought Linda Ford into the fold, to help me think through the changes I'd be facing. She asked tough questions like: What does hiring a CEO mean to you in the context of your personal life story? What are the two to three top things you still want to lead? Are there any things that are off-limits for the new CEO—that they cannot change?

She'd given me these questions as a homework assignment, but I had no idea how to answer them. What *was* off-limits? How could I even begin to think about that? What kind of changes would a new CEO want to make, anyway?

"Linda, can we just talk about it when I see you?" I said.

"All right, Scott." She knew I was punting, that I wasn't ready to focus on the deeper issues. I wanted to just get it over with and hand charity: water over to someone who would take better care of it than I could. By late September, I decided to call each board member personally and tell them of my plans.

"We need to hire a rock star," I said to longtime member Gian-Carlo Ochoa. "The stakes are higher now."

"Scott, you sound like you're really done," Gian-Carlo said. "Look, we're going to be 100 percent supportive, but I'm not sure who is going to be able to fill your shoes. Who are we going to find?"

"I don't know. But the time is now."

It was also time to tell my leadership team. We'd recently made two new executive hires, and there was a lot of team-building work to be done. So Lauren scheduled an executive offsite meeting for late September, and we sat down together to talk about how I would break the news.

"Remind them that this is about continuing to become as strong as possible as a team," Lauren said. "It's not about you or your transition. It's about the team."

She said something else about focusing on how appreciative I was of all their hard work, et cetera. It all made sense, but honestly, I was so burnt out that I just wanted to get this conversation over with and start the next chapter of my life.

On the morning of September 30, we all met at a tiny conference room in a WeWork space. Six of us crammed in together at a rectangular table—Gumbley, Lauren, Sabrina, Christoph; our two new hires, Matt and Amy; and me. We went over plans for the fourth quarter goals for each department. All I could think about was unburdening myself of my news, but I didn't say a word all morning. I was just trying to gather the courage.

Finally, after lunch, as everyone sat back down around the table, I spoke up.

"Guys, I've made a decision," I said somberly. "I've asked the board to help me hire a CEO."

The room was quiet. Lauren looked at the others to see how they were responding. Sabrina, who'd seen me suffer through our brutal fundraising year, was the only one who didn't look shocked. Nobody spoke.

"I believe in the future of charity: water," I continued. "But I've been doing this for almost ten years now. I don't want to manage people anymore. It's not what I do well. I think it's time for a professional CEO."

People were shaking their heads like I was putting everyone on. I think someone even joked, "What? Get back to work!"

"I'm serious," I said. "I'll stay on full-time and contribute alongside each of you, doing the things I do best, but we need a new leader. We're just not growing anymore."

Somehow, I had expected applause. And something like: *Congratulations, Scott. You had a great run, but yeah, it's been painful working with you lately. We're excited to help you hand off the baton!* Instead, I got crossed arms and audible grumbling.

"I'm sorry," I said, looking down, "but I've made up my mind. I'm doing this."

Amy spoke up first. "I didn't come here to work for a new CEO," she said. "I came to work for you."

Matt piped in with more of the same, and that pretty much set the tone for the reception of my big announcement. This would be harder than I thought.

"Guys, it sounds like Scott's really struggling here," Sabrina said. "Maybe we should at least listen."

In the debating back and forth, a voice of reason finally emerged.

"Look, first of all, it's Q4," Christoph said. "There's no way you're going to open up a CEO search in the fourth quarter. Let's focus on finishing the year strong. Why don't you take the month of January off? Go spend some time with your family and think things over."

I was tired of arguing. "Okay, fine," I said. "We'll press pause until Q1." Christoph had a good point. The last three months of the year? Maybe this was not the best time to put the organization through a massive change.

"But I'm serious," I said. "This *is* happening."

The year ended as dismally as I'd expected. We closed out 2015 having raised only $35 million. In 2014, we'd served a million people, but this year we'd be able to help only eight hundred thousand. I took it personally. In my mind, that meant two hundred thousand people would continue walking for dirty water and dying, all because I couldn't find the money to help them.

In the midst of it all, Vik decided to step down from her role as creative director. She didn't have a plan yet. Maybe she'd work a few days a week as a consultant, or help out with special projects. But she was tired of feeling like she was doing a dozen things poorly.

It was a painful year for us both. Then, in late December, a friend stepped up with a bright spot. He offered me and Vik his retreat home in Redding, California.

"You can have it for the entire month of January," he said. "Bring your whole family."

It was a beautiful mountain escape—countless bedrooms, four fireplaces, a pool, views of Shasta Lake a mile below—and we'd have it all to ourselves. Vik and I had never taken a month off from anything, so we brought her grandparents along to help with Jackson. We had this vision of the two of us hiking among the redwoods, reading, praying, cooking, drinking red wine, and talking about our future and our family.

A month on the lake would be a chance for Vik to recharge and clear her head before we came back to New York, found her replacement, and rethought her role. For my part, I'd already made up my mind that we'd start the CEO-recruiting process in February. And yet, it gave me hope to think that Vik and I might come back as new people, with fresh perspectives. I couldn't wait to get away with her.

But then, once we got there, I couldn't wait to get *away* from the mountains. We landed in California a couple of days after Christmas, but instead of sunny skies, we got freezing rain and fog. In fact, it rained, hailed, and snowed the *entire* time we were there—a record month of rainfall for Northern California. The house, which sat at the top of a hill, practically had its own weather system. The roof leaked, and the fog was so thick that you couldn't even see the lake in the distance when you looked out the large picture windows to the deck. The patio furniture was completely soaked, and gusty winds knocked over the umbrella stands.

Jackson, who'd gotten old enough to walk and boss his grandmother around, was bored and whiny and getting into everything. We were constantly chasing after him and telling him no—afraid he'd destroy this beautiful house. Then we all got sick. Someone sneezed or blew their nose every thirty seconds. I was miserable and bored. With nothing to do, I started thinking about all the ways we were blowing it at charity: water. I obsessed over all the things I wanted to fix *right now*. What was I doing stuck up here in the mountains for *four weeks*?

One night, Vik called down to me from the balcony. I was lounging on a big couch on the first floor, trying to distract myself with a book.

"Hey, guess what?" she said. "I'm pregnant again."

"Wait, really? You're serious?"

"Yeah." This time, she knew better than to doubt the pregnancy test.

I ran up the stairs to hug her. We'd talked about trying to have another baby, but again, neither of us had thought it was going to happen so fast.

"Honey, this is amazing!" I said. "They'll be exactly two years apart."

"Yeah, I guess," Vik said. "I can't believe I drank so much wine this week."

She laughed, but she looked sad. I could tell it wasn't about the wine.

"I guess . . . I don't know about work now," she said. "Being pregnant makes me so tired all the time. And I was hoping to regain some energy on this trip, not have less of it at the end."

"Babe, you are so talented. That can never be taken from you," I said. "I know this isn't easy, but I'm excited that we're pregnant."

She smiled and hugged me. I knew she was facing the hardest decision she'd ever have to make—whether or not to walk away from charity: water for good.

"Vik, please don't worry. We'll figure it out."

"Okay," she said.

The next day, I called my mom and dad to give them the good news about the baby. Mom hoped for a girl to round out our family. Dad asked if I was still determined to step down as CEO.

"Dad, we had a bad year. I just don't think I'm the right guy to lead charity: water anymore."

"Scott, I was in business for thirty years," he said. "And let me tell you, no business grows for thirty years straight. You have good years, and you have bad years."

"I know, Dad," I said. "But when *I* have a bad year, people don't get water."

"Well, that's true," he said. "Let me ask you this: Did you compromise your values in some way this year?"

"No, of course not," I said.

"Did you cut corners?"

"Absolutely not."

"Did you do anything you weren't proud of?"

"*No*," I said, a little fired up about what he might be insinuating.

"Dad, look—outside of revenue, it was one of the best years in the history of our organization. Our programs were more effective, our employees gave their best every day, our turnover rate was the lowest yet. A lot of things went well this year. We just raised a lot less money."

"I see," Dad said with a patient tone. "So maybe you're focusing on the wrong things?"

He was totally right. I'd been focused on the numbers. I was so consumed with our multimillion-dollar shortfall, so caught up in cash flow and growth, that I couldn't see the bigger picture, or even feel good about the accomplishments we'd had in 2015. After all, we'd helped *eight hundred thousand* people get clean water. Where had my optimism gone?

For the next couple weeks, I spent a lot of time going to church in Redding, thinking about my life and about the organization. Dad was right. There were so many wins this year that I'd been ignoring.

Like back in April, when our team spent a week in Ethiopia, capturing how the daily life of a thirteen-year-old girl named Selam changed when her community got clean drinking water for the first time. We turned her story into an eight-minute virtual reality film that was seen by tens of thousands of people. It helped us raise both awareness and money.

Or, in September, when I turned forty and celebrated with a birthday campaign that raised $400,000—enough money to drill wells in forty villages in Ethiopia.

And I'd forgotten one of the most important achievements we'd had as a team this year: we were finally moving the conversation forward on sustainability. In November, we'd installed three thousand sensors at wells across Ethiopia—no small feat, considering we had to make them ourselves.

In the last three years, we'd built numerous prototypes and ended up with several duds. The challenge was unique: Our sensor needed to be made of UV-resistant, food-grade plastic that was durable enough to sit out in the open blazing sun and not get broken by people or animals. It had to measure chaotic water flow—not just water going evenly through a pipe, but water splashing up and around. And the batteries needed to last ten years without having to be changed.

Most important, our sensor had to reliably transmit to us all the data it was collecting. So, we specially sourced a universal SIM card from a start-up in Hong Kong that had preexisting roaming agreements with every telecom company in the world—that way, the SIM card could work wherever we installed it. But when we tested our first prototype in Ethiopia, the sensor couldn't connect to the local servers. We simply couldn't get any data out. It was a total disaster. And it wasn't just our problem: mobile roaming never worked right in Ethiopia. Whenever we flew into Addis Ababa, we never got that "Welcome to Ethiopia, data charges apply . . ." message that's supposed to appear on your cell phone when your plane lands.

It was frustrating, but our team refused to give up. Instead, we flew the SIM card company's owner from Hong Kong to Addis Ababa to see if he could find a solution. He plugged his laptop into the main server at Ethio Telecom, looked around, and announced, "There's a bug in here."

The roaming code was broken. So he fixed it—*for Ethiopia's entire national telecommunications system.* All of a sudden, phones everywhere started buzzing, and our sensor started chirping. Just like that, we solved mobile roaming for all of Ethiopia, for a country of more than 100 million people.

I was so proud of our team. Now we could get real-time information on every new well that had a sensor. Today, I can call a donor who gave up her birthday seven years ago and say, "Hey, Gelila, do you want to know how some of your wells are doing? Let's check in on one of them." We can zoom in on her well, pull up a photo and GPS, and see that, on Tuesday of this week, more than a thousand gallons of clean water came out of the well—a well built for her birthday seven years ago.

We can also see if her well stops working. For example, today, we're at 90 percent functionality in Ethiopia—a huge improvement over the 60 percent status quo. But to address the 10 percent of wells that are broken on any given day, squads of local mechanics roam around on GPS-enabled motorbikes, fixing problems as they arise. Imagine if a technician from a local Apple or Samsung store showed up at your house every time your phone or laptop gave you problems. "Um, hi," you'd say. "How did you know it was broken?" Our teams are tipped off by the sensors and show up unannounced. They're local water heroes.

That month in the mountains of California made me realize that maybe 2015 had been a good year after all. Our staff, interns, and volunteers gave everything they had. Nobody took their foot off the gas. The problem had been my perspective. Why did I think I could just quit? Maybe, instead of feeling sorry for myself, I needed to step up.

Besides, 2016 would be charity: water's tenth year. It would be pretty lame to give up in year nine. I had to at least finish out the decade with my head held high. Like Dr. Gary, I would commit to another year, do my best, and then decide about the following year when the time came.

Vik's time in the mountains brought her to a different choice.

"Scott, I just can't get excited about the idea of going back to charity: water," she said. "I'm really trying to get to the place in my heart or soul where I first felt that passion for my job. But I just can't.

"I think for me, the risky thing to do is to leave," she continued. "Maybe I need to start a completely new journey and force myself to find something else that I love. Maybe I'll freelance or write a book or even start a branding agency one day."

For as long as we'd known each other, our identities had been completely tied to our work. It was always me and Vik and charity: water against the world. I couldn't even imagine her not being there by my side. But Vik needed a break even more than I did. She wanted to focus on being a mom, and then see what was next.

When we returned to the office in February, I told my team that I was fully signing up for year ten. That I was bursting with ideas and ready to try to solve our growth problems.

"Scott, nobody actually thought you'd really go," Sabrina said with a laugh. "We all knew you needed a few weeks off."

Right away, I promoted Lauren to the role of chief operating officer. I needed her to take over more of the day-to-day responsibilities, so I could spend less time in internal meetings (where I contributed little value) and more time telling our story, raising money, and working on the next big ideas for charity: water. Lauren was charity: water's most senior employee besides me and Vik, and I've always depended on her to get things done.

Vik's last day was February 26, 2016. It felt like the end of an era. At around 5 p.m., we threw a party for her at the office. It was actually sort of a roast, which was more Vik's style. We all gathered around the flex space, a large, comfy area with couches, beanbags, and big TV screens. Vik's team went up to the microphone one by one, giving speeches and talking about the times they'd been "Vik-timized," called out by their boss for messy desks or sloppy work. The staff made a beautiful book for her, filled with funny, brash emails she'd written and photos of her at the office and in the field. The celebration ended with a string of thank-you videos from longtime friends and donors like Michael and Xochi, and Ross.

At the end, I got up to speak. As our first and only creative director, Vik had been the architect of charity: water's brand. Her style and taste were—and still are—present in everything we do, from the fonts on our annual reports to the colors of our office chairs and our enduring yellow Jerry Can logo. If charity: water was born out of my search for redemption, Vik sculpted it into the mature yet playful brand it is today.

"So . . ." I said slowly into the microphone. "I have a special going-away gift for you. Vik, can you come up here?"

She walked up to stand by my side and gave me a "What are you up to now?" look. I handed her a small black box, and she opened it to find one hundred business cards. They read, VIKTORIA HARRISON, COFOUNDER.

"Oh my gosh, Scott," she said.

"I've thought of doing this before, and I probably should have," I said. "I want to honor your nine years of service to the organization. You built our brand, and you always demanded creative excellence— which, as Michael Birch said, was the only reason he emailed me back, so many years ago."

It was the first time I'd ever made her cry during a speech. But I wanted to give Vik a platform to be able to speak on behalf of the organization with real credibility, and not just as an "ex–creative director" or the "wife of the CEO." I wanted her to know that she'd never be an ex-anything. She'd always been my cofounder.

Now we'd made it official.

40

The Spring

SPRING 2016

In our tenth year, I had to face the fact that we'd never actually built a $43.4 million charity. Charity: water reached that number in 2014 because a few big donors had had a really good year and decided to drop a lot of money in our laps. In reality, I'd built a $30 million organization, with about $13 million worth of surprises.

Thanks to our Well members, we'd figured out how to fund our overhead account. Thanks to Christoph and his team, to the Google Award, and to the work of countless partners, we'd made serious breakthroughs on sustainability in the field. But if we wanted charity: water to survive long term, I desperately needed to figure out how to fix our *donation* sustainability problem. We needed a monthly giving program—something like the Well, but for water projects.

Charity: water actually had a monthly program—of sorts. If you went to our website to make a donation, you could check a tiny box and "choose to give monthly." Around 150 people a year had done that, but it didn't add up to much, and we'd never put any promotion or strategic thinking into it. Worse, the people who did tick that box got nothing in return. No reporting on their wells, no thank-yous, no personal experience. We needed to start over and give them something much better. I didn't know what that was yet, but the more I learned about other nonprofit monthly giving programs, the more I knew what I *didn't* want ours to look like.

One day, I went online looking for inspiration and found a non-profit that "sponsors" children in the developing world. After I answered some questions online and chose a child to sponsor, a checkout window popped up that read, "An item has been added to your basket."

"What?" I said out loud. "An *item*? A child is not an *item*!"

This was a huge organization with seemingly infinite resources. As far as I knew, its membership program actually worked. And yet I couldn't help but think that by billing the whole thing as a "shopping" experience, they were missing the point. You don't tell donors that they've added a child to their "basket." You say something like "Samuel is ready to join your family," or "You have chosen to help Miriam."

This is why I'd never felt connected to those traditional programs. I loved the idea of continuity, but I always wondered, *Am I really helping this* exact *child? Does it really cost exactly $38 a month in perpetuity to meet all her needs?*

And while child-sponsorship programs are pretty good about providing regular updates, most monthly giving programs are notoriously bad about it. Once you sign up, and your automatic payments start rolling in, you get ghosted. All communication ceases. Too many charities follow a "set it and forget it" model, where they hope that you won't notice the money leaving your bank account for theirs, month after month.

I wanted us to do the exact opposite. Instead of ignoring our donors, we could intentionally remind them of their generosity. Regularly thank them. Recognize them. Tell them how grateful we were.

When I pitched the idea to Well members, they had a lot to say about monthly-revenue models. I learned that most of us have about ten different things we subscribe to (Spotify, Apple Music, Netflix, HBO, Dropbox, newspapers, magazines), and of course we expect stuff in return for those subscriptions (music, entertainment, cloud storage, the latest headlines).

I certainly didn't want to send our donors more *stuff*—a T-shirt, coffee mug, or tote bag. Instead, I had a better idea. And in May 2016, I shared it with our staff.

"People are already familiar with monthly subscriptions," I said. "But we're going to create a subscription program like no other. I want us to sign up a million people to give an average of $30 a month. And for your $30? You receive *no* tangible value in return."

At first, I got a lot of blank stares. *What is he talking about?*

"In our program, 100 percent of the value of the donation is passed along to the people who really need it. And in return, we'll *inspire* our donors!" I said. "We'll give them exclusive content—stories from around the world of wells being drilled, biosand filters being constructed, women like Helen getting clean water and feeling beautiful for the first time. We'll show our donors the impact they're making month in and month out."

Our team started to get excited about the possibilities.

"What if we highlight the seven members in North Dakota, and the seventeen in Illinois," someone riffed, "and maybe, one day, we can connect them all."

"Yeah. Let's invite them all to New York for a summit! Kind of like Warren Buffett does for his Berkshire Hathaway shareholders."

"We can make videos just for them, introducing the new countries and local partners we're working with. We can bring them closer to the people they're helping."

"I love these ideas," I said. "We'll build a community of generosity!"

For weeks, we debated what to call our community. "The Reservoir," "the Village," "the Harbor," and "the Anchor" were just a few of the names floated around. I liked the triple entendre of "the Channel"—meaning water, a constant flow of information, and a place where our donors could "tune in" to the work. But in the end, we agreed on "The Spring." It felt simple and uplifting. Spring signals a time of rebirth, of possibilities bubbling up.

We decided to launch The Spring on our tenth anniversary. To celebrate a decade's worth of work and invite people in, we'd also make a short movie. I hired my old buddy Jason Russell, whom I'd met in Uganda ten years before on that first visit to Bobi Camp. Jason was a powerful storyteller, and had just started a new media company with his wife, Danica. Back in 2004, he and his friends had started a non-profit called Invisible Children and traveled around Uganda with video cameras to create a groundswell of activism in America. Their work helped to enact legislation that aided Ugandans in their fight against warlord Joseph Kony.

In April, Jason and Danica and I spent weeks crafting a script that we hoped would move people to action. For several days, I was holed up in charity: water's "Think Tank" conference room with Tyler Riewer, our brand and content lead, and Jamie Pent, our videographer, breaking down ideas and filling up the whiteboard in a scene straight from *A Beautiful Mind*. There were scribbles and arrows everywhere: *This story could go here. We'll move that part over there. Get rid of this.*

We shared our outline with Jason and Danica. Then we debated, sweated the details, and merged our visions until we had a blueprint for The Spring's launch: a twenty-minute video that told the charity: water story in one dramatic narrative. It would cost about $50,000 to make.

When I pitched the idea to our execs and staff, I got a lot of push-back. Our vision was too long, too expensive, totally unconventional, and totally unrealistic.

"Scott, a *$50,000* video?" Gumbley complained.

"Nobody is going to watch a twenty-minute video," Lauren said.

"They will if it's good!" Jason and I argued back. Ten years in, I believed more than ever that people respond deeply to human stories. I once spoke at four services at a church in Miami, with almost no response from the crowd. The trip seemed like a total failure. Then, four years later, a $100,000 check arrived at charity: water from the estate of a man I'd never met. He'd heard me speak at that church and was so moved by the stories of people in need that he went home and changed his will.

Over the years, I'd seen people cry and give $1 million after a speech that was just an hour of me talking and clicking through a bunch of photos. I firmly believed that a $50,000 twenty-minute video was totally worth it.

But as our deadline approached, I started to panic.

"This film—it's just not good yet," I said to Jason two days before we were supposed to launch. "In fact, it's really not good at all!"

"Scott, it'll get there," he said. "This is going to work."

I wasn't so sure. The Spring film and membership launch had to be perfect. This was our tenth anniversary; everyone was watching. The whole thing felt overwhelming. We had long nights, endless re-shoots, and voice-over recording sessions that lasted until 2 a.m. At one point, Jamie and I went from office to office, microphones and laptops in hand, looking for a completely quiet space. After a while, we gave up and just recorded intermittently, whenever the HVAC unit cycled off.

Finally, after weeks of frantic work, we found the right pace and edits, and took the video from a B-minus to what felt like a solid A. Or, at least that's what I hoped.

Before releasing it to the world, I sent the Spring video to friends and family.

"I'd love it if you could watch this with your kids, and let me know what you think," I wrote to Dr. Gary and Susan Parker. Their son, Wesley, was nineteen now, and their daughter, Carys, was twenty-two. Would a couple of college students sit through a twenty-minute video for a charity? I wondered.

The next day, Susan wrote to say that they'd watched the whole thing. Afterward, Carys and Wesley were so moved that they'd jumped up and said, "We have to join The Spring! We're joining right now." Having Dr. Gary as one of our first members was a special honor for me. And the Parker kids signed up for their own memberships, independent of their parents.

"My children aren't jaded, but they've seen a lot," Susan said. "They grew up on a hospital ship in Africa, so the stories in The Spring aren't new to them. Yet you've really caught their hearts."

That's when I knew this could be big.

On August 29, a week before our anniversary, we launched the video and The Spring monthly giving program. We splashed it across charity: water's website home page, promoted it on all our social media channels, and sent emails to everyone we knew. We set a goal: one thousand new members to The Spring in one month.

Over those next few days, I got up constantly from my chair to check the digital dashboard on the wall outside my office. It was thrilling to see new sign-ups being recorded in real time. Our staff finally just moved the dashboard closer to my door, so I could turn around in my chair to look. Every couple of hours, they'd hear me yelling, "We got *another* one!" (I'm sure Ross would have lectured me about focusing too much on the small wins, but some things never change.)

By September 1, we really did have reason to celebrate. We'd brought on 1,099 new subscribers to The Spring, beating our goal. And that twenty-minute video that nobody was going to watch? It got 989,000 views on Facebook, and another 21,402 on YouTube. At the time of this writing, it's at 2.5 million views and counting.

The Spring video is still the most successful piece of content we've ever created. The Spring membership has also grown, to more than 20,000 members from 94 countries. They give an average of $30 a month. And the community continues to grow each and every day. Thanks to The Spring, we can better plan our water programs around the world. We don't have to start at zero every year. And we don't have to have troubling conversations with partners in the field about commitments we cannot meet.

On September 7, 2016, the staff threw a small party at the office to celebrate charity: water's tenth anniversary and the success of our Spring launch. But I missed it—I was at the hospital watching the birth of Emma Viktoria Harrison. She was the best birthday gift I'd ever received.

Before Vik and I had children, a friend said to me: Imagine you're standing on an island, looking at water on all sides. You think that this little piece of real estate, which represents your capacity for love, is all there is. Then you have your first child, and a bubbling happens off in the distance and a giant new island appears. You realize that the new island was part of your heart all along, just submerged. And then you think you could never love another child like this one, but you look off to the left, and a brand-new island appears: your second child. And your heart expands even more. You're not borrowing from or shutting down other parts to feel more love. It's an additive process, like reclaiming land from the sea.

That's how I felt after Emma was born: that I had more to give, more ability to love, more capacity to feel—and more pain over the fact that children were dying because of bad water. Letikiros and many others I'd met had made this real for me. Having Jackson and Emma strengthened my resolve that no child should ever have to drink dirty water.

41

—

Someone Like You

NEW YORK, DECEMBER 2016

I have a friend who used to run a famous cancer charity. Sometimes we'd run into each other at conferences, and I once had to follow his talk.

He went onstage, in front of a thousand people, and said, "Raise your hand if you've had cancer? Go ahead and keep them up. Now, how about a family member? Okay, how about a friend?"

At "friend," every hand in the audience was up. He then began his speech.

I have to admit, it made me jealous. If I were to go up after him and say, "How many of you have gotten deathly ill from drinking dirty water? Okay, how many of you know someone who died from water-borne disease?" or "How many of you have walked eight hours to get water?"

Crickets.

I've actually tried it. Sometimes, if it's a huge group, I'll see one or two hands in the audience, people who've immigrated to the United States from the places we work. But most Americans don't know any-one who has died from schistosomiasis or diarrhea, or who's gone blind from trachoma. They've never seen a child drink from a brown river and throw up on herself over and over again. They don't know teenagers who've hanged themselves over spilled water. It's hard to relate.

To celebrate the end of our tenth year, we wanted to create an even stronger connection between our donors and the recipients. Somehow, we wanted to eliminate the distance between New York City and Africa, and bridge that gap in a meaningful way at our 2016 charity: ball gala.

Back in August, as we were finalizing the Spring film, a small group of friends and Well members came to the office for a gala brainstorming session. Every year, we try to outdo the innovations of the previous year's gala, but in 2016 the bar was set exceedingly high.

In 2015, we'd invited four hundred guests to a sit-down dinner in the Metropolitan Museum of Art's Temple of Dendur. After the meal, we strapped virtual reality headsets on everyone and simultaneously brought them into a thirteen-year-old girl's life in Ethiopia for eight minutes. People in tuxedos and evening gowns were weeping when they took their headsets off, and we raised $2.4 million in one night. For our tenth anniversary, I knew we had to come up with something even more creative and exciting.

"We're returning to the Met Museum," I told the group. "And we want to give guests a chance to transform one single life. But we're not sure how to create that one-to-one connection—that's our challenge here."

David Gungor, a musician and local pastor, riffed on an idea that got us excited.

"Think about your own life in the last ten years," he said. "What were your biggest problems? What kept you up at night, worried for your family? Now imagine sitting down at the table at charity: ball and finding a video message from someone like you in Uganda. And learning that this person's biggest problem in the last ten years was dirty water."

The idea bounced around the room, getting bigger and more exciting with each person's input. It boiled down to this: if our problem was getting people to relate, what if we could say to them, *Look, here's someone like you?*

Someone Like You was a great concept, but to truly personalize it for every gala guest, we'd have to shoot four hundred photos and four hundred video stories of four hundred villagers in a single community that did not have water. Then we'd have to match up every villager in a meaningful way with each and every one of our four hundred guests— all while developing The Spring program, launching our holiday campaign, and putting on the gala itself. Even more daunting, we'd have only three months to pull the concept off. It was an *insane* idea. But that never stopped us before. We were all in.

We zeroed in on Ethiopia pretty quickly. Christoph's team identified a handful of villages to scout, and our partners at REST helped us narrow it down to a remote community called Adi Etot, in the northwestern part of the country. Two months out of the year, during the rainy season, Adi Etot is flush with water. Teff fields sway in the breeze, golden rows of corn stretch across the horizon, and a natural spring seeps from a ravine at the center of the community. For a little while, collecting water is easy. But as the dry season approaches, the women and girls of Adi Etot must spend two to six hours a day collecting water from two alternate sources: a faraway spring or a nearby dirty riverbed.

For fifteen days in early October 2016, a small team of charity: water creatives made Adi Etot their home. During the first week, they camped in the village, drank coffee and ate meals with residents, and got to know people's stories. Christoph and I flew out and joined them for the second week, where every day was spent in production.

Tyler Riewer conducted interviews with young single mothers, couples with children, students and teachers, farmers and aspiring entrepreneurs. Lauren and Ali Troute, our producer, sat at a table with their laptops, a list of questions, consent forms, and translators from REST. A generator whirred nonstop as they interviewed a long line of people from ages four to ninety, before sending them off to Paul and Jamie to be filmed. Finally, the residents were led over to Jeremy Snell, our freelance photographer, who took beautiful portraits of each and every person. The working days began at 5:30 a.m. and didn't end until the sun went down.

As I walked from station to station, I knew that the people of Adi Etot would talk about this time for generations—*that week when a bunch of crazy Americans came with their questions and their cameras, and soon after, we had clean water.*

We came home with hard drives full of content. The next step was to find points of connection between each villager and each one of our four hundred charity: ball guests. Sabrina and her team created a spreadsheet to match guests with a counterpart in Adi Etot. Sometimes the commonalities were really specific: A pregnant donor was matched with a pregnant woman in Adi Etot of around the same age; or a couple who'd been married for forty years was connected to a couple in the village who'd been married for the same length of time. But for some, it was just "You're a teacher and he's a teacher," or "Hey, you both like to take long hikes."

Our team worked like crazy to finish the videos. Everyone was exhausted and cranky from managing so many moving parts. Lauren would push me to decide on details like the timing of my gala speech or the logistics around the "ask," and I'd snap at her, "I'm not ready! I need more time to think." She'd snap right back, "Fine. But the production will suffer if you keep pushing the deadlines!"

Then, just to make it a little more difficult for everyone, I decided that I wanted to cap the whole thing off with a live drill from Adi Etot. I imagined guests sitting down to dinner and learning about the person they'd been matched with. Then, from the stage, I'd invite them to change that person's life *right now*. And we'd watch together as four hundred people got clean water for the first time *in that very moment.*

Charity: water had never actually done a live drill before. When you're dealing with satellite equipment, drilling rigs, and unpredictable groundwater in remote locations, a million things can go wrong. So we'd always just filmed the drill and then immediately uploaded the video via satellite to New York.

When I ran the live-drill idea past Michael Birch and a few other Well members, their eyes lit up. I knew that if we pulled this off, it could be huge. I couldn't get the idea out of my head. A live drill would be the pièce de résistance for the gala—a powerful moment that people would remember, embrace, and share. It would also turn out to be a technical nightmare.

On December 5, the morning of charity: ball, 150 volunteers sat around our office customizing 400 iPads with the help of our engineering department. Ninety blocks north, in the Temple of Dendur, our event producers were running around with walkie-talkies, setting up the lighting and audiovisual systems and testing the satellite feed.

Four thousand miles away, Ali, Jamie, and Tyler were with REST's drilling team in Adi Etot, pointing their broadband global area network (BGAN) satellite units toward the sky. But nothing appeared on our side. When we'd tested the link earlier, at the charity: water office, we'd gotten picture and sound in sync four out of seven times. But here in the Temple, hours before the moment of truth, our eighth and ninth tests failed completely. The sky in Ethiopia had grown too cloudy to transmit. We'd get picture but no sound, or we'd connect briefly and then the signal would drop. Tyler, who'd be on-camera live from Adi Etot, had been practicing his speech all night and was a nervous wreck.

By 6 p.m. we decided to just cross our fingers and hope for the best. It was 2 a.m. in Ethiopia. Our crew in-country settled in to sleep on blankets on top of their Land Rovers, next to the drill site. They'd wake up in a few hours to go live.

With guests starting to arrive, I went to find a place where I could sit alone and pray. I felt as ready as I ever do before these moments— which is to say, not at all. But I wanted to stop for a few minutes and thank God for giving me this opportunity—really, for giving me ten years of opportunities.

Just a year ago, I'd burned out to the point of quitting and then somehow had found my way back. Now I couldn't wait to tackle year eleven.

As I quietly prayed, I thought about how dramatically my perspective had changed over the last ten years. There was a time when my mother's illness felt like such a burden. Now I saw it as a gift. It taught me that, just like my father, I could endure pain, try harder, and find solutions where others saw only problems. I used to look back at the decade I spent in the clubs with shame and disgust. But I've realized that those experiences gave me skills (making people feel included, special, and united around a joyful experience) that I still use every day.

Tonight, I was doing the same thing I'd been doing for years: throwing a huge party. My endgame was the only thing that had changed.

The Temple of Dendur feels truly sacred at night. It's a massive four-story room with views of Central Park through a wall of tilted glass windows, and we'd lit the whole place up with candles. The Temple itself is a sandstone Roman-era shrine to deities who ensured the prosperity of the community—the patrons of the people. As I looked around the hall from the table where Vik and I sat, I saw a lot of charity: water's longtime friends and patrons in the room. Michael and Xochi, Shak, Neil, Matt, and Marissa. And newer friends, like Ryan and Molly, Julie and Brian.

No one knew what we had planned for the evening, which was all part of the excitement. A little after 9:30 p.m., after the dinner plates had been cleared, I got up to speak.

"Right now, about four thousand miles away from this stunning room, high up on a plateau in Shire, Ethiopia, is a community called Adi Etot, where the people are just waking up," I said. "Several weeks ago, I joined our team in Adi Etot to listen to their stories. We heard about their hopes and dreams."

Behind me, a two-story screen projected photos of the people we'd met.

"Here's the oldest man in the village, a priest named Assefa Gebre-medina. He's either ninety-one or ninety-eight—nobody could seem to agree—and he told us he's never had clean water before, but that he wanted to taste it before he died."

I clicked to the next slide. "Here's the youngest baby in the village," I said. "She hasn't even been named yet! She's almost the exact age as my daughter. Her mother told us that she bathes her only every other week. But if she had clean water, then her baby could take a bath every day."

The screen cycled through images of the rocky ravine where the women of Adi Etot waited with donkeys and Jerry Cans for a trickle of dirty water. And then, the place where they had to dig in the dry season when the streams disappeared.

"We know that sometimes when you give to charity, it can be hard to imagine the exact person you're helping," I said. "But not tonight. Because every single person in Adi Etot has a story. And every one of you is about to meet your person."

Each guest had an iPad in front of them at their table, with their name displayed on the home screen. I asked everyone to pick up their iPad, swipe left, and use the code "together" to unlock the experience and meet their person.

I watched as guests thumbed through their tablets and discovered with surprise that they'd been matched with a unique person in Ethiopia. One friend, Monique, a jewelry designer, teared up after seeing a video of her person and recalling a trip she'd taken to the field with us many years before.

After about ten minutes, I told everyone that tonight we were going to raise money to drill a well for Adi Etot.

"It's going to cost $12,000, which breaks down to $30 per person," I said. "Now, if anyone is unable to give, Vik and I will make up the difference. But I'd really love to see 100 percent participation tonight."

It was fun to look across the room and see so many shocked and confused faces: *Just $30? That is too low. It doesn't even cover the cost of my dinner!*

But those who knew me well were chuckling, and warning the others, "Just you wait. He's not done with us yet."

"Are you ready?" I said. "Let's do this!"

The giant screen behind me switched to a grid of the four hundred faces of the villagers. As donations rolled in, each person's face turned from black and white to color. We raised $12,000 in about three minutes. I could hardly contain my excitement.

"I knew you guys would do that," I said. "So, in good faith, we've already dispatched a charity: water rig to Adi Etot, and yesterday it began drilling the well *you just paid for.*"

Clapping and cheering broke out across the room.

"Our partners in Ethiopia have been drilling through the night, and a few hours ago, we learned that they found clean water two hundred feet underground," I continued. "Guys, people in this village have been waiting their *entire lives* for this moment."

My palms got sweaty and my heart rate doubled. I had no idea if this was going to work. There were so many things that could go wrong. But it was 10:12 p.m. in New York and 6:12 a.m. in Ethiopia. Now or never.

"Can we please open up the satellite link to Ethiopia?" I called out, waiting and praying that we'd see Tyler and the people of Adi Etot appear behind me on the giant screen. I held my breath.

And then, there they were.

Standing on a high plateau in the morning's first light was Tyler, a drilling rig, and a sea of people wrapped up in white blankets and looking awfully cold, but visibly bouncing with energy. Everyone in the Temple clapped and cheered. These were *their* people.

"I'm standing here in the middle of Adi Etot, along with nearly every single one of the four hundred people you met tonight," Tyler began. He sounded great! The video was clear. And his speech delivery was pretty confident, considering the fact that our feed was only one way. The whole time he was talking, he had no idea if anyone in New York could see or hear him. He was driving blind.

"The next step here is to flush the well," Tyler continued. "Let's watch together." As the camera panned and the drill team fired up the rig, I prayed that we'd see water. What none of us knew at the time was that the rig's compressor had run out of oil. It had one more flush in it, and then it was done. We literally had one shot here.

It was so quiet in the Temple that I could hear the ice clinking in glasses. And then, suddenly, on-screen, as everyone was watching, a stream of water shot thirty feet into the air. It looked like a geyser erupting. The kids in Adi Etot were jumping up and down and rushing toward the water, letting their blankets get wet. The women sang and danced. From the oldest man, who thought he'd never see clean water, to the youngest child, everyone on that mountaintop was celebrating.

I looked out from the stage at all the guests. They were clapping, too, and some were even crying. They cheered so loudly it filled the Temple and bounced off the walls. I couldn't hear anything else. But I could see our donors smiling at one another and mouthing the word *amazing.*

They could *relate.*

Tears streamed down my face. I looked over at Vik, who was wiping her eyes. Every person in this room was now connected to someone like them a world away. Now it was time to make a bigger ask.

"I know that many of you came here tonight prepared to give more than just one person clean water," I said. "I want to see if we can do the same thing for one hundred thousand people living in three hundred villages all over the world. To do that, we'll need to raise $3 million."

I then announced that a group of eighteen donors had already put up $1 million to help us reach our goal—but it would be unlocked *only* if we could raise the first million.

"Vik and I will pledge $10,000 of our own money to start," I said. "This isn't a competition, and we're not selling you anything. We're just offering you a pure opportunity to help as many people as you can."

A giving counter lit up the giant screen behind me.

"We have fifteen minutes to raise $3 million," I said. "Let the giving begin!"

There was so much joy in the room as the numbers rose and rose . . .

from $10,000 to $20,000 then $150,000, then to $1 million. People kept pledging and then pledging more. It was the best party I'd ever thrown in my life.

Less than fifteen minutes later, we had raised a total of $3.1 million. We'd done it: one hundred thousand lives changed in a moment. Remembering what Ross had taught me, I looked around the room, inhaled deeply, took a mental picture of the scene, and stored it away in my heart and mind.

I was so proud of our team. *This is what charity: water is all about,* I thought. Tonight, we didn't just help another 310 communities get clean water. We also brought great joy to 400 people here in New York. We proved that pure giving—the kind that comes from deep within your heart, the kind where you expect nothing in return—can be a powerful and life-changing experience.

Tomorrow, I would go back to work and try to do it all over again.

You Are Invited

I recently got a chance to visit charity: water's very first project. It was the well we funded on my thirty-first birthday and then built in the IDP camp of Bobi, Uganda.

The war had ended years ago. The sprawling camp of 31,000 people had cleared out, leaving a small village of about 500. And while our old well was banged up and dented from a decade of use, clean water still flowed. It was incredible to see. Christoph and I calculated that the handle must've been pumped about 50 million times.

When I looked around at all the kids in the village who were ten and younger, I realized that they'd never had to drink dirty water in their lives. A simple piece of infrastructure had broken a cycle of disease and despair for generations to come.

When I go on trips like this and meet with the people we serve, they often talk about their lives as having two distinct periods: "before the water" and "after the water." I know that's true for me as well. Almost everything about my life is different now, "after the water." And I've learned a thousand lessons along the way.

I've learned that no one is beyond redemption. Even if you think your past might disqualify you from a better future, I promise you, it's never too late to make a change. One day, you'll look back, connect the dots, and see how your past was a necessary part of the journey.

I've learned that the most painful moments are often the ones that define us. There have been so many days when I've wanted to quit charity: water, run away, and hand the keys to someone else. But instead I stay. We tackle our problems. And we grow stronger. I will always look back on the lawsuit we endured with profound gratitude, because if we hadn't had our butts kicked and been challenged to improve, charity: water might not exist today.

I've learned that there are no shortcuts. I'd always thought there would be a finish line for our organization. That we'd raise all the money we needed and end the water crisis for good. But we obviously haven't moved on to charity: education, charity: health, or addressed all the other problems I wanted to solve at the start. For so long, I measured myself against this impossible trajectory and always came up short. It's taken me ten years to figure out that our work is not about the finish line. It's about the race. It's about keeping a steady pace and putting in the kind of effort and creativity that gets results.

There's an old rabbinic saying that I love: "Do not be afraid of work that has no end." That's how I've come to see this journey. If your work is in the service of others—if you are compassionately pursuing an end to the suffering of people less fortunate than you—then your work will simply never end. The idea of endless work used to scare me. But not anymore. Now, it inspires me.

My hope is that this book inspires greatness within you. And action.

Maybe your "do something" looks like partnering with charity: water as we seek to bring water to communities in need. Maybe it's finding a different cause that motivates you or starting a nonprofit of your own. Whatever it is, my hope is that you will give your time, your talent, and your money to make things better for others, to end their needless suffering—because so much of it really is needless.

Let me finally say something about hope. I live in a country where unemployment is at 3.9 percent, yet there seems to be a collective deficit of hope. The times feel caustic. So many people are angry, defeated, and fearful for the future. But in a recent address to a TED conference, Pope Francis said something that I can't get out of my head: "A single individual is enough for hope to exist. And that individual can be you. And then there will be another you, and another you, until it turns into an *us* . . . and when there is an us—there begins a revolution."

At last count, charity: water has funded more than 28,000 water projects that will help 8.5 million people get clean water—people who will never have to experience what it was like "before the water" ever again. We still have so much work to do. Yet every day, I wake up hopeful that we *will* solve this problem in my lifetime. I believe that together we can bring life's most basic necessity to the 663 million people who still don't have it.

I'm just one guy, who built one charity—but it's made a little dent in the water crisis. Next year, we'll make a bigger dent. This is how the problems of the world get solved: One by one. By me and you and us.

*

To join The Spring now and help us to bring clean and safe drinking water to people around the world every single month, visit charitywater.org/thespring.

To donate your next birthday, to sponsor an entire water project, or to learn more about The Well program and the visionary families who support the staff salaries and operations of charity: water and make our 100 percent model possible, visit charitywater.org or email thirst@charitywater.org.

You can connect with me and charity: water on Twitter and Instagram here: @scottharrison @charitywater.

Finally, I'd love to hear from readers. Write me anytime at scott@thirstbook.com.

Acknowledgments

On a recent trip to Ethiopia, a village elder stood up to make a speech. About two hundred people from the community sat shoulder-to-shoulder behind him as he began speaking in English with a grand sweep of his hands. "What can I say for you?" he said, welcoming us. "You have boarded airplanes. You have come across oceans. You have gotten on more airplanes. You've been in cars. You've walked long distances. And now you are here. With us."

In that spirit of gratitude, I'd like to honor some of the people who have walked with me and charity: water on this journey.

What can I say for Viktoria Harrison, my amazing wife. You put up with this project for eighteen months, letting me sequester myself in remote cabins and houses—often in beautiful, quiet places—while you took care of two energetic children. Your editing and candid feedback were so helpful, and you never held back. I couldn't have brought this book to life without you, and I'm grateful for the space you allowed me to make it happen.

What can I say for Lisa Sweetingham, my amazing cowriter. You were my thought partner, and we went deep together—more than I often wanted to—but you were always there to push, prod, and discourage me from taking the easy way out. You listened to hundreds of hours of podcasts and speeches where I was less than eloquent. You sacrificed precious weekend time with Bruce and the kids. I'm grateful for your help and our partnership, and for your determination to make this the best it could be. You made an instant fan of Vik (not an easy feat), and I can't wait until we all can spend more time in Africa together again.

What can I say for Kathy Robbins, my agent. You believed in this project from the first time we met, and worked hard to make sure it landed in the right home. More than a few times, you talked me off the ledge and gave me confidence. Vik and I are so fortunate to have you in our lives.

What can I say for Derek Reed, my editor at Currency. Your insight and guidance were crucial to making this book something we could all be proud of. And if not for your constant pruning and cutting, I'd probably have written a book twice as long, one that would only be useful as a doorstop. As Stephen King once said, "To write is human, to edit is divine," and you've proven it.

What can I say for Tina Constable, my publisher. When you told me at our very first meeting that you were a Spring member, I knew you were passionate about the cause and about bringing this story into the world. Your faith in me, and in this book, is deeply appreciated. Thanks also to Campbell Wharton, Carisa Hays, Ayelet Gruenspecht, Megan Schumann, Robert Siek, Philip Leung, Songhee Kim, and everyone else at Penguin Random House who touched this book.

What can I say for all those who helped make *Thirst* a reality: Baas Creative, Matt Pamer, Lauren Letta, Chris Barton, Ali Troute, Brad Lomenick, Michael McKeon, Johanna Rojas, Anna Stock-Matthews, Teresa Otto, Jason Keramidas, Alyson Nakamura, Cubby Graham, and the teams at Derris and Hilsinger Mendelson. Kari Reeves, Jessica Jackley, Andrew DeCurtis, Brantly Martin, and Alisha Gorder for taking the time to read and give valuable feedback on early versions of the manuscript.

What can I say for Michael and Xochi Birch. You guys are in a league of your own. You've been charity: water's guardian angels for more than a decade. You've come with your children to see our work up close, in person, in ten different countries now. You never complained about bumpy seventeen-hour drives through the jungle, "zero-star" $5-a-night hotel rooms with no running water or electricity, long speeches in the rain, creepy spiders, and plenty of upset stomachs along the way. Somehow, you both keep coming back. I'm grateful for the people you are and for your radical generosity that inspires others to follow in your footsteps.

What can I say for those of you who gave me a quiet place to write when I most needed it. Thank you Philip Truelove and the Greenwich Hotel, Steve and Lynne Foote, David and Tina Segel, Jayne Bentzen, Molly and Ryan Graves, and Angela and Ty Popplewell for opening up your homes, guest houses, and hotels.

What can I say for our past and present charity: water board members. Mike Wilkerson, I'm so glad you agreed to that first meeting more than a decade ago. Gordon Pennington, I'll never forget our time in Wolfsburg. Vance Thompson, your humor, wit, and wisdom kept us alive in those early years. Brenda Koinis and Grazia Ochoa, you believed in this crazy idea before it even had a name. Brook Hazelton, Brant Cryder, Gian-Carlo Ochoa, Ryan Graves, Shannon Sedgwick-Davis, Chi-Hua Chien, Al Gordon, Luke Beauchamp, Ije Nwokorie, Sam Lawson Johnston, and Valerie Donati, I'm grateful for your contributions and support, and hope we can continue to serve together for years to come.

What can I say for the staff and volunteers at charity: water. Your contributions of time and talent have never been motivated by money. You came and worked with charity: water because you truly believe that using your talent to benefit others is more important than using it to benefit yourself. You are the ones who built the organization. I feel so lucky to have worked alongside you, and to continue to fight for clean water alongside you.

What can I say for our local partners, fighting for change across twenty-seven countries. You're the ones out there right now making it happen. You're the local heroes leading your communities and countries forward, using clean water as a tool to bring health, education, and economic opportunity to all. You inspire us every day, and we'll do our best to make sure your important work keeps moving forward.

What can I say for the amazing charity: water fundraisers. You've run marathons and climbed mountains; you've jumped into freezing cold water; you've biked across countries; you've donated birthdays, weddings, anniversaries, and bat and bar mitzvahs; you've given up all your Christmas gifts. And most important, you've helped bring clean water to millions of people, and inspired so many others with your passion and creativity.

What can I say for those whose game-changing financial contributions have gone above and beyond to help propel the organization forward: Neil Hutchinson, Virginia Clay, John and Maia Vechey, Kenny and Esther Feng, Joe and Aimee Patanella, John and Ann Doerr, Marissa Sackler, Casey Wasserman, Greg and Yukari Pass, Neven Subotic Stiftung, Philip and Jennifer Carmichael, Joe and Sharon Kemper, Atlas Copco, Michele Sullivan and Jennifer Zammuto at the Caterpillar Foundation, Comic Relief US, Martin Gore, Jonathan Kessler, Depeche Mode, Hublot, EastLake Community Church, Jacqueline Fuller, Lacey and Google Foundation, Humble Bundle, Mosaic Church, Nautica Enterprises, Saint Laurent, Emergen-C, Amazon Smile, Steve, Pam, Kyle, and Matt at Smile Generation and the Pineapple Fund.

And to many others who have made invaluable contributions of time, talent, and money. Craig Hagelin, you were one of the very first to believe in me. Bob Watman, I think you wrote the very first overhead check. Alex Hurst, David Terban, Jeremy Snell, Paul Pryor, Esther Havens, Shelly Taggar, Alan Boss, Dan Kinder, Fredrick Weiss, Matt Oliver, Michele Helman, Shawn Budde, Robert Valentine, Rick Smolan, Philip and Donna Berber, the Bezos Family Foundation, Ride for Water, Emma Snowdon Jones, Pete and Devon Briger, B. Ray and Juanne Thompson, Bill Simmons, Rich Roll, Willard Brown, Miguel McKelvey, Brooke Hammerling, Shakil Khan, Rael Dornfest, Greg

Phelan, Michelle Kydd Lee, Dell EMC, Focusing Philanthropy, Ross and Laurie Garber, Gary and Mona Marshik, Chris and Grace Pretorius, Steve Sadove, Saks Fifth Avenue, David and Aviva Schwarz, Select Equity Foundation, The Macallan, Raj Shahani, Kristen Bell, Nathan Fillion, Seth Godin, Chris Guillebeau, Susan Peirce Thompson, Will and Jada Smith, HRH Beatrice York, HRH Eugenie York, Amit and John and the Bryan Cave team, and finally, our generous landlord Eric Gural and the team at Newmark Knight Grubb Frank.

What can I say for all the followers of Jesus in my life, and my extended church family around the world. You've reminded me that God's kindness and patience made my journey possible. And that today, more than ever, I am a sinner saved by profound grace. Thank you for encouraging me to be the best husband, father, friend, and colleague that I can possibly be. And encouraging me to live a life that points toward heaven, a life that shares with others, gently and respectfully, the great hope that I have.

Finally, what can I say for all of our Well members. You have our back. You are the reason we are able to come to work each day and provide for our families. You selflessly support the staff at charity: water, you pay for our office rent, our copy machines, our phone bills—you make our 100 percent model possible. Your generosity has inspired more than one million people to give to charity: water's projects in the field. And now, more than eight million lives have been changed for the better because of you. I'm so grateful for each and every one of you.

Well members at time of printing:

Abdur and Ana Clark Chowdhury

Ahrendts Couch Foundation

Aimee and Joe Patanella

Ajaz Ahmed

Alastair Cairns and Ellie Kurrus

Alex Tew

Alexandra Lenas Parker and Sean Parker

Alexios Vratskides and Natasa Vuckovic

Amy and Drew McKnight

Amy Nicolo and Ian Jones

Andrea and Mark Spears

Andrea Piana

Andrew and Dori McCall

Ann and Howard Dahl

Anna and Timm Oberwelland

Annabel Teal

Anoop Dhakad and Chitra Narasimhan

Bellamy and Nick Wojtaszek

Ben and Claire Goldhirsh

Ben and Heather Grizzle

Betsy and Dick DeVos Family

Blake and Heather Mycoskie

Blake MacDonald and Julie Billings-Nguyen

Bob and Sara Stevenson

Bodie Jahn-Mulliner and Sylvester Rishoj Jensen

Brad and Shanda Damphousse

Brandon and Natasha Beck

Brian Kopper and Julie Norris

Brook and Erin Hazelton

Cara Cutter and Dennis Phelps

Catherine O. and Tony Hawk

Chandra Jessee

Cheri DeVos Family

Chi-Hua Chien and Sohi Sohn Chien

Chris and Crystal Sacca

Chris and Michelle Clothier

Christian Jochnick

Chuck and Joan Harrison

Colin Corgan

Connie Hagelin

Corinne and Dan Goldman

Courtney Nichols Gould and Gordon Gould

Craig Clemens and Sarah Anne Stewart

Curtis and Shirley Chambers

Dan Springer

Daniel Ek and Sofia Levander

David and Eli Gardner

David and Mary Rutter

David and Sarah Kowitz

David and Traci Osborn

David Eun and Rochelle Yu

Denis and Meredith Coleman

Denis O'Brien

Devon and Pete Briger

Devon Biondi and Ryan Sarver

Dick Hillenbrand

Elaine and Norm Brodsky

Emily Moyer and Eric Jensen

Esther and Kenny Feng

Ethan Beard and Wayee Chu

Frances and Stephen Rowland

Frank and Tatiana Moretti

Gary and Liz Vaynerchuk

Greg Harper

Hannah and Katie VanderWeide

Harman-Mayes-Sooch Family

Heidi and Jon McNeill

Holly and Reggie Bradford

Jacomien Mars

James and Suzanne Jesse

Jane and Mark Wilf

Janita and Meyrick Douglas

Jason Fried

Jayne Bentzen

Jennifer Stengaard Gross and Peter Stengaard

Jeremy and Ruth Burton

Jim Kreissman

Jimmy and Natalia Furland

Joe and Sharon Ritchie

John and Kathy Hayes

John and Maia Vechey

Jon and Sarah Dahl

Jonathan and Lizzie Tisch

Julie and Mat Miller

Justin Shaffer

Karen Ray

Karin and Stephen Sadove

Kathryn and Todd Chaffee

Katleen Van Roost and Roberto Hoornweg

Ken and Teri Hertz

Ken Howery

Kerrilee and Martin Gore

Kevin and Maria McEvoy

Kevin Kwan

Kristen and Rob Bell

Kristin and Stephen Mugford

Kristina and Reid Tracy

Kuldeep Malkani

Laura and Scott Malkin

Lynne and Steve Foote

Maria and Nathan Bosshard

Marissa Sackler

Mark and Nancy Duarte

Matthew and Sarah Hasselbeck

Michael and Xochi Birch

Michael Wilkerson

Mike Dillard

Mikkel Bülow-Lehnsby

Molly and Ryan Graves

Monique Péan and Stephen Glass

Nathan Hubbard

Neil and Shannon Young

Neil Hutchinson

Pamela and Stephen Thorne

Penny and Steven Gundry

Pierre Andurand

Rebecca and Tyson Strauser

Saint Laurent

Sam Davis and Shannon Sedgwick Davis

Shakil Khan

Simon Sinek

Steve Kuhn

The Ive Family

The Maurice Marciano Family Foundation

The Muller Family

The Perry Foundation

William Connolly

Winston Fisher

For more photos and videos of the people
and places of *Thirst* please visit:

THIRSTBOOK.COM

Enter the code:

TOGETHER